Kathleen Clarke

Revolutionary Woman

'A remarkable work of enormous historical value'
RTÉ

'Fascinating ...a richly staisfying read'
THE IRISH TIMES

Kathleen Clarke

Revolutionary Woman

Edited by Helen Litton

THE O'BRIEN PRESS
DUBLIN

This edition first published 2008 by The O'Brien Press Ltd.
First published 1991 by The O'Brien Press Ltd,
12 Terenure Road East, Rathgar, Dublin 6, Ireland.
Tel: +353 1 4923333; Fax: +353 1 4922777
E-mail: books@obrien.ie
Website: www.obrien.ie
Reprinted 1997.

ISBN: 978-1-84717-059-0

British Library Cataloguing-in-Publication Data
Clarke, Kathleen, 1878-1972
Kathleen Clarke : revolutionary woman. - 4th ed.
1. Clarke, Kathleen, 1878-1972 2. Women revolutionaries - Ireland - Biography
3. Revolutionaries - Ireland - Biography 4. Ireland - History - 20th century 5. Ireland -
Politics and government - 20th century
I. Title
941.7'082'092

4 5 6 7 8 9 10
08 09 10 11 12 13

Photographs: Courtesy of the National Library of Ireland (KE 235, Tom Clarke),
(KE26, Eamon de Valera in uniform), (KE23, Ned Daly in uniform), (KE53, Seán Mac
Diarmada) and cover image (P12 - Prisoners being led away, Album 252).
Other cover images: Tom and Kathleen Clarke (composite photograph), 1901 (courtesy
of E.Clarke), Marcella's Cosgrave's armband and Pledge signed by women of Ireland,
Lá na mBan, 1918 (courtesy of the Kilmainham Gaol Collection).

Printed and bound in the UK by J.H. Haynes & Co. Ltd, Sparkford.

Contents

PREFACE TO SECOND EDITION

When this book was first published, in 1991, I hoped that it would be an addition to the corpus of first-hand material dealing with Ireland's nationalist revolution, and the 1916 Rising in particular. It was indeed widely welcomed as offering a close and unique view of the events of that time, and also as a woman's story, a rarity for early twentieth-century Ireland.

As a grand-niece of Kathleen Clarke, I was given the manuscript of her memoirs by her son, Dr Emmet Clarke, because she had wanted it published after her death, and he gave me every assistance while I was working on the edition. I was able to use the extensive Clarke archive, which has been dispersed since his death in 2005, and I also relied on the memories of the extended De hÓir, O'Nolan, O'Toole and O'Sullivan families, for which I am very grateful. Thanks are also due to the University of Limerick Archives, and Dublin City Council Archives. The original manuscript is now with the Daly Collection in the University of Limerick.

I did not change anything in the manuscript itself – this is the voice of Kathleen Clarke, stubborn, energetic and driven by a fierce commitment to a cause, particularly after her husband's death. I reduced the number of chapters, and removed some repetitive material; the memoir had been written over several years, starting in 1939. I added footnotes to explain references which might now be obscure to a reader, or to enlarge on family information. I was also able to use quotes from the extensive correspondence between Kathleen and Tom during periods of separation, and these are found in square brackets in Chapter 2. A new epilogue has been added, giving more detail on her later life.

Particular thanks are due to Michael O'Brien and Ide ní Laoghaire of The O'Brien Press, and to Síne Quinn, who oversaw this reprint. I am grateful for their belief in the importance of this memoir, and their determination to keep it in print. I believe this production is a worthy memorial to its author, and hope it will continue to consolidate her contribution to this period of Ireland's history.

Helen Litton, 15 February 2008

PROLOGUE

One of the reasons for writing these memories was a promise which I made to Reverend Father Albert Bibby [OFM Cap., who attended several of the 1916 executions] when he visited me to say goodbye before leaving for the USA, where he died. On leaving me he said: 'Now, I want you to promise me you will write your memoirs, as I think you know more than anyone alive about the Rising and all connected with it. Will you give me that promise?'

I answered that I had thought of doing so, but that I was up against a difficulty: if I write I must tell the truth as I know it, and some of those who are up in the skies in the minds of the people might not remain high. Would I be justified in causing some disillusionment?

His answer to me was: 'My dear child, so far history has been a falsification of the truth. It is time the truth be told.'

So far as I could, I have tried to tell the truth without causing disillusionment, as I would fear the effect of that on young minds. During those years of struggle for freedom, I could keep no documentary evidence of any kind lest it fall into enemy hands. In fact, prior to the Rising I had been trained to memorise all the details. After the Rising, my home was continually raided by some form or other of British military forces. The few letters and things I did manage to keep I had put away in storage. From 1914 to 1922 events were moving so rapidly that I hope I may be forgiven if after such a lapse of time I am not correct in the sequence of some of them.

The events themselves are as vivid and clear in my mind as when they happened; some of them could not be eradicated.

Kathleen Clarke

1
A Revolutionary
Childhood

1878-1898

Early years – Uncle John Daly's imprisonment –
Aunt Lollie's stories – father's death – Uncle James
returns from Australia – Kathleen sets up own business
– Uncle John released from prison after hunger-strike,
elected Mayor of Limerick

When I rose joyfully on my sixth birthday, Good Friday, 11 April 1884, I did not realise that before the day ended I would learn of an event which was to influence my whole life profoundly. It was a lovely sunny April morning, and everyone was wishing me a happy birthday. One of my presents was a big beautiful lifelike doll, which to my surprise could open and shut its eyes. I am sure I was one of the happiest children in Ireland that day. I was bursting to share my happiness with everybody, so with my sister Eileen I rushed off to show my doll to all our neighbours. We were made welcome everywhere, and my doll admired. Wildly excited, we ran home to tell Mother all about it.

We had left a cheerful happy home, but the home we returned to was a grief-stricken one. My mother Catherine, my aunt Lollie and my grandmother were crying bitterly and trying to comfort each other. I did not quite understand what it meant when I was told the reason for their tears, that Uncle John had been arrested in England, but seeing the grief all around me killed the joy in my birthday.[1]

My father, Edward Daly, arrived from England next day with further news. On learning of his brother's arrest, he had resigned his position as Chief Superintendent in St George's Private Lunatic Asylum. He had then called to the home of James F Egan in Birmingham, where Uncle John had been staying. There he learned that Egan also had been arrested, and that his wife, who was English, was in a terrible state. The garden of their home, Lake House, had been dug up by detectives and bombs found there. Egan always maintained that he had no knowledge of their presence, and he believed they had been planted there. James Egan was a very fine type of Irishman, but did not belong to the revolutionary element, although he was a close personal friend of Uncle John; that he was a friend of John Daly was sufficient for the British.[2]

After sympathising with Mrs Egan, my father left for home. He took with him Uncle John's luggage, which included a long cardboard box containing a doll which Uncle John had bought for my sister Eileen, his godchild. He never thought it would be of interest to Scotland Yard.

Early on Easter Sunday morning a jarvey, or sidecar, as they were then called, pulled up outside our house. As I watched from a front-room window, four men jumped off the car and rushed to our hall door. The house resounded with their knocking. Aunt Lollie opened the door and asked them their business, in her cool stately way. They told her they were from Scotland Yard and wished to see my father. This, I am sure, gave her a shock, but she preserved her calm manner and informed them that my father was resting, being very tired after his arduous journey of the previous day. She then showed them into the room where I was.

They said that what they really wanted was a long cardboard box which my father was known to have removed from James F Egan's house in Birmingham, and had had with him on his arrival in Limerick. They were not satisfied when my aunt assured them that it only contained a doll for one of her nieces, and they insisted on seeing it. When she brought it in and opened it they looked at the doll but did not touch it; to me they seemed nervous. I was amazed when, despite my aunt's protests, they stated they must take it away as evidence. I was bursting with questions I dared not ask, fearing I might be sent out of the room; I kept so quiet I think Aunt Lollie was not conscious of my presence. What did they want Eileen's doll for? What was Scotland Yard? Why were they nervous? What was evidence? I was wildly excited. They took the doll, handling it very carefully, and went off on the sidecar. It was returned, after months of constant demands from my aunt, with the skull removed. Years later I was to realise that they had thought the doll was a disguised infernal machine, or what we now call a time bomb.

Uncle John and James Egan were charged with being dynamitards; the charge was later changed to treason felony.[3] Lack of evidence did not save them from being convicted and sentenced, Uncle John to penal servitude for life, and James Egan to twenty years' penal servitude. They were sent to Chatham Prison. Some years later, the Birmingham Chief of Police lay dying, and in a statement to the press confessed that John Daly had been convicted on perjured evidence, and that he could not die in peace with the knowledge of it on his mind.[4] Neither man was in fact guilty of the crime he had been charged with.

This confession did not secure their release; they had to suffer many more years of imprisonment, subjected to all the indignities, brutalities and torture which British prison officials had devised especially for Irish political prisoners. Tom Clarke, who was a fellow prisoner, has given a taste of what they had to endure in his *Glimpses of an Irish Felon's Prison Life*.[5] Once in jail, contact with the outside world practically ceased for Irish political prisoners. They were at first allowed to communicate with their families only once every six months, and in later years once every three months. Nothing could be discussed in these letters except family matters, either in or out; if there was an attempt at anything further it was blotted out, or the letter was stopped altogether by the prison governor.

They were never sure of getting a letter or a visit at the due time; these could be stopped for the slightest misdemeanour, such as trying to talk to one another or to any other prisoner. They sometimes suffered the added punishment of solitary confinement in underground cells, with bread and cold water the only diet, for periods ranging from three to twenty-one days. They had to leave their clothes outside these freezing cold cells at night, lest they use them for warmth. Uncle John told me once that when Tom came out after one such twenty-one day period, he was a walking skeleton; his food had consisted of one pint of cold water and eight ounces of bread per day.

The arrival of a letter from Uncle John sent a thrill of anxious expectation through the family. If it arrived in the morning post there was a general rush from the bedrooms and we arrived downstairs in all stages of dishabille to hear the letter read. It was always read by Aunt Lollie, and conveyed little more than the fact that he was alive. My grandmother cried bitterly on these occasions. Poor grandmother, he was her favourite son, suffering through loving his country, a love she had instilled in him. She was a grand woman, whose sorrow for her son's sufferings was deep, but whose pride in the fact that he could suffer and, if necessary, die for Ireland's freedom was greater.

She was a very devout Catholic, and took great pleasure in teaching us our prayers. At bedtime we knelt around her and repeated the prayers after her. The first was always for Ireland's freedom, and when Uncle John was imprisoned the second was for his release. Then we prayed for all the relations alive and dead, ending up with 'God make a good child of me.' She was the kindest and most generous-hearted woman I ever met, with a fine broad outlook on life; she could see good in everyone and everything but England.

Aunt Lollie (Ellen) was my grandmother's only daughter. Her uncle, a teacher who prepared boys for university, had imbued her with a love of learning, and had given her a thorough knowledge of the history of Ireland, France and England, and a fair knowledge of the history of the USA and other countries. She was, for her time, a highly-educated woman, with a wonderful memory, and could give day and date for everything. From her store of historical knowledge she would keep us children entranced for hours; she had a wonderful way of recounting things so that we seemed to live the events all over again, and she wove history into the most beautiful stories for us. She would dwell particularly on the Fenian period, in which she had taken an active part; this she painted in the most glowing and romantic colours so that all our early enthusiasm was centred round the Fenians.

She did not confine her stories to Ireland; I remember crying at the story she told us one night about the little children imprisoned in the Tower of London. Often, when we should have been in bed, my mother would catch us sitting in our nightgowns on Lollie's bed, listening to her with rapt attention. Mother would say, ' Have you no better sense, Lollie, keeping the children from their beds with your rambling?', but the effect of that rambling in later years brought us through one of the most difficult periods of our history with our heads up; we knew our history.[6]

At the time of Uncle John's arrest, in 1883, my mother and aunt were carrying on a very successful dressmaking business, which employed many girls. I remember one very amusing incident in connection with that. Aunt Lollie was a rather unusual character, and it was her practice, when a large order such as a wedding was completed, to invite all the girls to tea. If it was summer, tea would be in the garden, where there was a lovely swing put up by my father. It was worked by pulleys, and one could go very high in accordance with the way the ropes were pulled. This day, the girls came into the garden for tea, and afterwards started to amuse themselves. One nervous girl got on the swing, and another gave the ropes a pull which sent her flying high. The poor girl lost her head with fright, let go the ropes and with a wild scream fell off and over the garden wall on to the roof of a greenhouse in the next garden, scattering glass everywhere and scaring the wits out of the owner, who happened to be in it. Both were unhurt, except for a few scratches, but the plants did not come off so well.

Living with us at that time was a boy called Jim Jones, the son of a ship's engineer who had smuggled Uncle John out of Ireland in 1867, when he was on the run. When Jim was ten months old his father died, and his mother went to the USA to earn a living. My aunt and grandmother undertook to care for the boy until his mother was in a position to send for him; they felt they were repaying a debt. His mother never did send for him, for which my aunt was very thankful; she idolised the little boy, and in later life he repaid all the care and love she lavished on him.

When the Amnesty Association was started in Limerick some time after Uncle John's imprisonment, Jim Jones was made Honorary Secretary. Though only a boy in years (although at least ten years older than any of us), he had all the enthusiasm and energy needed for the position. He adored Uncle John, who was a stimulus to his ardour if one was needed. He did all the work in connection with the Association in our house; I watched everything he did, and felt very proud when he allowed me to put the stamps on the letters he was sending out. Later he allowed me to fold the circulars for the post – I am sure I plagued him with my pleading to be allowed to help. In my imagination I was helping to free Uncle John and, of course, Ireland.

One evening in 1886, when I was about eight years old, a telegram came from the governor of Chatham Prison, saying: 'Brother ill, come at once.' It was a horrible shock to the family. It was too late to get a train to Dublin that evening, so my father and Aunt Lollie went by the first train next morning, leaving about 7am. When they arrived at the prison, Uncle John was still alive, but not out of danger. They were allowed to see him daily while death hovered around, but as soon as he took a turn for the better the prison doors closed around him again. They returned home very troubled.

While they were away, my mother gave birth to her eighth

daughter. She had been ill before they left, but as they feared Uncle John might die before they reached him, they had to leave her, and dared not delay. A nurse came, and took charge. Since it had been early morning when they left, none of the family was awake or up except myself. Even as a child, I could not sleep if there was anything disturbing going on; I had been listening to all the talk about Uncle John, so I got up when I heard my father get up. When he and my aunt had gone I went and sat outside my mother's bedroom, wondering what was wrong with her. Hearing the odd moan, I feared she was going to die, and was feeling very miserable. I wished I dared go in to her, but I was afraid of the nurse, who passed me a few times looking very stern, but took no notice of me. After what seemed like years, the nurse came to my mother's door, walked over to me with a bundle in her arms and said, 'Here is a baby sister for you, take good care of her.' She put the bundle in my arms and returned to my mother's room.

A few minutes before, I had been in such depths of misery, hearing my mother moaning and knowing that my father and aunt had gone to a dying uncle. I had been suffering as only an imaginative and sensitive child can. Now, here was joy in my arms, a lovely wee baby sister [Annie]. How I loved her; I was almost afraid to breathe, she was so tiny. Holding her, I forgot all about my misery, and felt very resentful when the nurse returned and took her from me, but then I had all the pleasure of going to wake my sisters and tell them of the arrival of a new baby. Looking back now, I can imagine what my father must have suffered having to leave my mother at such a critical time.

About a year later, a beautiful monument was erected in Limerick to the memory of the Manchester Martyrs, Allen, Larkin and

O'Brien, in St Lawrence's Cemetery.[7] It was to be unveiled on a certain Sunday, and arrangements were made to run trains into Limerick from all the surrounding districts. A big procession was organised, to march through the city to where the monument was to be unveiled. The British authorities proclaimed [banned] the unveiling, and hundreds of police were drafted into the city to enforce the proclamation. The police barracks were not large enough to accommodate all the police that had been drafted in, so a four-storey unoccupied house opposite ours, in Cecil Street, was requisitioned. Several loads of hay were put in for the police to sleep on, and several barrels of stout, all of which I and my sisters watched with great interest.

The city was in a tense state of excitement. Would an attempt be made to unveil the memorial? was the question on everybody's lips. Police were posted in every corner of the city, but so far as they could see the proclamation was being obeyed. This state of tension hung over the city that Sunday, as the funeral of a member of the Amnesty Association passed the police barracks in William Street. It was the custom at that time for relatives or close friends of the deceased to wear black armlets, generally supplied by the undertaker. This funeral was a big one, and hundreds of men walked behind it. My father and Jim Jones pinned a black armlet on each man's arm, and every man was aware of what was intended. When the dead man had been buried, the armlets were removed and pinned together; with this improvised covering the monument was veiled and then unveiled. The banned ceremony had been accomplished.

When the police got a hint that they had been outwitted they rushed to the cemetery, but there was nobody left there to wreak their vengeance on. They returned to the city, where they indulged in indiscriminate baton charges all day and late into the night. Everywhere, drunken police let their fury loose on the populace. Throughout this excitement my sisters and I were compelled to remain indoors, as my mother considered it too dangerous for children to be out. This annoyed me; I wanted to be out in the fun, as I thought it! That evening, we were sent to bed at the usual time. When all the others were asleep, I awakened Agnes, and induced her to dress and steal out with me to see what was going on in the streets. I told her that the grown-ups were playing cards in the sittingroom and would not hear us slipping down without our shoes on, and out the door.

When we arrived in George's Street (now O'Connell Street) the sight that met our eyes was one of horror. People were lying on the ground, battered and bleeding. As we came into the street a baton charge started, into which we were swept with the mad rush of people from the police. Fear gave wings to our feet, and we did not stop running until we arrived at Arthur's Quay, off George's Street. Down this we rushed, and stepped into the first open door we saw. There we stopped, petrified with fright. We could hear the screams of the crowds thundering by as the police charged. Finally, after I do not know how long, all was quiet. Timidly, we ventured out; the streets were dark and deserted. In a panic, we hurried home to find it dark and silent, as everyone had gone to bed. When we knocked on the hall door, it sounded loud enough to wake the dead, but it failed to wake the living. We kept knocking until a window in my father's room was opened, and he asked, 'Who is there?' 'It's me, Papa,' I said, and I heard him exclaim, 'God, Kate, it's two of the children!' Both of them came down to let us in and ask how we happened to be out when they thought we were safely in our beds. We got a good scolding and the promise of a good whipping next day, which they forgot to administer.

I remember my father as a very tall, handsome man, with very deep blue eyes with long dark lashes, finely-pencilled eyebrows, beautiful skin and a golden-brown beard. He was quite bald on the top of his head, due to severe neuralgia contracted after he had been imprisoned in 1865, at the age of seventeen [for suspected Fenian involvement]. He was the most refined and gentle man I ever met, kind and generous to a fault, and like Uncle John he had a deep and passionate love for Ireland. He had married very young, with little to marry on, but the marriage was a very happy one. He grieved constantly over his brother's imprisonment, and worked very hard in the Amnesty Association with the hope of procuring his release, but he did not live to see him freed.

About two years after Uncle John's first illness in prison, a telegram again came from the prison governor summoning my father; his brother was dangerously ill. Aunt Lollie and my father went off again to the prison, where they found Uncle John on the point of death from poison administered by prison officials. The officials claimed this had been accidental; a doctor's prescription marked 'Not To Be Taken' had been given him to drink. Uncle John believed there was malice in it. Again they were allowed to visit him daily until he was out of danger, then once more the prison doors were closed down on him.

On their arrival home, my father and Aunt Lollie were met with the news that their mother, my grandmother, was dying. My aunt rushed up the stairs to see her mother and met the priest coming down, having anointed her. He stopped to ask how she had found her brother, and she told him the story. He said, 'Don't be talking nonsense, woman, why would the prison officials deliberately poison him?' 'Well, Father,' she said, 'the prison officials admitted it, but said it had been a mistake made by a warder.' My grandmother did not die on that occasion; she lived to the age of ninety-seven, a rebel against England to her last breath.

The delicacy resulting from his youthful imprisonment, under the dreadful conditions prevailing in prisons at that time, was largely the cause of my father's death in 1890, at the age of forty-one. To show their sympathy, the people of Limerick gave him the largest funeral that had ever been seen there. Every shop and factory closed, and where employers refused to close, the employees walked out. Every window-blind along the route was drawn. The funeral passed into what is now O'Connell Avenue, along O'Connell Street and Patrick Street, and over Athlunkard Bridge. From there it turned into Mary Street, over Thomond Bridge by the Treaty Stone and up the Strand, then it went over what is now Sarsfield Bridge. At this stage, from Sarsfield Bridge back to Thomond Bridge was one unbroken line of marching men. The funeral continued up Sarsfield Street and William Street, to St Lawrence's Cemetery.

The procession moved very slowly through the many miles of streets; there were repeated halts to allow each man to pay his last respects by bearing the coffin on his shoulder for a little way, so the coffin was never in the hearse the whole way. It was the biggest spontaneous tribute to a man that I have ever seen; there were several bands, and I heard Chopin's 'Funeral March' for the first time. (A letter coming from Australia to congratulate me on being elected Lord Mayor of Dublin, in 1939, threw my mind back to this event; the writer, Seán O'Shea, wrote: 'I cannot believe it is close on fifty years since I saw the funeral of your father, the famous Fenian, going through the streets of Limerick. I have seen and taken part in many processions since then, but none made a greater impression on me than the tribute that great populace paid to your father on that occasion.')

My father left nine daughters, and his death ended the childhood of the three eldest, Eileen, Madge and myself. Our mother was prostrate with grief, as were our aunt and grandmother, and this forced on us responsibilities not normally placed on children's shoulders. Jim Jones was a pillar of strength to us during that difficult period.

My father had yearned for a son, but that wish was not fulfilled until five months after his death, when our brother Ned was born. It was hoped that my mother would accept him as some compensation for her husband's loss, but at first she did not; she seemed resentful that there was no father to whom she could present this little son. Then, gradually, she became absorbed in him. He was very frail, and perhaps this drew her to him more than a robust child would have done, or perhaps she sensed what the future might bring him and wanted to save him from his uncle's fate. Fate decided otherwise, and though her cup of sorrow was filled to overflowing, she bore it bravely when, twenty-five years later, he died facing a British firing squad for his participation in the 1916 insurrection. To others he might be Commandant Edward Daly, to her he was her idolised only son. Agnes and I felt that we reared Ned, for we tramped five or six miles a day to Shelbourne Farm, owned by a cousin, to get milk from a first-year milker supposed to be free of disease. Mrs Mac, as we called her, kept it for him.[8]

In 1895, Uncle John was nominated by the Limerick Amnesty Association as a candidate in the parliamentary elections. Maud Gonne (later Mme Gonne MacBride) came to Limerick to help; she had worked with the Amnesty Association before. There was only one other candidate, and Miss Gonne used her persuasive powers on him to get him to withdraw and leave Uncle John unopposed. This he did. It was the first time I had met Miss Gonne, and I thought her the most beautiful woman I had ever seen. She called to see my grandmother, as the mother of John Daly, and was charming to the whole family. She was as fascinating as she was beautiful, and the Limerick men went mad about her.

When Uncle John was elected to parliament the prison authorities were notified by telegram, and they conveyed the information to him. The British immediately declared him disqualified on the grounds that he was a felon, but even as a free man he would not have taken his seat in the British parliament, any more than John Mitchel or O'Donovan Rossa would have done. The Fenians were against Irishmen going into the British parliament.

Two of my father's brothers, James and Michael, had emigrated to Australia in their youth, about 1857, at the time of a gold rush. They did not find any gold, but they reached a position of wealth and affluence by sheepfarming, racing stables, coastal trading and many other activities, on the island of New Caledonia. Michael is said to have gone through three fortunes, and married three times; James was very much more thrifty and held on to his money. Never once did they lose touch with their mother. On hearing of Edward's death, James Daly, having provided amply for all his family, returned to Ireland to care for all of us, and his wealth certainly made life very easy for us. Shortly after Uncle James's arrival, Jim Jones died, in July 1894; he had been ailing for some time. His death was a great grief to us, as he had been our 'big brother'.

Uncle James took great pleasure in providing for all our needs. He was a great supporter of the anti-Parnellite Party.⁹ We did not like that; we were Fenians, and had no liking for Irishmen who became members of the British House of Commons. One day a member of that Party called to see Uncle James, and the maid showed him into the sittingroom where my mother was taking a nap. His entrance woke her, and she became flustered at seeing a strange man. He introduced himself by saying, 'I'm Tim Healy', whereupon she sat up and said, 'Are you that awful man that uses such bad language?' 'Yes, Ma'am,' he said, 'I am that awful man.' She was very angry with Uncle James for bringing that awful man into the house.

I was very fond of Uncle James, and appreciated all that he was doing for us, but was very disappointed when he refused to do something I asked for. I was passionately fond of music, and after my father's death my mother could not afford to pay for music lessons, so I got hold of the instruction books Eileen and Madge had had and set myself to learn to play the piano. I wanted a musical career, and asked Uncle James to help me towards it. He refused, the only thing he ever refused me; he said he had spent a fortune on his eldest daughter for music and it was money thrown away. Even to this day I feel regret at not getting a chance at the one thing I loved. I had studied so hard to learn without a teacher, and I can read any music put before me.

Well, I did not feel like being dependent on Uncle James forever, so I asked him to have me apprenticed to dressmaking to enable me to make a living. He agreed to that, and paid a big fee to what was then called a court dressmaker for my apprenticeship. At that time the field in which girls could make a living was very restricted; dressmaking would not have been my choice, had I the wide choice of employment girls have today, but I was very successful at it. The lady who ran the business was a very grand person and had a large staff.

One of the staff, a machinist, was a good honest girl but very rough in her language when things went wrong with her. Whenever she started to use bad language she would look at me and say, 'For God's sake, child, go out of the room, I can't swear when you look at me.' I never could understand why I had that effect on her.

When I was about eighteen years of age, I decided to start dress warerooms on my own. I had saved a little money out of what I had earned, enough capital, I thought, to start with, and I felt quite competent to do it. The family thought otherwise; they said I was too young and not experienced enough, and that people would not have confidence in one so young. I ignored all they had to say and went on with it. I rented rooms in Cecil Street to start with, and by degrees and very hard work I succeeded in building up a very good business. It was soon too big for the rooms I had, so I rented rooms in O'Connell Street. I increased my customers and enlarged my staff continually, and was in a fair way to having one of the best dress warerooms in Limerick when I gave it up in 1901.

Uncle John was released from prison at 12 noon, on 21 August 1896, on ticket-of-leave. He had been in prison since April 1884. He was released following a hunger-strike which he had begun when he had given up all hope of release, but he had given no hint to his fellow-prisoners of what he had decided to do. Fearing that if the prison authorities knew of his intention they would find some way of circumventing him, he started by reducing the amount of food he consumed every day, until one day he fell in the prison yard during exercise, from weakness. Tom Clarke was right behind him and stooped to lift him. 'My God, John,' he whispered, 'what is wrong?' Uncle John answered, 'It is release one way or the other, Tom.'

The warder ordered Tom and another prisoner to carry him to the hospital. On the way Tom tried to reason with him, and begged him not to go on with it, but it was no use; Uncle John had made up his mind that his imprisonment was going to end. Tom was in a terrible state; he feared the prison authorities would let his friend die, and he would never see him again.

In the hospital, Uncle John refused all food. Every kind of tempting food was left beside his bed, but he would have none of it. Then they started forcibly feeding him, but that was no use either. He defeated them. One day the doctor said to him, 'Give this up, Daly, and you will be released.' He answered, 'I'll believe that when I see the signed order for my release.' A few days later, according to Uncle John, the doctor brought the signed order for his release for him to see. He then gave up the hunger-strike, but was too weak to be released for some time. He had to be fed and nursed for several weeks before he could walk, and as soon as he could walk he was released.

The family knew nothing of what was going on behind the prison walls, but were notified that he would be released on a certain day. Uncle James went over to England and met him at the prison gate, but found him so weak that he decided he was not fit for the welcome being prepared for him, and took him to France for a short while. On his arrival in Dublin, he got a very good reception, but on his arrival in Limerick the people nearly went mad. Tar barrels burned and illuminations blazed everywhere, and the celebrations were carried on far into the night.

It took him some time to recover from the effects of the hunger-strike. When he was well enough, the question arose of how he was going to live. He would not live indefinitely on Uncle James. Big changes had taken place in the world since he had gone to prison, enough to bewilder him, and for a time he could not think what to do. He went on a lecture tour in England for the Amnesty Association, with Miss Maud Gonne, and this gave him the idea of going to the USA on a lecture tour to earn sufficient money to re-start life. He got in touch with his old friend and comrade John Devoy, who undertook to organise the tour for him.[10]

He left Ireland in October 1897, and was met by Devoy and other friends in New York. The tour was a great success. As a Fenian organiser he had travelled all over Ireland and knew people in every county. Fenians were everywhere in the USA, and they flocked to his lectures; they were pay-at-the-door, not collections. At this time Clan na Gael was disrupted by a split in which Uncle John had had no part, so both sides went to his lectures, and he utilised the tour to promote unity amongst the various sections, emphasising that the best way to celebrate the coming 1798 centenary was to unite by 1898. John Devoy worked very hard to make the tour a success, and accompanied him to many of the lectures. Uncle John was not long back home in Ireland when he got the news that his aim had been achieved; Clan na Gael had become united.

On returning to Ireland, he landed at Cobh on 14 May 1898, leaving for Limerick the following day. At St Patrick's Well railway station he was met by a group of the 1798 Centenary Committee, who had a carriage waiting to drive him to Limerick. At the entrance to the city he was met by a procession with bands and torchlight, and escorted through the city to Bank Place. Here he delivered an address from the window of the Trades Council rooms, to a wildly enthusiastic audience.

Soon after his return, he decided to start up a bakery for a living. He had no knowledge of the business, but induced an old friend, a foreman baker named James Prendergast, to come to him as foreman. He started the bakery in 26 William Street, and with the willing and loyal help and cooperation of my sisters he made a great success of it. A sensation was caused by his name appearing over the shop and on the vans in Gaelic. A ballad extolling the excellence of John Daly's bread was written by an old ballad-singer who sang it up and down William Street, the favourite street for ballad-singers at that time.

When the bakery was established, Uncle John tried to induce me to give up the dressmaking business and go into the bakery. I refused, for I was reluctant to give up my independence, and in the bakery I would be under the control of two older sisters. Furthermore, I was making a lot more money than the bakery could pay me, and I felt I had worked too hard to establish my business to give it up. Uncle John was very angry with me.

About this time, he applied for membership in the Shannon Rowing Club, of which Uncle James was a member; throughout the summer we spent a good deal of time on the river, as most Limerick people did then. To our surprise, he was blackballed. When he let it be known publicly there was great indignation in Limerick over it. This resulted in a subscription list being opened, to which no-one was allowed to subscribe more than one shilling, the object of which was to buy a boat and present it to Uncle John. The money was subscribed in a week or two, and the boat was built in Limerick and presented to Uncle John. A huge crowd turned out to see the presentation, which took place on the riverside in front of Cleeve's factory.

During all this time, Uncle John never forgot for one moment his fellow-prisoner, Tom Clarke. He talked about him continually, at home and elsewhere, and spoke about him in every speech or lecture he delivered. He fretted all the time about him, and worked in every possible way to bring about his release. He did one thing which his soul abhorred, but the Amnesty Association advised him to do it because if he did not, he might be keeping the remaining prisoners longer in prison. As a ticket-of-leave man, he had to report to the police once a month in person; this he could not bring himself to do, but when leaving the city he notified them by letter where he was going. This was as far as he would go, and he ceased doing that when Tom was released.

Listening to all Uncle John's stories of his wonderful prison comrade, Tom Clarke, we had formed a picture of a noble, courageous, unselfish character, one who showed unwonted sweetness and restraint under the most terrible provocation during his imprisonment, and who had become dearer to Uncle John than a brother. The joy of his own release had been dimmed by the fact of his comrade being left to endure his sufferings alone. I mean by this that, although there were still other Irish political prisoners in that prison, they did not take the risk of punishment by endeavouring to communicate with each other, or with Tom Clarke. Tom, Uncle John and James Egan had taken these risks, despite punishment, all through their imprisonment, so when Egan and Uncle John were released, Tom was virtually alone.

Uncle John formed what I think was the first Labour Party in Ireland, and they contested the local elections for Limerick Corporation. They were elected the largest party in the Council, and Uncle John polled the highest number of votes in the city, making him senior Alderman, with a nine-year term of office. The Corporation elected him Mayor of Limerick for 1899, 1890 and 1891, but he would not go forward again after that, as he was beginning to feel the strain.

One of his first acts as Mayor was to order that the British Royal Arms be removed from the front wall of the Town Hall. It caused quite a sensation. The police were in a quandary; the Mayor was then Chief Magistrate of the city, and if they interfered with his orders they might get into trouble; if they did not, they might get into trouble too. The Royal Arms came down. Uncle John never acted as Chief Magistrate.

2
Early Married Life

1898-1911

Meets Tom Clarke – courtship and marriage – they emigrate to USA – they return to Dublin – open tobacconist shops

I AM NOT NORMALLY A BELIEVER IN DREAMS, but one night early in 1898 I had a dream so vivid that it has remained clearly in my memory. I dreamt that it was Good Friday, and that I had gone to the Jesuit church in the Crescent, Limerick, to attend the three hours' agony service. Except for the candles on the altar, the church was in complete darkness. I went up the centre aisle and turned to the right. I stumbled over a chair, but continued going until I reached the extreme right, where I went into a seat and knelt down.

I was not long kneeling when the church door opened, letting in a ray of sunshine straight up the centre aisle. Someone came in and walked up the centre aisle; turning to the right, he stumbled over a chair as I had done, came over to where I was kneeling and knelt down beside me. It was a man I had never seen before, yet he leaned towards me and said, 'Ah, I knew I would find you. You thought to escape me.' There the dream ended. I thought I had forgotten all about it, but when I met Tom Clarke my dream came vividly before me. Apart from the colour of his hair, he was the man in my dream, yet I had never seen a picture or photograph of him.

Tom Clarke was released from Portland Prison in October, 1898, at the age of forty, having served fifteen years. He was met at the prison gate by his brother, Alfred, and some old friends who lived in London. Little notice was otherwise taken of his release; Uncle John had not known of it in time to meet him.[1] Limerick was in fact the only place that showed any interest in his release, or appreciation of what he had suffered for his country, and Limerick Corporation voted him the Freedom of the City.

He was to receive this honour on 2 March 1899, and he came to stay with us. It was my first time meeting him, and I was keenly disappointed. His appearance gave no indication of the kingly, heroic qualities which Uncle John had told us about; there was none of the conquering hero which I had visioned. He was emaciated and stooped from the long imprisonment and hardship. In his prison cell he had had for a table a tree-stump, fastened to the ground, and for a chair another, smaller, stump, also fastened to the ground at such a distance from the table that it was hard to reach; for a time, he found difficulty in sitting at an ordinary table.

He stayed with us for a few weeks. As I came to know him, his appearance receded into the background, and the man Uncle John had portrayed was revealed. By the time he left Limerick, to join his mother and sister in Kilmainham, we had become intimate enough to agree to correspond with each other.

In the summer of 1899 Uncle John invited Tom to come and

spend a month with us in Kilkee, Co Clare, where he had taken a lodge (he wanted him with him all the time, he loved him so) and Tom and I hailed this as a golden opportunity to meet. We became engaged to be married during the first week he was with us, and received Uncle John's blessing but not my mother's or my aunt's. They were very much opposed to the engagement, though neither of them had anything against him as a man. What they objected to was for me, whom my aunt called 'the flower of the flock', to marry a man without social or financial position. Tom had no means of livelihood at the time, and his prospects of getting one in Ireland were not very encouraging. My mother pleaded with me to give up the idea, saying that when poverty comes in the door, love flies out the window, that I did not know what poverty meant, that she would save me from it. I was deaf to all her entreaties; my decision was made.

My mother still hoped to change my mind, and placed every obstacle she could think of in the way to prevent Tom and I being together. We had to use the utmost ingenuity to get a few moments to ourselves. We woke early in the morning, before any of the family was awake, and walked to Look-Out Cliff to see the sun rise. At least, that was the reason we gave, though some mornings it was raining and there was no sun to see; still, when there was, it was well worth seeing. We had to steal out in our stockings, for if any of my sisters heard they would want to come too (and sometimes did, to our disgust), but the joy of those rambles over the cliffs remains a beautiful memory lighting the way for me still.

There were sixteen of us in the lodge, and some evenings after tea the whole family would start for a walk to the cliffs. My mother and aunt would walk at each side of me, thinking by guarding me this way they would prevent Tom and me going off together. It didn't work; usually before the cliffs were reached night would have fallen, and under cover of the darkness I would slip my guards and disappear with Tom. We took care not to be found until near the end of the journey, when we would rejoin the others and return home with them. At the end of the month he returned to Dublin.

[Kathleen and Tom continued their correspondence, but this time on a first-name basis: 'Dear Tom, ... It does seem very strange to be addressing you this way. If you felt the week long, I thought it would never end. Somehow Kilkee seemed to undergo a change...My reputation for early rising is gone completely.']

Tom planned to go to the USA at the end of the year to make a home for us, but before he left a vacancy occurred as clerk of the Rathdown Union. The Amnesty Association had him proposed for it, because they did not want him to leave Ireland. They got most of the members to promise to vote for him, but when it came to a vote he was defeated. His disappointment was very keen; so was mine. There was nothing for it now but to emigrate from the land he loved and had suffered so much for.

[Tom wanted to acquire a little capital to start in business on his own, so he wrote to John Devoy about arranging a lecture tour in the United States. However, the proposal was turned down, and he wrote to Kathleen in despair, offering to release her from the engagement: 'I built everything upon that tour – hopes, plans, and everything for me...I built my hopes of having a home on that.' She replied: 'Things may look black at present, but if they looked as black again I cannot take back what I gave. As it is I am very glad it happened the time it did – for if you had not high hopes you would not, I know, speak to me. You'd go off to America leaving me the humiliating thought I had given my love unasked, unsought – so you see there is a bright side to everything if we could only see it.'

[They hoped to marry in the near future. Kathleen wrote to him (23.1.1900): 'I sometimes get a terribly sad feeling over me when I'm with them all in the diningroom, when I think of how soon I may be wishing them all good-bye. None of them, as far as I know, have any idea of it but Agnes...Yet it is surprising how very fast the sadness passes away when I think of who I'll be parting with them for.' However, her mother was still opposed to the marriage: 'Mama does not like the idea of my going at all... It seems to puzzle her...how I could be willing to leave everyone I ever knew for what she calls almost a stranger. I told her you were no stranger to me...']

By August 1900, Tom was in New York, working as a pattern-maker at the Cameron Pump Works, a trade he had learned in prison. Another position became vacant in Dublin, that of Superintendent of the Abattoirs under Dublin Corporation. The Amnesty Association again got busy, and approached the Aldermen and Councillors to secure the position for Tom. The majority of the members promised to vote for him. The Association cabled to Tom: 'Abattoir, presence wanted Dublin, ten days, September 13th 1900.' To this Tom replied: 'Unless absolutely certain, I have a job here, I do not want to resign.' A subsequent cable said: 'Resign, presence necessary, twenty-eighth, McGinn.' Well, he did resign as urged and came back, delighted and charmed at the possibility of being able to marry and settle in his own land. Alas for his hopes! At the meeting held to fill the position the Council decided on ballot voting, and he was defeated. Back he had to go to the USA, where his job was being held for him.

Tom was very eager that we should be married, and go back together, but Uncle John, now Mayor of Limerick, did not favour this. He gave us his reasons, and though they were very good I felt a bit rebellious. However, he had been so good taking my father's place towards us that I could not go against his wishes. He told me he had accepted an invitation to be speaker at the St Patrick's Day celebration in New York in 1901, and that I could accompany him and be married in New York.

[They were parted again, and Kathleen wrote to Tom: 'I feel very miserable since you left...I was so sure of going with you that I can't get over it just yet... A few friends stopped me in the street to congratulate me. They heard I was married. I laughed at them and said I heard so myself. I suppose it was my giving up business that put about the report.' She had left her dressmaking business at the end of September, hoping that she could accompany Tom back to the States. Tom's sister Maria, who kept house for him in New York, was very surprised that he came back alone: 'Her first question was "Where's Kathleen?" and she had been getting everything ready for you....I am not going to pull long faces and say how I feel about the disappointment – Everytime I think of it, I try to console myself with the thought – "Well, it won't be long till she's here, anyway"...']

However, before March 1901 I became involved in a street accident case, in which I was the principal witness, and could not go with Uncle John. The injured lady was the wife of James F Egan, now Sword-Bearer to Dublin Corporation, and Mr and Mrs Egan promised to accompany me to New York when the case was finished and take Uncle John's place at my wedding.

[The legal action (taken against *The Freeman's Journal*, owner of the van) seemed to drag on forever, and Tom and Kathleen were very frustrated by the endless delays. Extracts from her letters give the course of events:

'24.12.1900...Mrs Egan is at home over a week, but had to bring a trained nurse with her. *The Freeman's Journal* offered them £1050 and pay all expenses, but Mr Egan wouldn't accept it...The trial is coming off on the 12th January.'

'15.1.01...I was terribly nervous when I came out of the witness box. I went to the waiting room where Mrs Egan was and the first thing I did was roar crying. I couldn't help it. O'Shaughnessy, who examined me, badgered me so much.'

'29.1.01...*The Freeman's Journal* have threatened to have the Egans' case tried over again.'

'9.2.01...to arrive before Shrove Tuesday I should have started to-day. You can't be married here during Lent except on St Patrick's Day. So it is either to go in time for Patrick's Day or wait until after Easter...[I'm] having them all laughing at me for being what they call in such a hurry. I can't very well blame them for that though they don't understand, I suppose. I'd do the same if the case was anyone else's.'

'6.3.01....if there is a new trial granted it may not come off until next September. The very thought of it sets me crazy...'

'5.5.01...*The Freeman's Journal* people were refused a new trial last Tuesday. I could hardly believe it when I heard it. I began fixing everything up and looking up the dates the boats were leaving...']

The Egans and I sailed for New York in July, 1901. Though I have crossed the Atlantic many times since, I have never experienced anything like that trip. Fierce gales raged all the way, and I was ill enough at times to wish the boat would go down. On our arrival in the bay at New York, we could not go in owing to fog, and had to anchor outside all night. Other ships were in the same plight, so there was little rest with the foghorns and ships answering each other. Morning brought sunshine, and I started to forget all the miseries of the journey.

Tom and his sister Maria were on the landing-stage to meet us, and we travelled on the L-Train to the Bronx, where they had a lovely apartment. We had to change trains at 129th Street, and in the confusion and excitement over the strange way of travelling I forgot my handbag, and left it on the seat of the train. It held all the money I possessed, quite a large sum, and though it was reported immediately I never recovered it. I thought the L-Train was wonderful; I had never imagined anything like it.

Mr Egan left us at 42nd Street to meet some friends in the Vanderbilt Hotel. He undertook to get my luggage delivered to the flat, and said he would join us later. Mrs Egan and I waited all evening in the flat, but neither Mr Egan nor my luggage turned up. What was I going to do? All my wedding clothes were in my trunks, and our marriage had been arranged for the following day (16 July). Tom, Mrs Egan and I stayed at the Vanderbilt Hotel for the night, and Tom arranged to call for me early in the morning, as I wanted to go to Mass and Communion. After Mass we went up to the flat, where Maria had breakfast ready for us, but no trunks had arrived.

The wedding was postponed until the evening, but still no trunks, and I decided to postpone the wedding no longer. Maria was aghast at the idea of my being married in the clothes I had landed in, as they were all black, and she said it would be very unlucky to be married in black. She offered me a loan of the clothes she had bought for the wedding, where she was to be bridesmaid; they were all white, and I accepted the loan. She was very small, and her frock barely covered my knees, at a time when frocks were worn almost touching the ground. What did clothes matter, anyhow; off I went to the church with Mrs McFadden from Boston, and her two daughters, old friends of Tom's. At the church, we were met by Major John MacBride, not long back from the Boer War, who acted as best man. Other friends at the wedding were John Devoy, his sister Mrs MacBride, Mr and Mrs James F Egan, and Michael J O'Brien, later the historiographer of the Irish American Historical Society.

Tom had planned a honeymoon in Atlantic City, but we had to abandon this owing to the loss of my luggage, which did not turn up until the end of the week. This did not worry me, because New York was as new and interesting to me as anywhere else in America, and I was too happy for trifles to annoy me. By the time my luggage did turn up, it was time for Tom to return to work; he had only had a week off.

The flat Maria had prepared for us in the Bronx was a charming one, large and airy, but to me, straight out from cool Ireland, the heat was prostrating; July is one of the hottest months in the year in New York. I found life in a flat very different from my home in Limerick; I missed the chat, the laughter, the noise, and sometimes the quarrels, of the big family. I had to learn to be very quiet, to make no noise, even the noise of walking round the flat, or the people in the flat below would be banging the ceiling for me to keep quiet. I had to buy soft slippers for moving around the flat.

Tom was away at work from 6.30am until 5.30 in the evening. He had secured the position in Cameron's through a Clan na Gael man, Maurice Allen, who was foreman there. It was a hard place to work in, as the workers were under as close surveillance as if they were in prison. If any man passed a remark to another, he might be asked by a supervisor what they had been talking about, and if the supervisor decided that what they had been talking about had no bearing on the work in hand, one or both of the men might get their dismissal on leaving work that evening. Workers were not then organised as they are now. After fifteen years of prison hardship, Tom was not fit for such work, but the pay was good and he would not give it up.

We moved from the Bronx to Greenpoint, Brooklyn, in order to be nearer his place of work. He had only to cross on the 23rd Street ferry, as Cameron's was on 23rd Street. This made his work-day shorter. He was also doing clerical work three nights a week, but this I prevailed on him to give up.

On moving to Greenpoint, Tom transferred to the Clan na Gael club there, and was elected its president. He became very active in organising its social activities on more thoroughly Irish lines; Irish language, music and dancing were put first on their programme. He published a journal under the auspices of the Celtic Club, called *The Clansman*, and it was a real propagandist Irish-Ireland publication. One article he wrote for it that I remember was on the Irish language, in which he said that a free Ireland without its language was inconceivable, and that the Gaelic League was doing invaluable work for Ireland in reviving the language, and deserved the support of every Irish man and woman.

Our first son was born in Greenpoint, Brooklyn, in 1902, and

Tom's joy over the little boy was great. The idea of having a son to follow him to carry on the fight for Ireland's freedom was almost too good to be true. At times he would say, 'God, Katty, wouldn't it be wonderful if he could grow up in a free Ireland!' He insisted on having him christened after his prison pal, John Daly. Soon after his son's birth, Tom sat for a civil service examination, for which he had been studying; as a full American citizen, he was entitled to do this. He passed the examination and we were both delighted, as we thought we were settled there for life. It was good to have a permanent position, and it would be much easier work. However, when he was called to the job a friend in the civil service, named Fitzgerald, advised him not to take it, as if he did there might be questions asked by the authorities. If it was discovered that he had been in prison, he might be deported. I asked whether they could do that to an American citizen; I presumed that when he had applied for leave to sit for the examination, his credentials were looked into. He had had to produce his citizenship papers; if these had not been satisfactory, he would not have been permitted to sit.[2] Naturally, I was fighting for the security this position would give us, but Tom said this friend knew what he was talking about. He thought it best to take his advice, with which I did not agree; personally, I thought Mr Fitzgerald was no friend.

When the baby was about eight months old, we got a rather bad knock out. Maurice Allen, the foreman at the Cameron Pump Works, had a row with the manager and was dismissed with one week's notice, having worked for them for thirty-five years. The manager then dismissed all the Irishmen who had been taken on by Allen, including Tom. It was something we had never expected. I had a little money saved, and with it we started an ice-cream and candy store; Tom got busy looking for a job.

Through a man named Billy Crossin, of Philadelphia, and another man named Teevins, of Boston, both high up in Clan na Gael, and through John Devoy, Tom was appointed to start the work of organising a weekly newspaper which the Clan had been thinking about for some time. It was a whole-time job, and took some months' hard work. When it was ready to start John Devoy was appointed Editor, and Tom General Manager. The paper was to be called the *Gaelic American*, and was to be devoted entirely to Ireland's interests. It was a work that was a real joy to Tom, and he put his heart and soul into it, as did John Devoy.

In my home in Limerick, John Devoy's name was revered. He and Uncle John had been old comrades in the Fenian organisation. When I met him first in New York I thought he was rather gruff and unsociable, but later I found I was wrong. I came to the conclusion, when I knew him better, that his manner was only a pose to cover intense shyness. In private, I found him sociable, simple and kind; he used to play 'bear' with his little niece, Eileen Devoy, when she was on a visit to him from Ireland. He was a man one had to know to like. His lifelong and unselfish devotion to Ireland endeared him to all the Irish in the USA who loved Ireland.

About 1902, England endeavoured to form an alliance with the USA, to be called an Anglo-American Alliance. With the help of the Secretary of State, a man named Hay, England's friends in Washington felt sure of success. Secretary Hay, it was said, had spent many years of his life, and a good deal of money, to secure this alliance. Clan na Gael decided to defeat it. John Devoy called for the support of his countrymen, and got it. All the Irish societies were brought together under the title United Irish American Societies, and Tom was Corresponding Secretary. He organised the Brooklyn Section, and co-operated with the Manhattan Central Council. John Devoy travelled all over the country organising opposition to the proposed alliance; he spoke at meetings every night, and travelled by day from town to town and city to city. He was not a young man then, but he did not spare himself. He had his reward, the only one he wanted; the alliance was defeated. One blow had been struck by the emigrant Irish against their country's enemy.

Again, in 1905, another attempt was made to bring about some kind of alliance between England and the USA, called an Anglo-American Peace Treaty. This treaty was supposed to operate only in peace-time, but Clan na Gael looked on it as another endeavour on England's part to get the thin edge of the wedge towards an alliance which would back her in war. Clan na Gael again stepped in, and the old Manhattan Central Committee leaped into action.

The German-American societies approached the committee, and asked to be allowed to co-operate. They offered to put themselves completely under the direction of the Irish-American societies who were organising the campaign against this proposed treaty, and their offer was accepted. The Irish-German combination worked well, and England's aims were again defeated; the proposed treaty was rejected.

The *Gaelic American* was well established by then, and John Devoy again travelled all over the States, organising, addressing meetings by night and travelling by day, writing articles for the paper while travelling. At the time, Clan na Gael were considered the best-organised force in the States, and politicians had to take heed of what they wanted.

When Tom was established in the *Gaelic American*, we sold our ice-cream and candy store and moved to 99th Street. John Devoy and his sister lived in the same street, and many other friends lived near, amongst them the American-born Irishman Daniel Cohalan, later Judge Cohalan. He was one of the few American Irishmen who went up the ladder of fame and fortune, and still remained true in word and deed to the cause of Ireland's freedom. His time and money was always at the disposal of that cause. He truly loved Ireland.

While we were living in 99th Street, I had a very serious illness. Tom's sister Maria came from her home every day to nurse me, and remained until Tom came home at night. One night he was late, and Maria had to leave before he arrived. He seemed very upset when he found Maria was gone. I sensed something was wrong, and asked him what it was. He tried to put me off, but I insisted on knowing. Very reluctantly, he told me that he had been responsible, with others, for organising a protest against a play called *McFadden's Row of Flats*, which was defaming the Irish. The protest, in which he was to participate, was to be made that night. He had counted on Maria being able to stay with me while he was away; I was so ill he did not like leaving me alone. We had a long argument over it. I said I would be all right for the few hours he would be away; if he did not go I would get worse with the worry of it, the worry of knowing his comrades would think he had let them down. They intended using rotten eggs and tomatoes in their protest, and were likely to be arrested. He yielded to my urging, but went in a very disturbed frame of mind, not knowing how he would find me on his return, and not even being sure of returning that night. He did return, though several of his comrades were arrested. When they were brought into court next morning, they were dismissed with a caution. Their protest was effective; the play was withdrawn.

As a member of Clan na Gael, Tom joined the military section called the Irish Volunteers, and became regimental adjutant. This body went regularly into the country for rifle practice. Sometimes baby Daly and I accompanied Tom on these jaunts, as a day in the country was a joy to me. I was not having good health in New York, so we decided to move to Brooklyn. We rented a flat at the end of Fulton Street L-Train line, which was almost country. It was while we were there that Tom started the Brooklyn Gaelic Society, with two Irish-American boys named Bennett. They rented a large room in a big building at the corner of Fulton Street and Red Hook Lane. The object of the society was the same as that of the Gaelic League in Ireland, the study of Irish language, history, music, games and dances. They held classes, lectures, debates and social evenings, meeting every Sunday night from eight to eleven. These meetings were Irish in every way and most enjoyable; I never missed one if I could help it, even though I had to take baby Daly with me. The meetings started with classes for the language, followed by a short talk or recitation, then dancing. The two Bennett boys were the most enthusiastic young men I have ever met; it was from their mother, a widow, that they had imbibed their ardent love for Ireland, a country they had never seen.

My attendance at these meetings came to an end when my little son Daly got diphtheria in 1905. We were quarantined for six weeks, as I would not let him go to the hospital, and Tom and I nursed him through it. The doctor had given us very little hope of his recovery, but he pulled through, though he was only a wreck of what he had been. He had been a fine, healthy child, full of life, fun and mischief. When he was well enough to travel, he and I came to Ireland for a few months; I found it hard to leave Tom but he insisted on our going, saying we needed the change. Indeed, he needed it too, but funds would not run to it.

My mother was wild to see her first grandchild, my sisters their first nephew, and my uncle to see the son of his old prison pal. Uncle John and my sister Madge were at Cobh to meet us and take us back to Limerick, where we stayed three months. During that time my uncle seemed to live for Daly. Dare anyone say a word to him! He would deny him nothing, a condition of affairs the lad took full advantage of. Our health improved rapidly at home, and when we left for New York we were both in good health.

Six months later, I was again in poor health, and the doctor advised country air and country life for me. On hearing this, Uncle John sent us money to buy a small farm, and we bought a small market garden farm, Manor Culverton, in Manorville, Long Island. Tom resigned his position on the *Gaelic American* and we started off gaily on our farming career.

We had not much knowledge of growing things for market, but we trusted to luck and hoped for the best. Luck was with us, for we had the first cauliflowers of the season from Long Island into the New York market, and got top price for them. We were equally successful with other crops. The work was hard, but we enjoyed every bit of it. I certainly would have been content to stay there forever; I loved the land and growing things and the joy of being together all the time.

We had a horse, a big rawboned animal, a cow, a pig and a car called a buggy. We needed eggs, so I undertook to rear fowl; about this I knew nothing, but found it very interesting. I discovered that hens have character; there were stupid hens, clever hens, flighty hens and reliable ones. One flighty hen wanted to hatch, but I did not want her to; I thought she was too flighty to make a success of it. We had a stand-up fight. I gave in, and put her in a hatching-house with thirteen eggs; it was a small thing on wheels, big enough for one hen, and we had bought a number of them with the farm. All went well for a week, then one day when I opened the door to put in food and water she flew out of the house with a loud squawk and away. She had had enough of it, she said; she was not coming back. I went after her, and round and round the farm we went on this hot July day; I was getting exhausted, and mad enough to wring her neck if I caught her. She finally ran under a toolhouse and out I could not get her.

I went into the house to sit down and think out what I could do. I hated the idea of her besting me, and the eggs being spoiled, and did not know whether to laugh or cry. Then I remembered reading about incubators and how they worked, and decided on an experiment. I went and sprinkled the eggs with warm water, turned them, and as they had already been exposed to the air for some time, I covered them with a down pillow. I repeated this for three days, and on the fourth day the hen came out from under the toolshed. She was weak from hunger, and allowed me to catch her. I fed her, and that night put her in with the eggs but not on them. She backed into a corner, so I uncovered the eggs and left a lantern shining on them. Peeping through the window next morning, not knowing what I would see there, I saw her sitting on the eggs and quite settled down. She remained to bring the whole clutch of thirteen eggs out, so my experiment succeeded. I was thrilled.

There were small snakes on the farm, called garter snakes, which we did not mind, but there were also large ones in a bit of swampy, uncultivated land which we did not go near. One day, I told Daly to go and tell his Daddy dinner was ready. Just as he got near Tom a large snake reared itself up between them, ready to strike. His Daddy shouted to Daly to run back home, and he proceeded to kill the snake with a spade he had. It took some time, and when it was dead he measured it and found it was six feet long. He was so shaken with horror at what might have happened to Daly that he did not leave it until he had it cut into little bits.

The farm next to ours was what was called a cordwood farm, and there were always large stacks of cut wood drying there. A train ran past both farms, and during a long spell of dry hot weather a spark from the train set fire to some of the cordwood. In a short while it was an inferno, and we were right in the midst of a forest fire, which is a most terrifying thing. The roar of it is worse than the angriest sea. When one occurred, at that time in the USA, every man in the district was bound by law to go and fight it. The way it was done in Long Island was this; a trench was dug a distance from the oncoming fire, across its track. The side of the trench nearest the oncoming fire was set on fire, so that when the forest fire reached the spot there was a clear space on which there was nothing to burn. When it reached that space it was likely to die out, unless there was a wind behind it that hurled it along to the next burnable space. When that happened there was another trench dug, and the same thing repeated, until the fire died out for want of something to burn.

As our farm was all cultivated the fire passed us by, except for one piece of swampy land, the big snakes' home; the fire caught that because it was dried up from the long drought. It was amazing and interesting to see the big snakes racing before the fire. I think the fire overtook them. Though the fire passed our farm, there was a risk of a spark falling on the house or outbuildings, which were all of wood, so

I had to stand guard with pails of water to throw on any spark. I also had to guard two small children, my son and Maria's child, Teddy Fleming. The men were all away at the fire; now and then they would come to the house for something to eat and drink, black as sweeps with smoke. I spent a very anxious time. The deafening roar of the fire and the huge clouds of smoke made me so nervous, I was sure we were all going to be burned. If the wind changed and blew fire and sparks our way, the house and all the buildings might all be burned, leaving us homeless. I still think of it with horror.

Some of the well-informed American journals began to talk of the inevitability of war between England and Germany for commercial supremacy. Germany was beating England out of many of the world markets, especially in some of the South American markets. It was suggested that war would occur within ten years. I could see that this talk of England being engaged in war in the near future was having an unsettling effect on Tom. Night after night, sitting down when work was done, he would revert to it, and the tragedy it would be if Ireland failed to avail herself of such an opportunity to make a bid for freedom. If she failed to do so, it would break the tradition of generations, and might end in Ireland becoming resigned to her fate as part of the British Empire. The thought of such a thing happening was to him intolerable; to avert that fate from the country he loved he was ready to sacrifice everything, self, wife, child.

By 1907, Tom was hinting that he would like to go back to Ireland and get things moving, but I would have none of it. I said, 'You have done as much as any country could expect of a man, and small thanks or appreciation you received.' 'Well,' he said, 'we don't do things for thanks or appreciation, but because they are right to do.' I replied, 'You must remember that though in the USA you are an

American citizen, if you go back to Ireland you will be a ticket-of-leave man, and the British could put you back to prison without trial if they found you getting busy to disturb the peace, as they would put it, and you are not of sufficient importance for America to interfere. I don't want to lose you. I am very happy where I am.' He dropped the subject that night.

Another night he started again, but I was still in the same frame of mind. I asked him how we would live if we went back to Ireland; he had not been able to get a living when he was there before. He was ready for that; he said his sister Hanna, who was in the tobacco and newspaper business in Dublin, would help him to make a start in business in that line. With the money we made on the farm and the sale of our goods we could make a start, and Uncle John was prepared to help us. Still I would not agree, and so we argued for many nights.

However, he moved me so much one night that I had to respond. 'Well,' I said, 'how about going back?' He became very excited and said, 'Katty, do you mean that? I want to go, but feared I would never get you to agree.' I told him that I did not want to go; I was very happy where I was, and thought that Ireland had treated him shamefully, but if it would make him happier to go back I would reluctantly consent. His happiness came first with me. I loved the thought of going home, but my fears as to what would happen to him outweighed that. I knew what going back to that prison hell would mean for him and for me. Of course, if we were going back to settle down to a nice peaceful life, I would have no fears; life would then be heaven for me.

Once he got my consent he made haste to arrange for the sale of our things and our journey home, fearing I might change my mind. When everything was sold, we went to stay with Tom's sister Maria, in New York, for the few days before embarking. Tom went to John Devoy and told him we were returning to Ireland, and the reason for it. There was not a more surprised man in the USA than Devoy. He promised him all the help in his power, a promise he kept faithfully. He also gave him credentials to introduce him to the IRB (Irish Republican Brotherhood) in Ireland, as Tom intended to start his campaign to prepare Ireland to take advantage of the coming war between England and Germany, and strike a blow for freedom, through the IRB.

We arrived in Ireland towards the end of November, 1907. My uncle and sister Madge were at Cobh to meet us, and with them we went down to Limerick. In a few days, when the excitement of our arrival was over, we sat down to think out ways of making a living. After a lot of proposals from the family, we decided to act on the suggestion of Tom's sister Hanna, and start a tobacconist and newspaper shop in Dublin. Uncle John would have liked to keep us in Limerick, but from the point of view of the work Tom intended doing, to prepare the country to take advantage of the coming war, Dublin was best suited.

[Tom left Limerick to look for a shop in Dublin, staying with Hanna and his mother at 176 Great Britain Street. Kathleen was pregnant again. He missed his wife and child very much, and wrote frequently. Kathleen wrote (18.1.08): 'Daly was in a seventh heaven of delight at getting that letter from you today. I had to sit down and read it to him...then he carried it around the house and held everybody up to tell them about papa's letter, the pig, the policeman and the funny conductor....I am getting a frightful size. I don't know where I am going to stop.' He finally found a shop in 55 Amiens Street, and wrote to her: 'I have struck what I consider the right thing

– a shop and back room; both in pretty good condition...rent free of taxes £36 a year...The location is a splendid one, in as much as there is always plenty of people passing and repassing – the crowd was as great on last Saturday night that one could hardly keep on the sidewalk.']

Before starting to fit up the shop, he took a trip to the North to see Séamus MacManus, hoping and expecting to get his help in starting a weekly or monthly newspaper, which was absolutely essential for the work he had come home to do. Séamus had been out in the USA some years previously, on a lecture tour which Tom had helped to organise for him; on leaving for Ireland again, he said he had to thank Tom for the success of the tour, and that if ever he wanted help in any direction or at any time he had only to ask. But Séamus in Ireland and Séamus in New York looked at things differently; Séamus in Ireland could not see his way to giving help of any kind. Tom returned from his visit very disappointed. He spent Christmas with us in Limerick, as the shop he had taken would not be ready to open for some time.

[After Christmas he returned to Dublin, and opened the shop early in February: 'Katty, the shop outside and inside is a perfect gem...Hanna went down last night to look at it, came back delighted – but was very emphatic in her disapproval of the big gold 55 on the window. ...Nobody did it in Dublin and everybody was talking about it...I told her that the points she was making...were the very points I was aiming at... I enclose copy of business card.']

Our second son, Tom, was born on 3 March 1908. When Tom heard the news he was overjoyed, but was unable to leave the shop to see him. Another son, he said, for a free Ireland.

[Tom wrote: 'I am a new man...this place is going to be a success –
At last luck seems to be setting in my direction – mind you, I have
had a few chunks of good luck in my day & the best share of it I ever
got was when I got Katty Daly...If you carry out your original idea
about the name – calling the baby after his dad – I will be delighted.'
The business seemed to do well: 'It's now 6 o'clock and I have taken
in just over £1. I may be able to do as good as last Saturday, which was
£2.3.0...You'd laugh if you saw me this eve. getting ready for my tea
and trying to eat it – when I took off the lid to rinse out the pot – a
customer – served him – went back to my teapot – put half the water
in – another customer – served him – went back to my teapot, just
got to it – another customer and so on. All the while I was eating –
but I do love the interruptions – several times this evg. I have had 1/2
doz. people at one time in the shop – it looks well.'

[Kathleen wanted to rejoin Tom as soon as possible, but her
family were reluctant to let her leave: 'Uncle John was speaking to
Madge about me going up. He said we could live in the back room if I
left the baby here but that if I had him, then I would make a huck-
ster's shop of the place...he and all of them seem to think that leaving
the baby for a year or a halfyear would cost me as little thought as it
would them. It irritates one. They put it down to pigheadedness
when I don't agree with them about the thing.']

In July I went with my son Daly to Dublin, leaving baby Tom in
Limerick, with the intention of getting a home together (up to then
Tom had been living in the room in the back of the shop). I was
about a month in Dublin, and had not yet procured a house, when
news came that my beloved sister Annie was dead. This was a great
shock, as when I had left Limerick she had seemed in perfect health.

We closed the shop, and went down to Limerick for the funeral. When we returned to Dublin I started house-hunting again, but before I succeeded Tom went down with the same thing my sister had died from, typhoid fever.

I shall never forget the kindness of the nuns in the Mater Hospital to him and to myself. They left nothing undone that could be done for him, and arranged for me to visit him any hour I could get there. His illness left me in an awful predicament, as I was quite unfamiliar with the business. My brother, Edward, came from Limerick to help me, though he knew as little as I did, and the customers and the stock agents helped us. Ned was a most delightful companion, cheerful and full of quiet fun. He would not let me be downhearted, took care of Daly and in many other ways helped me. I don't know how I would have gone through that period without him. All the time I was afraid Tom would die like my sister. When he had sufficiently recovered to leave the hospital he went to Limerick, and from there Uncle John took him to Crosshaven, Co Cork. Madge went with them, and they stayed there a month. Tom came back completely recovered.

[Early in 1909, Tom and Kathleen bought another shop, 75A Parnell Street, and in 1910 rented a shop with house overhead at 77 Amiens Street, leaving 55 Amiens Street.]

3
Laying the Foundations

1911-1915

*Irish Freedom newspaper – Pádraig Pearse – Seán
MacDermott – the IRB – the Irish Volunteers – Howth
gun-running – Cumann na mBan – Sinn Féin –
MacDermott imprisoned – O'Donovan Rossa funeral*

Though very preoccupied with the struggle to make a living, Tom
never lost sight of the purpose for which he had returned to Ireland.
He had been in touch with the Republicans, or as they were then
called Separatists, in the North. One of them was Bulmer Hobson,
with whom he had been in correspondence while in New York; he
had sent him an invitation to address a Clan na Gael Convention. He
seemed to vision Hobson as another John Mitchel.

Through Hobson he got to know Ernest Blythe, Denis
McCullough and Seán McDermott; Dr Pat McCartan and Diarmuid Lynch he had known in New York. All these gathered round
him, and some came to live in Dublin. P S O'Hegarty was also in
touch with him at a very early stage.

Seán MacDermott was organiser for Arthur Griffith's Sinn Féin when Tom met him first, and when Sinn Féin decided to contest a parliamentary election in North Leitrim, Seán was appointed local organiser. The candidate was C J Dolan. Seán worked very hard to get him elected, but did not succeed. When he returned to Dublin, he came to the shop to see Tom and tell him all about the election. He was full of fun and laughter, relating all the tactics they had resorted to to win the election. When he had finished Tom turned to him and said, in a very severe tone, 'Seán, I would rather lose an election than resort to tricks to win it. Our cause is too sacred to be sullied with electioneering tricks. No matter who else may indulge in them, we should not, neither should we participate in an election to the British Parliament.' Opening his big beautiful eyes and looking startled, Seán said, 'Tom, I never looked at it that way before. I see now you are right.' He held out his hand to Tom, saying, 'There's my hand on it.' They shook hands. 'I promise you never to take part in such proceedings again.' He kept his word, and later resigned his position as organiser for Sinn Féin.

Seán threw in his lot with the IRB, and was appointed organiser. He was a wonderful organiser, full of charm and magnetism, and very handsome. He never spared himself, he was here and there, in Dublin, out of it, all over the country. He was a very lovable character, and became Tom's loyal and loved comrade. He did all his organising under Tom's guidance; Tom being older and more experienced, he trusted him completely. Indeed, they trusted each other completely.

From the time Tom arrived back in Ireland, he was keenly aware of the necessity of a weekly or monthly paper, through which the young people would be educated nationally and their minds turned in the right direction, ie to encourage them to strike a blow for freedom when the inevitable war between Germany and England was being fought. Having failed to get the help he had expected from Séamus MacManus, he sought it elsewhere.

By 1910, he had succeeded in getting sufficient funds to make a start. The subscribers were Dr Pat McCartan and Uncle John. Tom formed a committee of IRB men to take charge; as far as I remember they were Dr McCartan, Bulmer Hobson, Seán MacDermott, Ernest Blythe, Denis McCullough and Tom himself. A monthly paper was decided upon. The policy laid down for it was that it was to be Separatist, and the principles of Wolfe Tone were to be its guiding ones, a policy from which it never deviated.[1] It was to be called *Irish Freedom*. Seán MacDermott was appointed Manager, and McCartan acted as Editor for a time; they had a small office in Findlater Place. The first issue came out in October, 1910.

Tom had very little time to give to the working of the journal, as we were running two shops at the time, but by common consent he had a veto on everything that went into it. Usually there was a meeting once a month, when selections were made from the many contributors, all free. Later they took an office at 12 D'Olier Street, and Bulmer Hobson took over the Editorship. It was a good team, and they worked in the greatest harmony until the start of the Irish Volunteers, when Bulmer Hobson took a line of his own.

From the start of *Irish Freedom*, the work towards the Rising began, and those connected with it had a fair idea of the ultimate aim. Most of the work was voluntary; men turned into the office after their day's work was done to give a helping hand, particularly on publishing day, and to do the dispatch work. Seán O'Casey was one of the voluntary workers in the early days, and P S O'Hegarty contributed an article nearly every month.

Generally speaking, apathy was the order of the day nationally at that time, though under the surface there was movement, a certain discontent with things as they were, among the young people. The majority of the older people were hopeless; they were wedded to the Irish Parliamentary Party, and lived on the hope of all that that party was going to do for Ireland. If one talked to them about fighting for freedom, they would point to the failures of the various risings, and how hopeless it was to try to fight the British Empire. The only way to get anything from England was through the Irish Parliamentary Party.

Organisations such as the Gaelic League, the Gaelic Athletic Association, Sinn Féin, Inghinidhe na h-Eireann [Daughters of Eireann] and other Nationalist groups (none of them revolutionary except, perhaps, Inghinidhe na h-Eireann) served the purpose of getting the young people thinking and questioning. Into these organisations members of the IRB found their way, and being men of good character, education and ability they gained the confidence of these organisations. They got into positions of trust and authority, and used their positions to inculcate the doctrine of freedom and separation from England in those with whom they came in contact. When Douglas Hyde, Agnes O'Farrelly and a few other members of the Gaelic League discovered that the revolutionary element had penetrated its organisation, they left as a protest. They had aimed at keeping it a purely academic organisation.

In July 1911 King George of England visited Dublin, and was given a spectacular British reception. To offset this, the IRB organised a pilgrimage to the grave of Wolfe Tone, in Bodenstown churchyard. Tom had to be there, so I had to take his place in the Parnell

Street shop. After the official reception for the King was over, the soldiers and sailors who had participated in it were dismissed in Phoenix Park. Those returning to the city via the North Circular Road route were met at the corner of O'Connell and Parnell Streets with a large poster outside our front door. On it, in large black type, was: 'Damn your concessions, England, we want our country.' It was the *Irish Freedom* poster for that month, announcing the heading to an article written by P S O'Hegarty.

Some soldiers and sailors stopped to look, then others stopped to see what they were looking at. In a short time, a large crowd had collected. They seemed very angry, and were getting more angry as the numbers increased. They started using threatening language, and one of the sailors took the poster off the hook it was hanging on and threw it into the shop. I walked out of the shop with the poster board and replaced it on its hook. Then I turned to the crowd and announced that I would have anyone who touched the board again arrested. The poster remained untouched after that, but the angry demonstration continued. Tom was a welcome sight when he walked into the shop on his return from Bodenstown, though by then the demonstration was over. I had been under a great strain throughout the evening, not knowing from one minute to the next but that the angry crowd would wreck the shop.

The first time Tom met P H Pearse was through Seán MacDermott. The IRB were planning the Robert Emmet commemoration to be held on 3 March 1911, and had rented the Rotunda to hold it in. Tom and Seán were discussing who they would invite to be speaker for the occasion, and Seán suggested PH Pearse. Tom asked whether he spoke well, since he did not know him, and whether he would speak on the lines of their policy. Seán said he was a beautiful speaker: 'If you give him the lines you want, he will dress it up in beautiful language.'

It was arranged that Seán would bring Pearse to the shop and introduce him, and that Pearse could then be asked to speak, and told the lines they wanted him to take. Pearse came with Seán, the proposition was put to him and he consented. Tom, myself and our children went to the meeting; Tom was anxious to hear how Pearse would handle it. For the first few minutes, we thought it was going to be a fiasco. Pearse was apparently nervous, and seemed to have difficulty in getting out a word. Then he recovered, and gave one of the most beautiful speeches on Robert Emmet I have ever heard. The language and delivery were perfect.

1912 was a year of comparative quiet, but under the surface things were moving steadily in preparation for the blow to be struck for freedom. The IRB was marshalling all its forces to secure a position of influence in all the nationalist organisations. They were educating them along the line that force was the only thing that got anything from England, and showing them the futility of the Irish Parliamentary Party in the British House of Commons. It was not easy to wean the old supporters from the belief that the Party could get anything they wanted from England, if only those hotheads would keep quiet; any little concession was hailed as a great victory. The young had little faith in them, and were easily led to the belief that the Fenian way to get freedom was the only one – to fight for it.

In 1913, the famous tram strike occurred.[2] The police acted in a savage and brutal way to the strikers. The Citizen Army then came into existence as a defence force against the conduct of the police. Jim Larkin, leader of the Irish Transport and General Workers' Union, was arrested and imprisoned for a time. On his release he went to the

USA, and James Connolly took his place. He and Tom became great friends, and kept friends to the end.

Towards the end of 1913, Tom got Pearse co-opted on to the Supreme Council of the IRB; his reasons were that as a speaker he would be very useful to them. After being co-opted, Pearse asked Tom for credentials to John Devoy to get a lecture tour organised for his school. Tom wrote to Devoy and it was arranged that he would organise the tour for Pearse. Devoy worked very hard for it, and it was very successful, netting him £1500.

The Ulster Volunteers were then established by Carson to resist Home Rule. This gave the IRB the chance they had been hoping for, and they immediately set to work to start the Irish Volunteers.[3] If Carson could have Volunteers, so could they. The British would not suppress Carson's Volunteers; then logically they could not suppress the Irish Volunteers. There were endless meetings to organise the start. Seán MacDermott and Bulmer Hobson did most of the work; Tom dared not show his nose in that, for to do so would make the British suspicious of it, but it was all done in collaboration with Tom behind the scenes.

To make for success, the Volunteers were to be composed of all sections of the community. There was to be no bar to any man joining; the only question to be asked was, 'Do you believe in Ireland's right to freedom?' They decided to rent the Rotunda for the opening meeting, and men well-known in public life were interviewed and asked to participate. The speakers were selected from among those who had agreed to be present, and the names of those to be proposed for the Provisional Executive were decided upon. They represented as far as possible every section of the community, but no man who was known to the British authorities as a revolutionary, such as Tom, was to be proposed. It was also decided that those who were in any way identified with the revolutionary element, such as Seán MacDermott or Bulmer Hobson, were not to take any official position on the Executive.

The meeting, held on November 25th, 1913, was a huge success. The Rotunda was packed and there was a big overflow meeting which some of the speakers had to address. The young men were wild to join. Hobson chose to ignore the decision about taking official positions on the Executive, and accepted the position of Secretary. This action came as a complete surprise to Tom, who had believed that Hobson was in agreement with all their decisions. It shook the complete faith he had in Hobson. However, the thing was done, and they had to make the best of it. Seán and Tom agreed that perhaps the Secretaryship was too important a position to leave in other hands than those of a member of the IRB. Let me explain that these precautions and safeguards were with the object of not arousing British suspicions about the real object of the Irish Volunteers; they really were intended to be the open arm of the IRB.

The Irish Volunteers received an enthusiastic response. Young men of every class, creed or political opinion joined up. My brother, Ned Daly, was one of the first to join. He was living with me at the time, having left the bakery business in Limerick, which he did not like. I never saw a happier young man than he was the night he joined. He told me it was what he had always been wishing for. He joined as a private in Company B, 1st Battalion, but he was very soon Captain, and later Commandant. He became completely absorbed in the Volunteers. Every moment outside his waking hours was devoted to them, he bought every book he could on military matters, and when not out with the Volunteers he was studying these books at home. He got the reputation of being the smartest turned-out Captain in the Volunteers, and one of the best loved.[4] I was told that he was very strict with his Company, but that they were very proud of him. So was I. It never occurred to me that his work and enthusiasm would lead him before a British firing-squad. Ned had been born on the last day of February 1891, and he and Seán Heuston were about the same age; they were the two youngest of the executed men.

In April 1914, the first meeting to start Cumann na mBan was held in Wynn's Hotel, Abbey Street, Dublin.[5] Miss Agnes O'Farrelly was in the chair. Amongst those present were Mrs Wyse Power, Madame O'Rahilly, Mrs Eamonn Ceannt, Mrs John MacNeill, Mrs Kettle, Miss Lily O'Brennan, Mrs Dudley Edwards, Miss Louise Gavan Duffy, Miss Carney, from the North, another lady from the North whose name I have forgotten, and myself. The next meeting was held in a room in a house in Abbey Street, near the hotel, and it was decided to continue meeting there until more suitable premises were acquired. At one of those meetings it was decided to start branches, the first to be called the Central Branch.

Mrs Ceannt and myself were appointed to start the Central Branch, and with a right good will we set to work and had a branch going in a very short time. We rented a hall from the Gaelic League, in 25 Parnell Square, and started with first-aid classes, with doctors giving us lectures and practice. By the time the split occurred in the Volunteers [see below], our membership numbered two hundred. A small committee ran the branch, and Mrs Tuohy was President. I had been proposed for it, but withdrew in favour of Mrs Tuohy, as she was older and more experienced than I was, and a great worker. Later, I became President.

The growth of the Irish Volunteers was very rapid, and its

proportions were such as to alarm John Redmond, leader of the Irish Parliamentary Party. He made an effort to get control; he demanded that he be allowed to nominate a number of members to the Provisional Executive of the Irish Volunteers, equal to the numbers that composed that body already. This would give him control, as some of the members already on the Executive were supporters of his.

Tom, Seán MacDermott and all the IRB were opposed to this. Their opinion was that though the refusal to agree to this plan would cause a split, it would at that stage be a small affair which would not do irreparable damage. Once John Redmond had made his demand, the split was there anyway, owing to the composition of the Executive. If the demand was agreed to now, in order to avoid a split, the split was bound to come later, as his nominees would make progress impossible, and the later break would split the country from end to end. Unfortunately, what they feared happened.

Seán MacDermott told me that Bulmer Hobson used all his influence and worked very hard to get Redmond's demand agreed to. Amongst those who voted to accede to Redmond's demand were John [Eoin] MacNeill and Sir Roger Casement. Tom was deeply disturbed by Hobson's action, as he had idealised him. It was through Tom that Hobson had been invited to the USA by Clan na Gael during the time we lived there. I had warned him more than once that he was idealising the man too much, though I liked Hobson. He was very kind, and seemed to like children; when my eldest son was recovering from typhoid fever he came and read stories to him any night he was free; I was very grateful to him for it. It took Hobson's own action to destroy the complete faith and trust Tom had in him; after that he dropped all association with him.

Uncle John was staying on holiday in Sandycove, Co Dublin, at the time, and Casement and Hobson called to see him. He was very angry with them for voting for Redmond's demand, and very nearly ordered them out of the house. Their visit was very short. Casement's action in voting for the demand destroyed what little faith Tom had had in him. It was through Hobson that Casement had come into things national, and Tom knew very little about him. Naturally, he had no cause to place much confidence in him; the fact that he had been knighted by England in recognition of services rendered made Tom suspicious of him. Casement was not long enough in nationalist things in this country to prove his genuineness.[6]

John MacNeill had been selected that year by the Wolfe Tone Memorial Committee, all IRB men, to deliver the oration at the pilgrimage to Wolfe Tone's grave in Bodenstown. Tom sent word to MacNeill that he wished to see him, and when he came told him that owing to his action in voting for Redmondites, he would not be permitted to speak at Wolfe Tone's grave as had been arranged. MacNeill expressed regret, but asserted that in voting as he did, he thought he was doing what the IRB wanted. He looked on Hobson as representing them, and was guided by his actions.

It was then decided that Tom should do the speaking, a thing he disliked, for he said he was no orator. What he did say was brief. Addressing the meeting, he said that the spirit of Wolfe Tone still lived, and was moving through the length and breadth of the land today. The tramp of marching men eager to grasp the rifle was evidence of that spirit. They were there to honour the memory of Wolfe Tone. They had with them Irishmen of different religious beliefs, symbol of the union of all Irishmen for which Wolfe Tone had worked. With the new spirit abroad, they hoped there would come the realisation of their ideal. They knew what Tone's name stood for amongst Irishmen, not only in Ireland, but wherever the sons of the Gael were to be found, and today thousands of eyes were turning to this sacred spot looking for signs that Wolfe Tone's principles were still a force in this country. They were there to do honour to Tone's memory, and no-one, he was sure, came to that graveside but with feelings of reverence. The time for speaking was rapidly passing (cheers), the drilling and arming of the people of Ireland was going to count, and was going to be the determining factor as to just how their nationalist ambition was going to be fulfilled.

At the end of the meeting, cables were read from the Adjutant-General of the Irish Volunteers in America, the man who had planned the Manchester rescue: 'The Irish Volunteers of America send greetings to National and Ulster Volunteers, hope for union of both to guard Ireland one and indivisible.' Another cable was from Colonel Richard Burke, one of the revered of the old-time Fenians still with us: 'Recognise the necessity that Ireland should take what she can get. Convinced that freedom ultimately depends upon return to policy of Wolfe Tone.' A third cable was from John Devoy, the man who more than anyone else helped to smash the proposed Anglo-American alliance: 'Best wishes for meeting at the grave of Wolfe Tone, the Protestant apostle of Irish nationality. The voice from the grave forbids partition, and brands as infamous any man who consents to exclude Ulster for even one day' (*Irish Freedom*, 14 July 1914). Seán MacDermott read the cablegrams.

Now that the Irish Volunteers were launched, the next thing was to arm them. The British Government had issued a proclamation prohibiting the importation of arms, but despite that Carson had a large consignment of arms brought in to Larne, Co Antrim, for the Ulster Volunteers, and he was not interfered with. If the Ulster

Volunteers could have arms, why not the Irish Volunteers? The question was how and where to get them. The British Government would do everything in their power to prevent arms coming in to the Irish Volunteers, so they would have to be smuggled in. Arrangements were made for a landing of arms at Howth, Co Dublin, the history of which has been written and published by the participants.

The landing was to take place on Sunday, 26 July 1914. To cover the landing of the arms, the Volunteers were ordered on a route march to Howth on that Sunday. As route marches of the Volunteers were common everyday affairs, it caused no comment or excitement; only the officers knew the real object of the march. However, as the men were all armed with batons made of hard wood, which was unusual, most of them guessed that something out of the ordinary was going to happen. We were living over the shop in 77 Amiens Street at the time, and I remember watching the marchpast of the Irish Volunteers that morning, feeling very proud of them and wildly excited, knowing what they were going for. Seán MacDermott was having dinner with us that day, and he and Tom would be going to Howth after dinner to see how things were. They had engaged a cab as Seán was not able to walk far; he dragged one leg, the result of an attack of infantile paralysis.

Before dinner was over, I looked out the window and noticed that the Howth trams passing were full of British soldiers with rifles. I told Tom and Seán, and they left their dinner and rushed off. The cab was waiting for them, and they got in and started for Howth. They found that the soldiers had got off the trams at the junction of the Howth and Clontarf roads, and were stationed there. The cab passed through without interference. They were in a state of anxiety to reach the Volunteers before the British soldiers.

They met the Volunteers on their return march; they had rifles, but no ammunition. Tom and Seán told them to drop their rifles in the hedges and ditches before the British soldiers reached them, and took two of the rifles and drove back to Dublin with them. They found that the soldiers were not marching; they were apparently waiting for the Volunteers. The cab passed through them again without interference. Tom and Seán came back to the house and left the rifles there, then took a couple of rugs and went back again to the Howth road. They filled the cab with rifles, covered them with the rugs and again passed through the British soldiers without interference.

Meanwhile, the Volunteers were hiding their rifles everywhere, in hedges and ditches and behind walls. On the last journey Tom and Seán made they saw the British soldiers and the Irish Volunteers lined up facing each other at the junction of the Howth and Clontarf roads. The Volunteers now had no arms, but the British soldiers had apparently expected an armed force. Had the Volunteers had rifles, even without ammunition, it is possible the British soldiers would have fired on them, and it would have been a holocaust.

My brother, Ned, was a very young Captain then. When he arrived home, after all the rifles they could find were stored, many of them in our house, it was after two o'clock in the morning. He was very tired; the march to Howth and back was long, and then there had been the continuous search for the rifles, but he was very gay, and ready to talk for hours. I made tea for him and Tom and listened to all he had to tell. He made us laugh describing the encounter with the British soldiers. When his Company reached the Howth road junction, they found the soldiers drawn across it, waiting for them. Ned told his men he would go forward and parley with the British officer;

meanwhile, they were to pass the word along for all to clear off quietly except the front line. The ruse worked so well that when the attention of the officer who was parleying with Ned was drawn to what was happening, by one of his men, very few Volunteers were left.

On the way back to barracks those British soldiers opened fire on people along the North Quay, without reason. Three people were killed, and many injured. The soldiers probably felt they had been outwitted and wanted revenge on someone. Looking back, I have often wondered how the British seemed to know of the landing of arms at Howth, and the hour to expect them, and had the army ready to meet the Volunteers on the way in from Howth.

After the declaration of war by England on Germany, in August 1914, activity increased on all sides. From the time Redmond's nominees were put on the Provisional Executive of the Irish Volunteers, the incipient split was there, but had not spread to the rank and file. Once war was declared, an open breach could not be avoided, especially after Redmond's speech on 20 September, at Woodenbridge, Co Wicklow, at a parade of the Irish Volunteers.[7]

For those opposed to Redmond's nominees, it was only a question of selecting the most opportune time to break with them, and on the night of 24 September a statement was issued, signed by most of the original members of the Executive, that Redmond's nominees would no longer form part of the Provisional Executive of the Irish Volunteers. The following day Redmond and Asquith were to speak at a recruiting meeting to be held in the Mansion House. There was great excitement over it; many wanted to attack the meeting, but Tom and Seán MacDermott advised against it.

Cumann na mBan, like the Irish Volunteers, was composed of all shades of political and religious opinion, and all were working in the greatest harmony when the split in the Irish Volunteers occurred. A meeting of the Dublin branches was summoned by the Provisional Executive to decide what action to take on the split. The meeting was held in the Commercial Club, in Upper O'Connell Street, and it was a very stormy one. On a vote for or against the Redmond side, there was a large majority for Redmond, so now Cumann na mBan was split too. Central Branch went down from about two hundred members to about two dozen; those who stood with the Irish Volunteers had, like them, to start to build again.

The members of the Central Branch who remained true to the Irish Volunteers were Mrs Eamonn Ceannt, Miss Lily O'Brennan, Miss Sorcha MacMahon, Mrs Martin Conlon, Mrs Joseph McGuinness, Mrs Tuohy, Mrs Reddin, Miss Maura McCarron, the two Misses O'Sullivan, the two Misses Elliot and myself. There were others, but I have forgotten their names. Unfortunately, our Secretary went with the majority. I asked Miss Sorcha MacMahon to act as Secretary; she agreed, and the other members approved. A more competent Secretary no organisation ever had; we became fast friends and still remain so, a friendship founded on love, trust and admiration (she later became Mrs Thomas Rogers).

One good thing as a result of the split, however, was that now every member of Cumann na mBan and the Irish Volunteers knew what they were working for, and that they might be called upon to make sacrifices in order to bring their work to a successful conclusion. Knowing it, they worked with a will and a cheerful confidence that was amazing. In less than a year, Central Branch had nearly as many members as it had lost over the split.

The work of the Irish Volunteers and Cumann na mBan was

going along steadily all over the country when *Irish Freedom*, *Sinn Féin* and other nationalist papers ceased publication, either through being seized by the police and forbidden by the competent British military authority, as in the case of *Irish Freedom* or, as in the case of *Sinn Féin*, by the printers being threatened with the confiscation of their plant if they printed it. For a time there were few, if any, nationalist papers in circulation. Central Branch, Cumann na mBan, then stepped into the breach, and carried out an idea proposed by me, ie to have pamphlets on revolutionary characters in our history written and published, and sold for one penny each. It was a great success, and they sold in thousands. The money to start was loaned from the *Irish Freedom* funds, and repaid. The first pamphlet was on Wolfe Tone, and I asked P H Pearse to write it. He said he did not know much about him, but he would read him up and write him for us.

The Executive of Cumann na mBan were very angry at our action in getting out the pamphlets, and two of the members were appointed to call on me. They demanded that the scheme be handed over to the Executive, as they thought it altogether too ambitious an undertaking for a branch. I told them that I had no intention of handing over to them, that the branch had made a success of it and would hold on to it. I pointed out to them that when the branch had asked the Executive some time before for suggestions for work which would keep branch members busy, the Executive had told them that every branch must work out its own scheme of activity. Central Branch had done that, and was going to continue doing so. Both ladies were very angry with me, and left with rather ruffled feathers.

Central Branch also ran lectures, classes in first aid, signalling and rifle practice, lessons in cleaning and loading rifles and small arms. Also, to help in getting money to equip the Irish Volunteers, we held whist drives, céilídhe (dances) or anything which would make money for the purpose. One night I was on my way to a lecture arranged by Central Branch. Being a little early, I turned into the shop in Parnell Street to have a word with Tom, and he introduced me to a lady who was talking to him. She was Miss Mary MacSwiney, head of Cumann na mBan in Cork city, so I invited her to the lecture, and she said she would be very pleased to come.

Meeting her made me late, so we took our seats in the back of the hall in 25 Parnell Square, but little either of us heard of that lecture. She would talk. She began by saying that she did not agree with seeking help from Germany. I asked why. 'Well,' she said,'I lived in Germany and I dislike the Germans. They are a tyrannical people, and if we accept their help we will be under their rule.' I said, 'Supposing we get guarantees that no such thing will happen? It has been our policy to seek help from any country willing to give it, to enable us to free ourselves.' She said, 'I don't care. I hate the Germans and we should have nothing to do with them.'

By this time the argument had got hot, so I took her by the arm and led her out, fearing if we stayed the lecture might be upset. In the entrance hall we had it out. I asked: 'Should it matter to us what the Germans were? All we asked of them was help to free ourselves from British rule, and I understood they were willing to do that.' 'Yes,' she said, 'for their own ends.' I asked, 'Does that even matter? Their object is to defeat England, and if helping us helps them to do that I cannot see why we should refuse their help.' It was no use continuing; she had her views and I had mine, and we both held on to them and parted in no friendly frame of mind. I thought her stupid and narrow. What she thought of me, God knows.

Another evening there was to be a lecture at Central Branch, and I was in a great rush to be on time. As I had no maid at the time, I had to get the children to bed before leaving. I was very nervous about leaving them alone, as the youngest, Emmet [born 1910], had a passion for fire and was rather wild. Whenever I had to leave them I was gripped with fear that he would start a fire and burn himself or the house. I had to be at the lecture, as it was I who had arranged it, and I was torn between the two things. With a quaking heart I decided to trust in God and leave them. I heard them say their prayers, put them to bed and sat down and talked to them. 'Now, boys,' I said, 'My duty to Ireland tonight is to go and make this lecture a success, and your duty to Ireland is to stay in bed until I return. You are not to light paper, matches or anything else. I will leave the light on. Will you promise to do your duty to Ireland?' They all promised most solemnly. When I arrived home some hours later I found they had kept their word. I was very proud of them and hugged them and gave them a lovely supper.

In October, 1914, Roger Casement decided to go to Germany to seek aid for Ireland. He did not consult any of the revolutionary group. His idea seems to have been to raise an Irish Brigade from among the prisoners-of-war in Germany, many of whom were Irish. When Tom heard this he was very upset. For one thing, he and the men working with him towards the Rising did not want men from Germany – they needed and asked for arms only. Casement, he heard, intended getting to Germany through the USA, so Tom sent word to John Devoy to have nothing to do with him, and to give him no help to reach Germany. Through his action in voting for Redmond's nominees on the Provisional Executive of the Irish Volunteers, he did not think him a suitable person to represent Ireland.

Casement had been in the USA before the war and apparently got to know his way about, so he managed to get to Germany. The explanation John Devoy gave to Tom at the time was that Casement got to Germany on his own initiative and got in touch with the German High Command. There he announced himself as Ireland's representative, with which under the circumstances Devoy thought it best to concur. As far as is known, the Irish Volunteer Executive gave Casement no mandate to do this.

When Tom got this information from John Devoy, he was very worried. He considered Casement was not sufficiently conversant with the actual situation in Ireland, that he did not know what the Supreme Council of the IRB wanted in their relations with Germany, and certainly did not know the extent of their control. He sent for Captain Monteith, who had been dismissed from his post in Islandbridge Barracks, his loyalty to the British being suspect. He told Monteith he wanted him to go to the USA and from there to Germany to join Casement. He gave him credentials to John Devoy to help him. An account of all this is given very clearly in Monteith's book, *Casement's Last Adventure*. In sending Monteith, Tom believed him to be the most suitable person available. He told him to tell Casement that they did not want men, they wanted arms only, but that if Casement insisted on trying to raise an Irish Brigade, to advise and help him in his approach to the prisoners-of-war. But Casement was not a man who would take advice or counsel from anybody.

Casement failed to get the Irish Brigade, but succeeded in concluding a formal treaty between Germany and himself. There were many provisions in it which the Irish at home and abroad did not approve of, in relation to the disposal of the Brigade (if raised) in the event of its not being used in Ireland. Article 7 read: 'The opportunity to land in Ireland can only arise if the fortune of war should grant the German Navy a victory that would open, with reasonable prospect of success, the sea route to Ireland. Should the German Navy not succeed in this effort, the Irish Brigade shall be employed in Germany in such a way as Sir Roger Casement may approve...In this event, it might be possible to employ the Irish Brigade to assist the Egyptian people to recover their freedom by driving the British out of Egypt. Short of directly fighting to free Ireland from British rule, a blow struck at the invaders of Egypt to aid Egyptian national freedom is a blow struck for a kindred cause to that of Ireland.'

A copy of this Treaty, which was never ratified by any Irish assembly, was published in the *Gaelic American*. According to John Devoy, in his book *Recollections of an Irish Rebel*, publication of this document was withheld by Casement for several months. It was eventually released by him when, in his opinion, the opportune moment had arrived. The treaty bore the seal of the Imperial German Government. Devoy says: 'With respect to the clauses setting forth that under certain circumstances the Brigade might be sent to fight in Egypt, we in America strongly objected to such a proposal, and our friends in Dublin were unalterably opposed to it. There was only one place for these men to fight, and that was Ireland.' Casement did not succeed in raising the Irish Brigade, and it seems to have had a very depressing effect on him.

After the declaration of war, things in Dublin became very hectic. For a few days traffic through a route to the North Wall was stopped, in order to leave a clear passage for the movement of troops to the North Wall for embarkation. They passed our shop in Amiens Street before turning into Seville Place. One morning I put my head out the window in a top room to see them passing, feeling sad that so many of them were Irish, going as I thought to be slaughtered for England. A soldier on top of a gunwagon looked up and saw me, and blew me a kiss. I nearly fell out the window with rage. If I had had a brush or any other weapon I would have thrown it at him. The only weapon I had was my tongue. He could not hear what it said, so I stuck it out at him, and then was shocked at the vulgarity I had been guilty of.

The British used every device to induce young Irishmen to join their army. Posters with inducements were pasted up everywhere. One poster I remember was: 'Join up and see the world, and be paid for doing it.' Some wag wrote under it, 'and see the next world', which was the fate of many. Thousands of our young men joined up, some on Redmond's advice, others possibly for adventure. It was heartbreaking to look on at. Walking along the streets, it seemed as if everyone was wearing a Union Jack. It seemed like mass hysteria.

Walking from our shop in Amiens Street, through Talbot Street, North Earl Street and O'Connell Street one day to our shop in Parnell Street, I was so disgusted and enraged at the display of Union Jacks that I could scarcely speak when I arrived in the shop. Tom looked up at me and said, 'Good God, Katty, what is wrong with you?' I told him what had upset me, and asked if there was anything we could do to offset this thing, as I was sure there were many people feeling like me. I stood a long time at the counter thinking, then I said, 'How would it be if I made a few hundred of those little orange, white and green badges made of ribbon, the kind the Clan na Gael used to wear at functions, and put them on sale at a penny each? There must be many who would like to show their colours in some form, as against the Union Jack.' Tom said it would be worth a trial.

I went out and bought the ribbon and set to work, and worked late into the night making them. I finished one hundred, and stuck them into a pincushion and laid them on the counter in the Parnell Street shop. There was not one left that night. Day after day I continued making them, and selling them as fast as I could make them. Liberty Hall then took it up, and asked me if I would give them the name of the firm which supplied me with the ribbon; it was especially stocked for me in colours, width and quality.[8] Gradually the Union Jacks disappeared, and the orange, white and green took their place.

Hostility to the British was hardening as British oppression was increasing under the Defence of the Realm Act (DORA). Under it men were arrested and imprisoned for the most trivial things. On 3 December 1914 police and detectives entered newspaper shops and seized the *Irish Freedom* newspaper, and at the same time the printers of Arthur Griffith's paper, *Sinn Féin*, were told their plant would be seized if they continued printing. When Uncle John heard about *Sinn Féin* he wrote to me and told me to go to Griffith and say that he was prepared to advance any sum of money he required to continue his paper. Other printers, who had not been threatened, could be got. I went to Griffith, very pleased with my mission, but my pleasure was short-lived. I got a mighty cool reception from Griffith, and Uncle John's offer was turned down, and not too politely. I came away hurt and indignant. I considered Uncle John had done a very generous thing, when I remembered that he and Griffith differed politically, and how unfair Griffith had always been to Uncle John in his paper. Uncle John was a Fenian, Griffith was not. The IRB brought out another paper to replace *Irish Freedom*, and called it *Eire*. This was also seized by the police.

Seán MacDermott was arrested in Tuam on 16 May 1915, and charged with making a speech calculated to endanger the peace of the realm. He was transferred from Tuam to Dublin for trial, and lodged in Arbour Hill Military Detention Barracks. As soon as we heard where he was, I was despatched to Arbour Hill to try and get an interview with him. I had never seen Arbour Hill Barracks before, and it seemed a very formidable and imposing place to me. I sought admittance with my heart in a flutter. The ponderous door was opened by a British soldier in answer to my ring, and he asked me my business. I stated it. He told me to come in, and he would see if I would be allowed to see the prisoner. He left me standing in the hall and went off.

He had been gone some time when an officer appeared, who looked me up and down for a while without speaking. Then in a loud voice he said, 'You wish to see the prisoner MacDermott. Why?' I said, 'Well, to find out if there is anything I can do for him.' 'In what way?' he asked. I said,'He may want food sent to him, he may want a change of clothing, and other things done for him which a friend may do.' He then asked, 'Are you related to him?' I said, 'No, but he has no relatives living in Dublin, and I as a friend am taking the place of a relative.' He then asked, 'Are you sure you have no other interest in him?' 'In what way?' I enquired, and he said, 'It seems strange to me that a friend should be so interested.' 'The truth is often strange,' I answered. 'Well, well, well, and so you want to see this young man friend, as a friend, hum-hum,' he said.

By this time I was very angry. To be cross-questioned in this way was a new experience. I was not angry so much at what he said, but at the way he said it, but I kept my temper and held my tongue. I feared that in answering the way he deserved to be answered, I might say things which could give him an excuse to refuse my request, though I was dying to lash out. We stood looking at each other. Then, as calmly as I could, I said, 'Listen, sir, I am asking for an interview with this man as a friend. Hearing of his arrest and being lodged here, and knowing he had no relatives in Dublin, I hurried here to see him as a friend in trouble. My definition of friendship is to give help in time of trouble.' He paused for a long time, then he said, 'I'll permit you to see him for ten minutes.' I said, 'Thank you'; the relief was so great I nearly burst into tears. I was going to see Seán and give him Tom's message. That was all that mattered.

I was then conducted to a small room at the right side of the hall door by the same soldier who had admitted me. When he left to go for Seán I did burst out crying for a minute, I was so worked up, but when I heard Seán's stick and the slight drag of the leg along the passage outside I put the brake on the tears, and did what I could to prevent him knowing I was in any way distressed. I gave him Tom's message, and arranged a way of corresponding that only ourselves could understand. I returned to the shop, in great glee at having accomplished what I was sent to do.

Seán was put on trial, charged with having made a speech calculated to endanger the peace of the realm. He was convicted on the evidence of a member of the Royal Irish Constabulary, who said he had made a mental note of what Seán had said. He was sentenced to four months' imprisonment. Francis Sheehy Skeffington and Seán Milroy were put on trial the same day, for offences under DORA, and sentenced to terms of imprisonment. I received many letters from Seán during his imprisonment, mainly concerned with business matters and the supply of clothes, etc, to him.

After Seán's arrest and imprisonment, Tom went to Arthur Griffith and offered him the Editorship of *Eire*, on condition he kept strictly to its editorial policy, which was the same as that of *Irish*

Freedom. Griffith accepted it, and agreed to the conditions. Tom offered the Managership of *Eire* to Seán T O'Kelly, as he had held that position on Griffith's paper, *Sinn Féin*, and he also agreed to accept. When *Eire* was seized later by the British authorities, the IRB brought out another paper called *Scissors and Paste*, a name which was suggested by Griffith. It was composed of cuttings from other newspapers, British and foreign. The British news must have been passed by the Censor. Still, its appearance in *Scissors and Paste* gave offence to the British authorities, and orders were issued to suppress it. The IRB then published a paper called *Nationality*, the last paper to be published by the IRB before the Rising. Arthur Griffith was still acting as paid Editor.

On 29 June 1915, there died in New York one whose career John Devoy called 'An epitome of the history of Fenianism', Jeremiah O'Donovan Rossa. Devoy cabled to Tom, 'Rossa dead, what shall we do?'[9] Tom cabled back, 'Send his body home at once.' He immediately began to organise the funeral, and said, 'If Rossa had planned to die at the most opportune time for serving his country, he could not have done better.' He planned to rouse the country by making the funeral a pageant representing all Ireland, and through it he hoped to revive all the glory and enthusiasm of the Rossa period. The story of Rossa was printed in pamphlet form, and a beautiful Souvenir Programme was issued.

To prepare for the huge funeral he formed a large committee, and divided this into sub-committees. Each sub-committee was in charge of a particular section. Commandant Tomás MacDonagh was General Commanding Officer and Chief Marshal. The general plan was formulated by Tom, but he and MacDonagh worked out the details. It was during this time that Tom and MacDonagh got to know each other intimately, and a friendship developed, based on mutual respect and admiration, which lasted while life did. MacDonagh almost lived in our shop while working out the details of the plan, as Tom's experience of large processions in New York was helpful.

The plan involved arranging where each section was to line up, its exact place in the procession, and its time for joining in. As men were pouring in from all parts of the country, this was a stupendous job. MacDonagh was perfectly competent for it, as results showed. I think it was the most wonderful procession Dublin ever saw, and the organisation of it was perfect. Tom looked on MacDonagh as a very clever, gifted man, straight and clear in thought and action as a man could be, and an able commander.

For a while, Tom was considering who he would select to deliver the oration at the graveside, and finally decided on P H Pearse as the best available orator. It was a choice between Pearse and Father Micheál O'Flanagan. When Pearse was made acquainted with this decision, he sent a note to Tom, asking how far he would go. The answer to Pearse was verbal, one which I delivered: 'Make it as hot as hell, throw discretion to the winds.' The reason for Pearse's query was that Seán MacDermott was in prison for a speech he had made, and it had been decided to refrain from speechmaking, the loss of such men as Seán MacDermott being too high a price to pay for a speech at such a critical time.

When word came from Mrs O'Donovan Rossa that she and her daughter Eileen were on their way to Ireland with Rossa's remains, Seán McGarry and I were sent off immediately to Liverpool to meet them and escort them to Ireland. Knowing we would be only one night in Liverpool, our luggage consisted of an overnight bag each. It was late when we landed in Liverpool, so we took a cab and told the driver to drive us to a hotel. At every hotel we called to, we were told they were full up. We sat in the cab to consider what we would do; we could not stay in the cab all night. Then it suddenly dawned on us, the reason all the hotels we called on had been full: we were not respectable, we had no luggage. It seemed so strange that they were all full, and it was the only conclusion we could come to. We had a good laugh, but still it was very awkward. We went back to the Station Hotel, which was very expensive, the reason for our not going there at first. In the morning we met the boat with some Liverpool friends, and returned to Ireland that night with Mrs O'Donovan Rossa and her daughter Eileen.

Before we left Dublin, Tom had given us strict instructions that if we were asked our nationality when embarking at Dun Laoghaire we were to say British, lest we would be stopped if we said Irish. This was quite a possibility at the time, and it was important that we be at the boat to meet the Rossas. We carried out the orders when the question was put to us on boarding. It was a hard thing for me to do, and the recollection of it still hurts.

On the arrival of Rossa's remains a day or two later, they were taken to the Pro-Cathedral and laid before the High Altar with a guard of honour of Irish Volunteers, for that night. Next day they were removed to City Hall, where he lay in state until the funeral. There was a guard of Irish Volunteers around the coffin day and night, and a continuous line of people to see and pay their respects to this grand old Fenian's remains. It looked as if all Dublin turned out to do so. Tom was elated. The purpose of the funeral had been accomplished, Ireland was aroused, the spirit of Rossa and men like him was around us, the spirit that called men to do or die for Ireland.

The funeral took place on Sunday, 1 August. It was most

impressive. A guard of Irish Volunteers walked beside the hearse and thousands of Irish Volunteers walked after it, followed by Cumann na mBan and many other organisations. From City Hall to Glasnevin cemetery the sidewalks were thronged with spectators. O'Donovan Rossa had served Ireland, living and dead.

On the morning of 18 September 1915, Seán MacDermott was due for release from Mountjoy Prison. A number of friends collected outside the prison gate to greet him. Tom and I were there, and took him home to Richmond Avenue. It was a glorious sunny morning, so we had breakfast in the garden, a thing Tom loved. Basking in the sunshine, Seán was thrilled with his freedom, the song of the birds, the peace of the garden, and the beauty of the morning. My memory goes back to that morning as one of supreme peace and happiness. Seán was a very lovable character, kindly, sweet-tempered, full of fun and laughter. He adored children, ours particularly. His own childhood was not too happy; his mother died when he was too young to remember her, and he always seemed to long for that mother's love which he had missed.

During the morning, he turned to me and said what happiness it meant to him to have us meet him and bring him home with us. He continued, 'I have never known a mother's love, and I have always longed for it. I have tried to picture what my mother would have been like. You fit that picture. When I see you with your children and the loving care you give them, I ache with the thought of never having known my mother. I missed all you give your children.' Tom smiled, and said, 'She gives them an odd spanking!'

When breakfast was over, Tom and Seán started discussing events since Seán had gone to prison, and matters connected with the papers brought out since *Irish Freedom* had been seized. Seán disapproved of Arthur Griffith being appointed Editor; he believed Griffith was so wedded to his own policy and ideas that he would, despite his promise, revert to his own policy and perhaps create difficulties for them. Seán said, 'I know Griffith better than you, Tom, I worked with him', and pointing to a copy of the latest paper brought out (I think it was *Nationality*) which had just arrived, he said, 'Look, even in this issue he has done it.'

Tom looked surprised; he had not seen the paper. He looked at the paper and saw what Seán objected to; it was an advertisement for a candidate in a parliamentary election. As they were against the policy of sending men to the British Parliament, neither of them would have accepted the advertisement. Griffith had not consulted Tom as he should have done. However, Seán agreed with Tom to keep Griffith on when Tom explained his reasons for appointing him, which were that Griffith had been deprived of his employment by enemy action, and though he differed with him, Tom believed Griffith loved Ireland sincerely and worked for it along his own lines.

Tom also stressed the fact that having Griffith and O'Kelly in charge of the paper would leave Seán free for more important work, now that they were approaching the crisis. Seán had no objection to the appointment of O'Kelly, but he disagreed with the action taken over the Gaelic League [now given a political stance under Pearse], which Piaras Béaslaí in his recollections reminds me of. Seán said, 'You know, Tom, the Gaelic League will die, and the death will be put down to our influence.' I gathered in listening to Seán that he thought a purely academic movement such as the Gaelic League would not live long. Tom's answer was, 'You are wrong, Seán, the Gaelic League must live. Its work is too important for the future of our country. A free country must have its own language, and the

Gaelic League is saving the language for that time. All our influence must be used to keep it alive.'

When the position of General Secretary of the Gaelic League became vacant, I think early in 1916, two IRB men were amongst those seeking the post. Seán T O'Kelly was one of them; Tom favoured him as a man he knew and could trust, and used all his influence to have him appointed, which he was. He sent Seán T to New York, with messages to John Devoy, and James Connolly's daughter Nora was also sent to Devoy.

4
Plans for the Rising

1915-1916

Kathleen's secret role in the IRB – Connolly disappears
– preparations for the Rising – Tom wounded –
Clarke/MacNeill conflict – MacNeill countermanding
order – the eve of the Rising

Some time before the Rising, Tom came home from a meeting of the
Supreme Council of the IRB, and told me that it had been decided at
the meeting to select some person whose discretion, silence and capa-
bility they could rely upon; one who would be made fully acquainted
with all their decisions. In the event of the arrest of all the members of
the Supreme Council, the custodian of their plans and decisions
would be in a position to pass on the work to those next in command,
thus preventing confusion and temporary stoppage. The person
selected must be one for whom there was little likelihood of being
arrested. I was very interested in all he was telling me; it was unusual

for him to mention anything that happened at their meetings. So I was very surprised when he informed me that the person selected was myself.

He warned me to do nothing which might draw the attention of the British authorities to me. He gave me the names of the first, second and in some cases the third line key men all over the country, with whom I could connect should necessity arise; these names I had to memorise. From that time on, after each meeting I was made acquainted with any decisions, changes, or anything of importance it was thought I should know.

I was informed, late in 1915, that word had been sent to John Devoy that if anything happened to the Supreme Council of the IRB, he was to communicate directly with me. He did this after the Rising. I was not a member of the IRB, but I had done work for them since 1909, and they had learned I was capable and could be trusted. For some years after the Rising I thought it wiser not to mention this to anybody. I did not want the British to know how deep I was in the confidence of the IRB. I had work to do, and did not want to draw the attention of the G-men [detectives] to me, though they kept an eye on me.

It was to my mind great foresight on the part of the IRB to have done this, as I was in a position after the Rising, when even all the key men whose names I had were arrested, of knowing where to take hold and keep things going until the general release of the prisoners. P S O'Hegarty has given me credit for the work I did during that period in two of his books. Years after the Rising Mrs Wyse Power, writing to Mrs O'Shea Leamy, said: 'I felt very sorry for Mrs Clarke; she suffered more than anyone, because she knew in advance what she was going to lose in 1916.'[1]

We decided to spend Christmas 1915 in Limerick. Seán MacDermott and my brother Ned came with us. We all had a feeling it might be the last one we would spend together. As it was, Tom and Ned had to return to Dublin the day after St Stephen's Day. Seán MacDermott, myself and the children remained in Limerick a week. When Tom arrived in Dublin, he found Tomás MacDonagh in a very angry frame of mind, waiting for him. During Tom's absence, Tomás had unexpectedly turned up at a meeting Pearse and Plunkett were holding in 41 Parnell Square. Pearse was proposing that he and Plunkett should launch a new weekly paper in which he was to write inflammatory articles, designed to rouse the country to fever pitch. The idea was reminiscent of what John Mitchel had done, and for which he had been transported.[2]

MacDonagh took great exception to what Pearse was proposing, and left the meeting very angry. He told Tom he believed the sole reason for the proposal was that Pearse and Plunkett resented the fact that Seán and Tom had more power than they had. I do not know if Tom agreed with MacDonagh's interpretation, but he certainly did not agree with the idea of a new paper.

Pearse had no money to start the new paper, so he and Plunkett had been obliged to await Tom's return from Limerick to get his consent to the proposal. Tom agreed with MacDonagh that the project was not a good one, and refused to approve it. His attitude was this: a Rising had been planned, and a paper on the lines suggested by Pearse would give the British authorities an excuse for arresting the leaders and all suspected persons. This would destroy all chances of a Rising.

On 19 January 1916, James Connolly's paper, *The Workers' Republic*, published an editorial calling for immediate action. Later

KATHLEEN CLARKE

that day, Connolly disappeared, and was missing for some days. This, I fear, will always remain something of a mystery. There are many versions of it; I will give mine.

I came to the shop to find Seán MacDermott, in a great state of irritation, talking to Tom about Connolly's disappearance. He had come from Liberty Hall (Connolly's HQ) where Michael Mallin had told him of Connolly's instructions, ie that if he (Connolly) ever disappeared, Mallin was to wait four days. If he heard nothing, he was to mobilise the Citizen Army and cause an uprising. Connolly had always been distrustful of all the group except Tom; I knew this from Connolly himself. His doubts seemed to have become an obsession; he feared that they would dilly-dally until it was too late to rise and strike a blow for freedom. In disappearing, he thought to force their hand; if the Citizen Army started, the Volunteers and the IRB would be forced to join them. Mallin, however, agreed with Seán's arguments, and very wisely did nothing. I never saw Tom so irritated or upset. Their plans for an all-Ireland Rising were not complete, and if the Citizen Army acted in the way Mallin had said, the Rising would only be a Dublin one. That day Tom could have wrung Connolly's neck.

Connolly was away three or four days. The day Seán got the news that he was back he rushed to Tom with it. I arrived at the shop to hear Seán saying 'Damn the fellow and his tricks', and he told me the story. Connolly returned from his retirement a disappointed man. Seán MacDermott and all the Military Council were very angry with him. They considered his action childish, and suspended him from the Military Council, but restored him to his position there on his giving an undertaking not to act on his own.

It has been stated that the IRB kidnapped Connolly. This I must challenge. Tom and Seán MacDermott were practically the heads of the organisation, and had more power in it than any other members of the Supreme Council, and from the talk I heard I am positive they had nothing to do with Connolly's disappearance. For one thing, Tom had too deep a respect for Connolly to agree to such a thing. I never saw two men in such a state of trouble and anxiety as those two men during Connolly's absence. If Connolly had been kidnapped, as has been stated, the IRB had nothing to do with it officially, of that I am certain. This does not exclude the possibility that an individual member or members might have acted in the name of the IRB, but I fail to see the reason for such an act. I know Seán MacDermott believed his disappearance was a voluntary act, from a remark I heard him make: 'That will teach him a lesson.' He was alluding to the fact that Mallin hesitated to take the initiative and act on Connolly's orders.

I had already known from Connolly himself that he distrusted all the members of the Irish Volunteer Executive, and most members of the Military Council, but why I cannot say. I was sent with a message to him one day, and when I had delivered the message he said, 'Sit down for a chat.' This was unusual, and I was astonished when he said he distrusted them all. I said, 'All? Surely you do not distrust Tom?' He said, 'No, he is the one man I have complete faith in.' Then I said, 'Surely Seán MacDermott is worthy of your trust.' 'Yes,' he said, 'but they are the only two I trust completely.' I think the only people he had complete trust in were those under his own control, the Citizen Army. He seemed to have an obsession that they would delay too long, and that the war would be over before the date of the Rising was decided upon. This was unjust and unfair to all the men concerned, who were only waiting for what seemed the most opportune time. I had a great admiration for Connolly, but I left him that day feeling sad that he had such a poor opinion of the men he was working with.

In January, 1916, there was a rumour that the Dublin Castle people were preparing to make a swoop on the Irish Volunteers one night. Word was sent to my brother, Commandant Edward Daly, to go to headquarters, and there he was told that it was decided to have the Volunteers stand to arms all night. He went off to arrange for those under his command to carry out the orders. Then Tom sent for me to come and take his place in the shop, as he wished to go to the Volunteer headquarters. He went, and took part in the work going on there, and though he was not on the Volunteer Executive he was recognised as one who had a right to be there.

Some time in January, Pearse came to Tom in great trouble. He told him that if he did not get £200 immediately the school would have to close down, as there was a court order for possession, either for rent or rates, I forget which, if the money was not paid at once. Tom said he would cable to John Devoy for it, but Pearse said it would be too late. On Pearse's urging, Tom borrowed from another source, and went with the money to Rathfarnham, very happy that he had been able to get it in time. He suggested to Pearse that as so much of his time was occupied with National work, it might be advisable to form a small committee of trusted people to look after the financial side of the school, thereby relieving Pearse of that worry. This suggestion, which arose from a desire to help Pearse, was received very coldly, and as if it were an impertinence. When Tom came home, he told me about it. He was very distressed at the way his suggestion had been received; he said Pearse had been practically insulting to him. He was surprised that Pearse should act so towards him, when he had given him so many proofs of his desire to help him.

The plans for the Rising were outlined to me some time before it, and for many years I remembered every detail clearly. Now, I only remember the broad outlines. The plans for the defence of Dublin were drawn up by Joseph Plunkett. The bridges giving entrance to the city were to be covered by armed men in the houses commanding them, to prevent British troops entering and to enable them to hold the city as long as possible. The approaches to Stephen's Green were also to be covered by armed men in the houses commanding them.

The Wicklow men were to join up with Dublin. When they could no longer hold the city, they were to fall back to North County Dublin, where the Meath men were to join them. The North men were to mobilise in Coalisland and make their way down the coast to join the Galway men. The Limerick men were to go to Kerry to cover the landing of the arms from Germany; from Kerry, the arms were to be distributed. The Limerick men were to return to Limerick and hold the railway, and if necessary destroy it to prevent the British troops using it.

When word reached the GPO on Easter Monday evening, when the Rising was under way, that Commandant Mallin had entered into St Stephen's Green park, instead of the houses, and had started his men digging trenches there, orders were sent from Commandant Connolly to Mallin to evacuate the park immediately, and take to the houses as planned. Mallin seems to have ignored the order until he was forced to withdraw by British snipers from the surrounding houses. Why Commandant Mallin went into the park, no-one will ever know now, but such a thing was never contemplated by those who had planned the defence of Dublin.

Early in January, 1916, I was told to prepare for a trip to New

York with messages to John Devoy. I was in the middle of preparations when it was called off, and Miss Plunkett went instead. It had been changed because Seán MacDermott said that I might not be able to get back in time for the Rising, and I had a definite place and work allotted to me in the Rising. I was delighted; I did not like leaving my husband, even for a short time. My part in the Rising was to organise the care and maintenance of the dependants of the men out fighting; at that time they thought they would be able to hold out for four or five months.

The prospects were fairly good; there were only about twenty-five thousand British troops in Ireland, mostly raw recruits in training. The military and police barracks were well stocked with arms for determined men to seize, when they were armed with weapons from the expected landing of arms from Germany. They believed that if they could hold out for four or five months, the Irish in America would be roused and would force the American government to come to their assistance, or at least allow the Irish there to do so, both with men and arms. At that time, the Clan na Gael were the best organised force in the USA, a force to be reckoned with, and they were always able to arouse other Irish organisations.

One night towards the end of January, I think the 30th, Miss Sorcha MacMahon and I were at my home, going into the accounts of the pamphlet scheme run by the Central Branch, Cumann na mBan. It was about 11pm when we finished, and she left for her home. When she had gone I rushed up the stairs to see how my son Daly was; he was very ill at the time. I stayed with him until I heard a knock at the door, and thinking it was Tom, whom I had been expecting, I went down to open it, wondering why he did not use his key as usual. But it was Miss MacMahon, not Tom, at the door. She said she had met Mr Clarke in Ballybough Road, and that he had asked her to come back and tell me he was going into McGarry's house and would be late getting home, but not to worry.

Sensing disaster, I said, 'Is he dead?' 'Oh,' she said, 'if that is how you feel I had better tell you what has happened. He has been accidentally shot in the arm by Seán McGarry, and is awaiting a doctor in McGarry's house.' I went over to McGarry's with her, and on the way she told me how the accident happened. On leaving my house she had decided to walk home, and went down the Ballybough Road. She met Tom and Seán McGarry and stopped to talk to them. She asked McGarry if he had got the pistol he had promised to get for her, and he took a small pistol from his pocket and started tricking with it. In fun he pointed it at Tom, who protested at his fooling, saying he would get clink in the British Army for such action. McGarry said, 'It's all right, Tom, it's not loaded.' Tom moved out of the way, as McGarry had it pointed directly at his heart. As he moved, a shot rang out and a bullet was lodged in Tom's elbow.

They went into McGarry's house and sent for a doctor. Very little could be done for Tom that night, as the bullet was lodged in the elbow joint. There was no bleeding, but the bullet had been fired at such close quarters that it was hot and burned as it went in. Next morning it was removed, with large splinters of bone from the lower arm, in the Mater Hospital. After the doctor's examination that night, Tom and I left McGarry's for home, accompanied by Seán McGarry and his brother-in-law Billy Monbrun. I set to work as soon as we got home and got all the hot water jars in the house for Tom's bed. Knowing he must be suffering from shock as well as pain, I thought bed was the place for him. I then asked McGarry and Monbrun to leave. I was very angry with McGarry.

When they were gone I got Tom to bed and gave him hot, strong tea, but the pain was so great he could not stay there. I made a big fire in the diningroom, as he seemed very cold, and drew a couch to the fire with rugs and pillows, but it was no use; the pain would not let him rest. He walked the floor all night in agony, and I was in an agony of mind watching him, unable to do anything to relieve him and fearing he would collapse any minute. At daybreak he persuaded me to lie down. To please him I did, and quite unexpectedly fell asleep, not waking till nearly 6am, a thing I have never forgiven myself for. He never recovered the use of his arm, the right one, but he learned to use small arms with his left one for the Rising. He had a strange love for McGarry, and though suffering through McGarry's carelessness he was all excuses for him. He hated to hear me damning him, which I often did.

The first visitor to our house next morning was Seán MacDermott. He had first been told that Tom was dead, and then that he was dying. His relief was tremendous when I told him the shot was in the arm, and that Tom was in the Mater Hospital to have the bullet removed. He did swear at McGarry. As he was leaving the house, he said, 'Do you realise what it would mean if Tom was killed?' I said, 'Yes, I do, I know what it would mean to me.' He said, 'I know, but that is not what I was thinking of. I meant did you realise that if Tom was dead, all our hope of a Rising was gone?'

When Tom was sufficiently recovered to travel, he went down to Limerick to recuperate and enjoy a visit with Uncle John. While he was there Seán MacDermott called in to the Parnell Street shop every morning on his way to the office, to know if there was any news from Tom. One morning he was in a very irritable mood, banging his cigarette on the counter, a habit he had when annoyed or worried. I joked him about it. He looked at me very solemnly and said, 'I wish to God Tom was back.' 'You will not have long to wait,' I said, 'he will be back for the St Patrick's Day parade. What's the trouble, Seán? Why not share it? A trouble shared is eased.'

He stood thinking for a while, then he said, 'As a matter of fact, Pearse's ambition is beginning to get badly in the way.' With that he left the shop, giving me no chance to question him as to what he meant. Seán was young and impatient, and was often irked by the constant demands of Pearse to which they had to yield. I remember hearing Seán say to Tom one day: 'It's not good enough, Tom, that he (Pearse) must get all the honours, even of other men's work; it's not fair.' Tom's reply was, 'Well, Seán, so far as you and I are concerned, does it matter who gets the honours or credit so long as the work is done?'

I have always felt that Tom was too modest; he thought too little of himself or what he had suffered. He never considered his brains or ability were anything out of the ordinary, although they were. In the group with which he worked, there were poets, writers, teachers, professional men of all kinds, all men of ability, but it was his brain which planned. P S O'Hegarty wrote, in his introduction to *Glimpses of an Irish Felon's Prison Life*: 'His life and his unconquerable will and his work and his energy made him easily the first of us and the best of us. And amid all the jokes and easiness that marked our intercourse, we all knew that we were in the presence of one who stood as the embodiment of Fenianism, an impregnable rock. More than any other one man he was responsible for the insurrection, for he was the mainstay of the group which from 1911 had worked and planned for an insurrection.'

By 1916, Tom Clarke was not the old man generally portrayed.

He was fifty-nine years old on 11 March 1916, but the prison with its brutalities and starvation had left him emaciated, and looking much older than his years. He had grown from boyhood to manhood in Dungannon, Co Tyrone. His mother was a Tipperary woman, and his father came from the Ballyshannon area. He was ten years old when his mother and father brought him from South Africa to Ireland. He was wildly excited, coming to a country which was interwoven into all his childish dreams and imagination, a land of romance, heroism, a fairy land, where everything was beautiful. There was to him no place in the world to compare with Tipperary and Ireland, as a result of his mother's constant talk of that wonderful place. The year he first saw Ireland was the year of the 1867 Rising.

Is it any wonder, and hearing all the talk of the Fenians' attempt to free Ireland, that he developed that all-absorbing love for Ireland for which no sacrifice was too great to make? Liberty, family, life, all were sacrificed for the freedom of that land. He loved his life as much as any man; he adored his wife and children. He took pleasure in the most trifling things, the first daffodil, the first rose, the sunrise, the sunset, the new-mown hay, the song of the birds, the catkins. A garden-lover, he was always happy in a garden, and nothing gave him more pleasure than working in a garden. But everything began and ended with Ireland and her freedom.

I wish I could give an adequate picture of him as I saw him, with everything in life made subservient to the one thing, the freedom of Ireland, but I have not the gift of word-picturing. He was completely lacking in personal ambition; looking back now, I can see that if he had not had that wonderful, selfless and unselfish nature he would not have kept that group working together as one man. They were all men of ability and ambition, and the natural rivalry among them for leadership would have been sure to create friction, possibly disunion. It was God who ordained that he was blessed with that spirit.

When he returned from the USA in 1907, I do not believe that any other man, however gifted, would have rescued the country from the state of apathy and indifference in which it was gripped. The people, especially the young, had lost faith in the Irish Parliamentary Party. Their period was a most flowery, oratorical one, but the grand speeches in the House of Commons, and dying for Ireland on the floor of the House, had ceased to stir. Neither oratory nor poetry would have roused the people at that time.

Into this phase of apathy came a man, Tom Clarke, full of enthusiasm, energy and faith in the cause of freedom for Ireland. After he had been tried in the hell and tortures of British convict prisons for nearly sixteen years, he was ready to take up the fight where he had left off when he had been sentenced to penal servitude for life. It was this man who gained the confidence of the youth and their admiration, filling them with enthusiasm and rousing in them the spirit of sacrifice for the ideal of Ireland's freedom. It was his undying spirit which, consciously or unconsciously, appealed to them, drawing them into the revolutionary movement, and when the Rising came they were ready, ready to fight and if necessary die for Ireland's freedom. The youth once aroused, or even only interested, the poets and orators did their part, and did it well.

I look on Tom Clarke as unique in our history. Men of outstanding ability and noble character have generation after generation laid down their lives for the freedom of our country, but he is the only one in that long history who, having spent long years in British convict prisons, came out from them with the spirit, the faith and the energy to organise and lead a rising for freedom.

Early in April, Tom and Seán MacDermott asked me to select sixteen girls, members of Cumann na mBan, for despatch work, girls whose silence and discretion they could absolutely rely upon. With the help of Miss MacMahon I drew up a list and handed it to Tom, and I have the intense satisfaction that all were true to the trust placed in them.

On Palm Saturday night, 1916, the Central Branch of Cumann na mBan held a *Céilídhe* [dance] in, I think, the Grocers' Hall, Parnell Square. Many criticised us for having it on such a night, but I been asked by Seán MacDermott to hold it in order to cover a meeting with men from the provinces. Miss MacMahon and I got busy to carry out his request, and we were the only two in the branch who knew the object of the *Céilídhe*. Seán came early, and asked me to stay with him until those he had to meet turned up, as he could leave me without apology. I asked if he would mind Miss MacMahon staying with us. He said, 'If you wish, I have no objection. She will of course understand when I leave you.' So we both formed a kind of bodyguard for him; many of his friends who would, I knew, have liked to speak to him passed into the hall, but with Miss MacMahon on one side of him and myself on the other they did not dare. I remember three of the Misses Ryan passing, Miss Kit, Miss Min and Miss Phyllis; I am sure they would have looked to speak to him, but he waved them on.

Con Colbert came into the shop to protest against a *Céilídhe* being held in Lent. He was deeply religious, and did not think it right. I could not explain the reason for it to him, so I told him not to be so squeamish and to dance while he could, as he might be dancing at the end of a rope one of these days. I fear I shocked him, and I was sorry the minute the words were out of my mouth. I was sorry for having being so flippant, but I was under a great strain at the time.

I had no intimate knowledge of the work of the other branches of Cumann na mBan in Dublin or throughout the country, but I did know, as a member of the Executive, that they all worked as hard as Central Branch, of which I was President.

On the Tuesday of Holy Week, 1916, Tom left the shop in Parnell Street to go to a meeting. I took his place there, and when he was not back by 11pm I closed the shop and went home, hoping to find him there. He was not, and after I while I began to worry. It was unusually late for him. Our house was at the end of the avenue, which was not well lighted, and I was always uneasy when he was late, fearing that some night the British might lay for him there and murder him. When he had not arrived by midnight I put on my hat and coat, and walked up the avenue hoping to meet him, but there was no sign of him. I kept walking up and down for an hour in a distracted frame of mind; now and then I went into the house to see if my sick son wanted anything, and to see if by any chance he had passed in without my seeing him. The last time I came out I saw him coming up the avenue, and went to meet him. He seemed so joyous and excited, telling me he had great news, that I had not the heart to mention my anxiety and fears to him.

On reaching home we settled down to supper, and during it he told me the great news, that the Rising had been arranged for the following Sunday, that a Proclamation had been drawn up to which he was first signatory. I said, 'That means you will be first President.' 'Yes,' he said, 'that is what it means.' Then he told me how the Proclamation was drawn up. Some time before, Pearse had been asked to draft it on lines intimated to him and submit it to the Military Council. He did, and some changes were made. When it was signed that night, it represented the views of all except one, who thought equal opportunities should not be given to women. Except to say that Tom was not that one, my lips are sealed.

Tom then told me that when he was proposed as the first signatory he had demurred, saying that he did not think that such an honour should be conferred on him, that he was not seeking honours. He was very surprised when Tomás MacDonagh rose and said that to his mind no other man was entitled to the honour. 'You, sir, by your example, your courage, your enthusiasm, have led us younger men to where we are today.' If Tom did not agree to accept it, MacDonagh would not sign his name to the Proclamation. 'No man will precede you with my consent.' Being very much touched by what MacDonagh had said, Tom agreed to sign. He was amazed that anyone should speak so highly of him, being a man with no personal ambitions, and no desire for honours. Honours; well, anyone could have them as far as he was concerned. He was the most selfless and unselfish man I ever met; in his home he was the personification of gentleness, joyousness and good temper. I saw him out of temper only a few times in the nearly sixteen years we were together.

At that meeting Tom, as first signatory, was President, Pearse was made Commander-in-Chief of Ireland and Connolly Commander of Dublin. No other positions were created; the other signatories were all members of the Provisional Government. The meeting had been held in Mrs Wyse Power's house in Henry Street. Seán MacDermott was sent from the meeting to see John MacNeill and explain the position to him, ie the expected landing of arms and the general plan, and also to ask him to stand in with them and put his name to the Proclamation, and to surrender his position as head of the Irish Volunteers to P H Pearse. He reported back that MacNeill had agreed to go in with them, and that he either signed or agreed to sign the Proclamation, I can't remember which. Immediately after the Rising, I was positive that Tom had said he had signed, but there has been so much denial about it that I am now in doubt. Pearse was to give the word to all the Commandants on the following day.

We talked well into the night, or rather morning. Tom was wild with excitement. I was feeling the world was tumbling around me, though I did not say so; I had no wish to damp his spirit. Though I knew the Rising had to be, I could see no military success. I saw the force that could be mobilised against our small strength, and my reason could not see how our small strengh could defeat that. It seemed to me the odds were too great, and as far as I was concerned I could see my happiness at an end. I felt Tom would not come through, and I think he knew he would not, but neither of us would admit it. I rather envied him. It would be the end for him, but I would have to remain and bear the separation as well as I could.

I asked him if they won through would he act as President? He said, 'If we win through it will take a long time. By then I fear I would be physically unable for the job, but if I am fit I shall certainly act. I have more knowledge and experience of our enemy, and if necessary the force and ruthlessness needed for the position.' After some further talk we went to bed. I woke in the morning with a feeling of the most profound depression. I could not shake it off, but hid it from Tom. He went to the shop as usual, as there was a close watch kept on it by G-men, and if he failed to put in an appearance they would get busy to find the reason.

When my brother came home to tea that evening he said nothing to me about Sunday, so I wondered if he had yet been informed by Pearse. Later that night I asked him a question about Sunday, and he knew nothing. I went and told Tom, and said it was very unfair to Ned to leave him in ignorance until that late hour. He was a Commandant, and would have to get his men mobilised and ready. It left him little time for preparation.

Tom was very annoyed when I told him. He believed Pearse had issued instructions to all Commandants as it had been agreed he should. He could not understand how it was Ned had not received them. He then had a long talk with Ned and explained matters to him. I could see Ned got a bit of a shock. Even though he knew the Rising would take place some day, this was very short notice. After that I saw Ned only a few times, once when he asked me to buy material and make six signalling flags for him, which I did.

On Holy Thursday, I was sent to Limerick with despatches.[3] I took my three children with me to leave them with my mother, so that I could be free to take on the duty assigned to me in the Rising. On arriving in Limerick I presented the despatches to the men there, and also a verbal message: 'Tell them that John MacNeill has agreed to sign the Proclamation and is quite enthusiastic.' After delivering both to Colivet and another man, who I think was Ledden, I was told that they were holding a meeting, at the end of which they would give me a message to bring back to Dublin. I told them that I had orders to take the mail-train back to Dublin that night, and that they must have the message ready by then. Someone would be at Kingsbridge Station to meet me, as the train would be arriving in the early hours of the morning.

Before train time arrived, Colivet, Ledden and another man, who I think was George Clancy, came in from the Fianna Hall at the rear of my mother's house, where the meeting was being held. They asked me to wait over until next day, as they had not yet reached a decision on the message I was to take back. I said that I thought I should obey orders. Colivet said they considered it more important for me to await their message than to obey orders to return that night. I agreed to stay, very reluctantly; I had a full day's work waiting for me on Good Friday.

The three men stayed for a while chatting before returning to the meeting, and told me some of their difficulties. Listening to them, it occurred to me that they were of a nature which should have been considered and settled long before. I was exasperated when, after waiting overnight, I still got no message to bring. I was told that they were sending a lorry to Dublin for some things, and that the message would go with the lorry. The trains on Good Friday ran on a Sunday schedule, and it was too late for the morning train when I got this message from Colivet. I had to wait for the evening train, and it was very late when I arrived home.

Cumann na mBan were in my mother's house in Limerick that day, making First Aid outfits, so I decided to give them a helping hand while I was waiting for the train. Though none of them except my sisters knew that the manoeuvres which were to take place on Easter Sunday were really a rising, they seemed to sense a crisis, which made them very anxious and troubled. To cheer them up I started to sing a popular pantomime ditty, 'One grasshopper jumped right over another grasshopper's back, and another grasshopper jumped right over another grasshopper's back.' It was sung in fugue form, and by the time the last girl joined in we were all laughing like idiots. A stranger coming in might have been excused if he thought he had inadvertently entered a mental home. It was all very silly, but it broke up the tension. My sisters knew the position, but were not depressed. On the contrary, they were in a wild, but suppressed, state of excitement and enthusiasm, and quite sure of success. It amazed them when they found I did not feel the same way.

When I arrived in Dublin, I went home to Richmond Avenue. Seán MacDermott was there with Tom. I gave them an account of what had happened in Limerick, and why I had disobeyed orders in not returning to Dublin the previous night. Seán asked me to get him some tea. Before leaving the room to do so, I said that I had not been impressed with the men I had met in Limerick. Seán turned on me in a rage, saying, 'For Christ's sake shut up, you are always croaking!' I said, 'I am very sorry, Seán, but I considered it my duty to let you know the impression they left on me. I had not met them before, and they struck me as slow and hesitating, especially for the work before them.' It was the first time in our acquaintance Seán had spoken to me in that way, but I understood the strain he was under and forgave him.

Later that evening Dr Pat McCartan arrived from Tyrone, and a man called De Burca from Carrickmacross for instructions and money for their requirements. Dinny McCullough also called for the same purpose. Before leaving he said, very solemnly, 'Tom, you carried this thing at a meeting at which I was not present. Well, let it pass now, but when this is all over, I'll have it out with you.' McCartan stayed the night with us, and left for Tyrone next day.

When McCartan had gone, Tom and I left home together. My sister Laura was with us. It was, we thought, the last time we would be together before the Rising started. We walked down Ballybough Road and Summerhill and parted at the corner of Parnell and Gardiner Streets, he to go into hiding until Sunday morning, and I to take up duty in the shop. Though both of us feared it might be our final parting, we dared not say so. We dared not indulge in goodbyes.

There was work to be done, and goodbyes would break us and leave us unfit for anything.

He went to stay in Seán O'Mahony's home, Fleming's Hotel in Gardiner Place, where he told me afterwards he had never received such kindness as Seán and Mrs O'Mahony showered upon him. I don't remember much of what I did that day; I served customers automatically. Ned came in for the flags he had asked me to get; I had taken them home to make them, and had them all ready for him.

About 9pm that night, I was alone in the shop when an unknown lady came in enquiring for Mr Tom Clarke. She said she was Pat McCartan's sister and had come from the North with an important message from Pat and Father Daly. My orders were not to let anyone know where Tom was staying, and not to go near it. I was in a difficulty; I did not know how important the message might be, and I could not leave the shop until closing time, 11pm. I told Miss McCartan that I could not tell her where Mr Clarke was, but that if she would go to my home I would give her a note so that the maid would give her tea and make her comfortable until I got home. I would then try to put her in touch with those she could deliver her message to. She agreed to go to my home and wait there for me.

I arrived home about 11.30, and after having something to eat I took her to a house on the North Circular Road where I thought some of the leaders might be. I could get no answer to my knocking, so I took her to Mrs Kissane's house in Hardwicke Street. She was a member of Central Branch, Cumann na mBan. The house was in complete darkness, and though I knocked very lightly the door was opened immediately. There was no light in the hall, but a man with a flashlight showed us into a room, also in complete darkness. Someone flashed a light on us and I saw Seán MacDermott, and by degrees the other occupants of the room, Tomás MacDonagh, P H Pearse, Joseph Plunkett, Diarmuid Lynch and Eamonn Ceannt. There may have been others, but those were all I saw. The room was so dark because they feared to draw attention to the house if it was lighted up, so they used only flashlights.

I explained to Seán my reason for bringing Miss McCartan along there instead of to Tom, then I told Miss McCartan that she could deliver the message to Seán MacDermott, as it was impossible to reach Tom Clarke. She told him that she had been sent by her brother and Father Daly to say that unless they got a guarantee that the arms were landed and the messenger had returned from Rome, they would not act in the North. I was watching Seán's face as she gave him her message. He had his flashlight on, and I never saw such sorrow in a face as he said, 'My God, that is the worst we heard yet.'

I don't know what message he gave her to bring back, but before leaving I asked Seán what was the meaning of the report in the morning papers about the arrest of a man found wandering on the Kerry coast. He said he was not sure yet what it meant. I then asked why Tom was not there with them, saying, 'I do not wish to worry you with questions, but I can see by you all that something dreadful has happened. That being so, Tom should be here.' 'Well,' he replied, 'we all realise that, but wished to leave him undisturbed as long as possible, knowing how badly he needs it.' I replied that he would not thank them for their consideration under the circumstances, and that I would not like to be in their shoes when they met him. I said I thought he ought to be there, and that it was unfair to him not to let him know at once whatever it was that had happened. 'It must be very serious to bring you all together at this hour. What is a night's rest under the circumstances?' I exclaimed.

I was very annoyed with them, and on my way home debated with myself whether I would or would not go and tell him, but the fear that I might be followed, or that by trying to gain admittance to O'Mahonys' at that hour I might attract attention to where he was, thereby doing more harm than good, caused me very reluctantly to abandon the idea. Next morning, Easter Sunday, I escorted Miss McCartan to Amiens Street Station and saw her off to the North. I went from there to open the shop, and remained there according to orders until 2pm, the usual time for closing on Easter Sunday. The Rising was to start at 4pm.

After opening the shop I looked at the *Sunday Independent*, and read there John MacNeill's orders to the Irish Volunteers.[4] I could not understand this, and was inclined to think it was not genuine, that it was some move on the part of our enemy to upset the planned movements of the Irish Volunteers for that day. Volunteers who came into the shop that morning did not believe it was genuine; they said MacNeill had never issued orders through the press before, and they would not obey it. They would only obey orders received from their officers.

I closed the shop and went home to my dinner, then waited to hear the first shot, which I expected about 4pm. I had strict orders not to leave the house, because messengers and instructions would be sent to me from the GPO, therefore I could not go out to seek information. I was in a state of suspense and uncertainty, listening for the sound of that first shot. I could not sit still; I wandered upstairs, downstairs, in and out of every room, and looked out of every window, hoping to see a messenger or someone who would tell me what was happening.

To my amazement, Tom turned into the avenue, accompanied by

Tommy O'Connor, who had been appointed with Seán McGarry as his aide-de-camp. Tom looked old and bent, and his walk, which was usually very quick and military, was slow. I rushed to open the hall door, overjoyed to see him, but fearful of the reason. He looked very ill, and seemed scarcely able to speak. Seeing this I asked no questions, but as soon as he was seated by the fire in the sittingroom I hurried out to get him an egg flip, with a good measure of whiskey in it, as he seemed very cold. He did not drink any kind of intoxicating liquor as a rule. I then prepared a meal for both of them, but he could not eat. He did not eat anything up to the time he left the house next morning.

Sitting around the fire that night, Tom told Tommy O'Connor and Seán McGarry, who had come to stay the night, and myself, what had happened. When the signatories to the Proclamation had met in Liberty Hall that morning, those who did not already know were told of Casement's landing and arrest.[5] Before he was arrested, he had managed to get a message to MacNeill asking him for God's sake to call off the Rising, that the Germans were fooling us. On receiving this MacNeill, instead of getting in touch with those he knew to be the leaders of the Rising, who were all in Dublin and could be reached easily, took counsel with others, among whom were his brother James (recently retired from the Indian Civil Service), Arthur Griffith and Bulmer Hobson. With them, he decided to send countermanding orders secretly all over the country, and orders to the Dublin Volunteers through the *Sunday Independent*. Their action in thus endeavouring to stop the Rising took the ground completely from under the feet of the leaders; Casement's landing was a complete surprise to them, and was the last thing they had expected.

In recounting MacNeill's action, Tom said, 'I could understand

MacNeill if, on getting Casement's message, he thought the Rising should be put off and came straight to us and told us how he felt about it, leaving the decision with us and withdrawing if our decision did not agree with his belief that the Rising should be abandoned. That would have been the honourable course. To send out countermanding orders secretly, giving us no hint of what he was doing, was despicable, and to my mind dishonourable.' According to what Tom had been told, it was by mere chance that Tomás MacDonagh had walked into the house where MacNeill was, with those he had been consulting with. Assuming he would be in agreement with them they told him what they were doing, but MacDonagh was a man of honour, a great soldier, a great soul. Turning on his heel he left them, saying, 'Gentlemen, I owe you no counsel.' He then got in touch with as many members of the Provisional Government as he could, and told them what MacNeill was doing. I think it must have been that meeting I had walked into in Mrs Kissane's.

The direct result of Casement's arrest was the sinking of the German ship, the *Aud*, with the arms. Tom said they could have overcome the loss of the arms, as their arrival had been really a gesture to create confidence. There were plenty of arms in the country, stored in police and army barracks, that determined men could get. What British soldiers were in the country were mostly raw recruits, and their number comparatively small. But the secret countermanding order, a thing they never envisioned, was the death-blow to their hopes.

Was it any wonder that every man broke down on being confronted with such a tragedy? Every hope they had had for a successful Rising had been destroyed, and by an Irishman. Twenty-four hours previously their hopes had been soaring. Their plans so far were good, no hitch had occurred, freedom seemed almost within their grasp. What was to be done in the face of this terrible disaster? They discussed the matter for hours, Tom all the time urging that they should strike that day as planned. Others argued that it was better to wait until Monday, and in the meantime send out orders all over the country telling the men not to demobilise, but to carry on according to original orders. Tom maintained that if they struck that day in Dublin as planned, news of it would reach the rest of the country faster than messengers. Those in the country would then assume that the orders they had received from MacNeill were forged, or anyhow not genuine, and would act on the original orders, signed by Pearse, as far as it was possible. If the Rising was delayed until Monday, Tom argued, the men in most places would be demobilised and unable to do anything, as the British military would by then be on guard to prevent any mobilisation.

To Tom's surprise, even Seán MacDermott was against him in the matter. Up to then Seán had seen eye to eye with him in everything. Tom pointed out that they were all likely to be arrested that night, and what they planned for the morrow might never take place. His efforts were fruitless; the decision was taken to send messengers through the country, and start the Rising on Easter Monday. Tommy O'Connor and Seán McGarry were to act as Tom's bodyguard, and were to stay in the house for the night. They decided that if there was a raid on the house, and any attempt to take them prisoner, they would not surrender. They were to fight and die rather than that. I had a pistol and knew how to use it, and if necessary meant to take a hand.

Before going to bed, we planned what we would do in case of a raid. The hall door was in the centre of the house, with rooms on each side, and the stairs faced the hall door. If a knock came, I was to go the door and ask who was there. If the answer was the police or the military, I was to say nothing but open the door, keeping close behind it. Tom was to be in the door of the room on the other side of the hall door, and Tommy and Seán were to take up a position at the head of the first flight of stairs. We were to fire at each man as he came in, and it was to be a fight to the finish.

After all our plans, no raid occurred, though someone did come to the house during the night and knocked gently. Before opening it, we all got into position, but it was only an old man named Ryan who had just heard there was going to be a rising. He came in shouting at Tom, asking was he mad, what was going to happen to his wife and family, hadn't he suffered enough for Ireland? It took Tom a long time to quieten him down and persuade him to go home, but he finally went, still protesting. I slept in my husband's arms for the last time that night, and slept soundly.

5
Easter Week and Execution

1916

*The Rising – the aftermath – Kathleen arrested –
visiting Tom in Kilmainham Jail before his execution*

Easter Monday was a day of brilliant sunshine, and this we hoped was
a good omen. After breakfast, the three men left for Liberty Hall. I
begged Tom to let me go with them; I said, 'Surely, if all your plans
are sent skywards and if, as you say, you will be lucky if the Rising
lasts as long as Robert Emmet's, it is not necessary for me to stick to
my orders.'[1] But he absolutely refused to let me go with them. He
said that I was to carry out my orders, that no matter how things went
the work entrusted to me would still be there to be done. It was terrible to see them go, but to insist on my own wishes would be making
things more difficult for Tom.

Earlier in the morning, I had said to him: 'I often told you that if it
came to a parting of this kind, I would become a poltroon. Am I one
now when I ask you if there is any way out with honour other than

what you are doing, going to certain death, with all hope of success gone? I feel I want to take you and hide you away, save you at any cost.' He said, 'That is only a very natural feeling just now, but you would not feel the same way towards me if I did pull out. No,' he said, 'there is no turning back; we must save Ireland, and this is the only way. Even if we did decide to call everything off, as you suggest, for the time being to reorganise and await a more favourable opportunity, we would be wrong. England will strike at once. We would all be arrested, some of us perhaps executed; the country would be disarmed and Ireland would have gained nothing. No, there is no turning back.' 'Well,' I said, 'that ends it, I have no more to say, but I had to put before you the thoughts running in my head, even though I feared you might think me a poltroon.'

When they were gone I could not keep still. I knew the Rising would not start until the afternoon, and while waiting to hear the first shot I worked unceasingly in the garden. I planted a hundred cauliflowers. It was a hot day and I was very tired, but I could not stop working until I heard that first shot which was to tell me the Rising had started. I heard a terrific sound some time in the afternoon, rather like an explosion, and I took it to be the first shot. I heard that Volunteers stationed at Ballybough Bridge had withdrawn from there after they had had a skirmish with British soldiers.

Miss MacMahon came from the GPO with messages, and gave me a graphic description of what was happening there. She said, 'Mr Pearse would make you laugh; he was going around the GPO like one in a dream, getting in the way of those trying to get things in order, and Mr Clarke said, "For God's sake will someone get that man an office and a desk, with paper and pens, and set him down to write".' There he sat writing most of the week, and brought out the

paper called *The War News*. Later on Monday evening Seán T
O'Kelly also came with messages from the GPO. He told me he had
been sent to release Bulmer Hobson from the house where he had
been detained for some days.[2]

On Tuesday, the lovely weather continued. Early in the day, a
Post Office official who was a neighbour called to tell me that he had
overheard a message, sent over a private wire at the telephone
exchange, to the effect that an airship was being sent over that night
to drop incendiary bombs on the GPO. Could I have word sent to
the GPO? Miss MacMahon arrived early with messages, and I sent
her back to the GPO with the message about the airship and the
bombs. The GPO was darkened that night.

When Miss MacMahon had gone, I went into the garden to continue my planting. The ground was very dry, so I had a can of water
to water in the plants. I had just laid it down when I heard a hiss,
which gave me a shock. I fell over on my face and was unable to rise
for some time. I did not know what the hiss was, but I examined the
watering-can as soon as I was able and found two bullet-holes in it,
one on each side. Where they came from I have never been able to
find out.

Some Volunteers from the North called during the evening, and
asked for directions to headquarters. Late that night I was surprised
when two of my sisters, Laura and Nora, arrived from Limerick,
accompanied by a young Co Limerick man named Eamonn Dore.[3] I
knew him coming into the shop with messages from Seán MacDermott to Tom. I wondered how they had come to Dublin, thinking all
the trains had been stopped. They told me they had got to Dublin
through the agency of a friend employed in the booking office of the
railway station in Limerick; a special train was to be run from

Limerick to Dublin to carry relatives of British soldiers, and he had procured tickets for them. They had met Eamonn on the train, coming to Dublin to participate in the Rising.

When they arrived at Kingsbridge Station, there was no conveyance to bring them to my house so they had to walk, a long weary walk. Eamonn Dore accompanied them, as they had to go through a part of the city they were not familiar with. They said that they had come on their own initiative to find out what was happening and to get instructions for Limerick; they were both members of Cumann na mBan. The Limerick Volunteers had been mobilised out in the countryside when they had received the countermanding orders from MacNeill; they decided to act on the orders and disband. They were confused when they received the later orders from Pearse, and did not know what to do; they returned to the city and did nothing. My sisters wanted headquarters to know the position in Limerick, and hoped to bring back orders to the Limerick Volunteers.

I got tea for them in the kitchen, as the only light we had was candles; the gas had been cut off. I gave them all the news I had, and when the meal was finished they started for the GPO. I would have disobeyed orders and gone with them, but I knew I could not walk the distance and would only hamper them. When they arrived at the GPO they were hailed with delight, and had a long talk with Seán MacDermott and Tom. They got no orders for Limerick, but one of them was asked to try and get to Cork, and get in touch with Terence MacSwiney. Seán said: 'If you get to Terry, he will act.' The message to him was, 'For God's sake go out and do something to cause a diversion in the South, to prevent the British troops massing round Dublin.'

When my sisters got back to me, they had time for a few hours' rest before leaving for the train, which was due to leave Kingsbridge Station at 6am. The friend in Limerick had got them return tickets, otherwise they would not have been allowed on the train. They had to walk to Kingsbridge, where their tickets got them on the train all right, but how where they to get to Cork when their tickets were for Limerick?

On enquiry, they found that one portion of the train was going to Cork. Nora, who had decided to get to Cork somehow or other, tore up her Limerick ticket. When the ticket checker came around, she sought in her bag for the ticket she knew she would not find, and pretended to get into an awful state about it. The checker asked if she had had it at Kingsbridge; 'Of course I had,' she said, 'I would not have been let on without it.' 'Well,' he said, 'I'll be around again, and if you have not found it by then you will have to pay.' When he got around again, of course she had not found it; he demanded payment, she paid with pretended reluctance and got to Cork.

According to Nora later, when she arrived in Cork she went to the MacSwineys' house, the only address she had, but there was no answer. A neighbour told her that the MacSwineys were away for the weekend. As she had never been in Cork before and knew no-one there, she was in a predicament. She then remembered that Seán O Muirthile had once brought a girl piper from Cork to Limerick, to play at some function, and this girl had stayed with the Daly family in Limerick. Nora could not remember her name, but chatting one day the girl had mentioned that she had a sister who worked at Thompson's in Cork.

On a chance, Nora went into the first Thompson shop she came to, and asked the first girl she saw serving there, 'Have you a sister that plays the pipes?' 'I have indeed,' she answered. 'Well,' said Nora,

'I met her in Limerick when she stayed at our house.' 'You must be one of the Dalys, then.' 'I am, and I wonder if you could direct me to the Irish Volunteer headquarters.' 'I could not,' the girl said, 'but if you go along to Jennings' shop, he will be able to do so.' When Nora got to Jennings' shop, she was told that he was at his home; he was getting married that day. When she got to his home, he was very nice to her, and sent a Fianna boy with her to the Volunteer headquarters.[4] There she met Terence MacSwiney and Tomás MacCurtain.

When she had delivered the message from Tom and Seán MacDermott, both men told her it was absolutely impossible to do anything. They were surrounded by British military, and were expecting an attack at any moment. The Bishop was advising them to surrender, but they did not want to do that. Nora was very disappointed; she had arrived so full of hope. From what Seán had said about Terence MacSwiney, she had thought that if she got to him everything would be all right.

Miss MacSwiney arrived before she left headquarters and insisted on Nora staying the night with her in her house. They were followed to MacSwineys' by G-men. There was a Cumann na mBan meeting that night which Miss MacSwiney had to attend; Nora asked if she might accompany her, as she did not like being left alone in a strange house, but Miss MacSwiney said she could not. Later that night, MacSwiney and MacCurtain told her that they would give her a message to Limerick in the morning. Having been followed the night before, she thought it well to disguise herself a little, and borrowed a costume from Miss MacSwiney to make a change. She feared that if she was recognised on the train for Limerick, she might be stopped by G-men.

On leaving for the train, she was told that the message from headquarters would be sent to Limerick by special messenger, who would come back with news for Cork. When she got to the railway station and went to the ticket office there was a detective inside the office window. She felt sure she was going to be nabbed. Getting her ticket, she hurried to the train. She knew her disguise was good, but could still feel a hand on her arm, either to question or arrest her, and thought it was all up when she saw the detective walking down the platform, looking into every carriage. When the train started and she was safely on her way home, the relief from the strain was so great that she burst into tears. It came as a great surprise to her later, when she heard that Cork had surrendered their arms.

On Wednesday morning, the *Helga* [a British gunboat on the river Liffey] started shelling Liberty Hall. The sound was very disturbing; I did not know what was being shelled or who or what was doing the shelling, until Miss MacMahon arrived from the GPO with messages and told me. When she had gone, I got out a shirt I had been making for Tom. It was made in a special way, so that he could put it on without hurting his injured arm. I thought the sound of the sewing-machine would drown the sound of the big guns. It did, a little. I worked on the shirt until it was finished; by then the big guns had ceased. In doing the shirt I was filling myself up with the hope that Tom would be back to wear it.

Late that night Seán T O'Kelly came with messages from the GPO. He was not in any great hurry, so we sat and talked over a cup of tea; it was after 11pm when he left. Afterwards I heard that he had not been able to get back to the GPO; the British had drawn a cordon around the city that night, and all approaches were guarded by British soldiers. He was not there for the surrender, but was arrested later in his home. The next time I saw him was on his release from a British prison camp.

On Thursday I got more messages from the GPO, but they were not cheerful. I ached to join them all there, and to be near my husband, but hesitated, fearing that by disobeying orders I would only add to their worries. I know now I would have been wrong to go. If I had been there at the surrender, and like the rest imprisoned, I would not have been free to do the work of caring for the dependants of those dead or imprisoned, the work which had been allotted to me. On Friday, I got no word from the GPO, and had no idea of what was happening. The suspense was terrible. My neighbours were, I think, too scared to come near me, possibly fearing they would be involved by doing so.

During the day a lady who lived on Richmond Road called, to know if I had any news of how things were going. She had a niece and a nephew out in the Rising; the nephew, Frank Bourke, was a teacher in St Enda's School. She was in a very anxious state about them, and said there were all kinds of rumours, some of which she told me. She was not relieved by my lack of reassuring news. However, we had a long chat which in some way seemed to ease her anxiety. Before leaving, she paid me what I considered a compliment, by saying, 'You are a fit wife for a revolutionary', though I am sure she did not mean it as a compliment; she lacked my enthusiasm.

That evening an elderly man, a neighbour, brought me a long brown paper parcel. He said it was a rifle which belonged to his son, who was out in the Rising, and would I hide it for him. If it was found in his house it would bring all his family into trouble, but I was so deeply involved that a rifle more or less found in my house would make little difference. I said he could hide it in his own garden, that I did not feel like taking it, but he was aghast at the suggestion; he said he might be caught doing so. He had brought it to me at great risk and I could do what I liked with it, and out he walked leaving the rifle with me. Without opening the parcel, I threw it in a disused ashpit and forgot all about it. Some years later, when rifles were scarce and difficult to get, I remembered it and had it dug up, only to find it was one of the dummy guns used by the Irish Volunteers in the early days, when they had no rifles. I had to laugh when I remembered the absolutely scared condition of the man who had left it with me.

That night I watched, from the upper windows of the house, the smoke and flames of what seemed to be the whole city in flames. I watched all night; it seemed to me no-one could escape from that inferno. The picture of my husband and brother caught in it was vividly before me, and their helplessness against that raging fire appalled me. I don't know how I lived through it, though death in that dreadful fire might have been more merciful than the treatment I saw meted out to them in Kilmainham Jail, while awaiting death there.

Saturday was a day of great suspense, much greater than Friday, with one rumour more horrible than another. It was said that a surrender had taken place. I refused to believe it. On Sunday morning the milkman arrived, about 9am, and told me that the Volunteers had surrendered. 'Nonsense,' I said, 'they would not surrender.' 'Well,' he said, 'I saw them with my own eyes this morning in the Rotunda Gardens, surrounded by British soldiers.' Yet even that did not convince me; it might be a group of Volunteers the British had captured that he had seen, I said. Perhaps I did not want to be convinced. He got very angry with me when I would not believe him, and walking away he said, 'It's damn cool you take it, anyhow!' It was only too true, what he had told me.

The day passed for me in quiet agony, and there seemed a hush over the city, the hush that is pregnant with disaster. I neither slept nor ate. Monday passed in the same way, except that I was now consumed with suspense as to the outcome of the surrender, and did not know if my husband or brother were dead or alive. On Tuesday, the suspense was so great that I could not keep still, and went into the garden hoping to kill time there.

I worked until an old lady friend called, and I had to go in to see her. I came in with my garden shoes and overall on, intending to resume work as soon as she had gone. While talking to her, I looked down the avenue and was startled to see a large detachment of British soldiers turn the corner from Richmond Road and march up the avenue. Their guide was a local mental defective. He was in front waving his arms, puffing and panting with his ephemeral importance, guiding them to our house. When they arrived, they drew up and surrounded the house in semi-circular formation, with their rifles pointing to the roof.

While they were coming up the avenue and arranging themselves around the house, I was busy. Never having experienced a military raid, I was not quite sure what they would do (though my Aunt Lollie had given me a description of a raid on her home in Fenian times, carried out by police). I had a fairly large sum of money in the house, some of it receipts from the shop for Saturday and Sunday, and some of it money held in trust for the dependants of those participating in the Rising.

I feared that if the soldiers got it, that would be the last I would see of it, but where was I to hide it? Time was short; any minute now they would be demanding admittance. Ah, sudden thought; I would give it to the old lady! She would scarcely be searched, even if I was. This was easier said than done. She was frightened, and I had to bully her into consenting. She was so terrified at the thought that she was quite helpless, and I was shaking with pent-up excitement. She had an old-fashioned bodice, buttoned from the neck down. I opened the buttons, put the money inside and rebuttoned it. Her ample bust was not noticeably increased by the added bulk.

The knock came at the hall door as the last button was buttoned, and though I had been shaking violently while expecting it, when it came it made me perfectly cool and steady. Opening the hall door, I was confronted with five revolvers held by five officers, who had arranged themselves in a semi-circular form around the hall door. They informed me that they had come to search the house in the name of His Majesty, the King. I looked coolly at them, and said, 'You seem to have sufficient force to carry out your order.' Leaving the hall door open, I turned back into the room where I had left the old lady. I was uneasy about her; I feared she might break down.

The soldiers came in and started to search the house. They brought Sarah, my maid, up from the kitchen, and put the three of us under arrest. They left a soldier on guard at the door of the room. In order to show them how little their actions disturbed me, I took up a Limerick lace handkerchief I had been making and worked on it throughout the raid. It was a pure piece of bravado, and the work done was very poor, but it seemed to have a soothing effect on the old lady and the maid, who had been a bit hysterical.

Suddenly an officer appeared at the door bawling, 'What is the meaning of having this in the house? Why has it not been reported?' I stopped work for the moment, as I was far from the door and could not see what he had in his hand. I said, 'Would you mind coming a little nearer and let me see what you are making such a rumpus about?' He came over to me with something in his hand. I had never seen it before, and did not know what it was, and I told him this. He told me it was a bomb, I think he said it was a Mills bomb, and told me where he had found it. I told him that if I had known it was there and what it was I would have taken good care not to notify the authorities, or leave it for him to find. He seemed very disconcerted at my reply, but apparently not being able to think of a suitable reply he left the room without a word.

Later he returned, to question me about my men. He wanted to know where they were. Were they out in the Rising? When had I last seen them? Was I in sympathy with them? I could have refused to answer, but felt it would be letting my men down not to show I was with them, so I said that they were in the Rising and that I was in perfect sympathy with them, and very proud of them.

He then announced that he was taking us all away under arrest. I protested against the old lady being taken; I said she had nothing to do with the Rising; she was just an old family friend who had chanced to call in shortly before his arrival, and she was far too old to suffer such treatment. I also protested against the arrest of my maid; she was an entirely innocent person who had the misfortune to be earning her living working for me. He was adamant; he was taking us all away under arrest no matter what I said. I told him I would reiterate my protest against the arrest of these people wherever they took us.

He ordered us to get out of the house and march down the avenue. I said, 'You must allow my maid and myself to dress suitably for the street.' He said we must go as we were. I told him if he did not permit us to change to street wear I would not stir one step. Just then I looked out the window, and noticed the soldiers jump to attention and salute three more officers who had come up the avenue. One of them seemed to be of higher rank than the one who was bullying me.

On a chance, I turned to him and said, 'Bring your superior officer to me.' To my surprise, he did, and it was the one I had noticed through the window. When he came in, he was very pompous, and said, 'You wished to see me, madam.' I said, 'Yes, this man here refuses to allow my maid and myself to dress suitably for the street, though he says he is taking us away under arrest. I demand to be allowed to do so, otherwise I shall not move one step from here.' Very curtly, he agreed to permit us to change, but insisted on the doors of our bedrooms remaining open and a soldier being placed inside each door while we dressed.

When I went to my bedroom, a scene of great disorder met my gaze. The contents of the wardrobe, chest of drawers and cupboards were dumped on the floor. It took me some time to find a coat and skirt to match, and a hat I could wear; my hats were all ripped up. When we were ready, we were marched down the avenue between two files of soldiers. At the end of the avenue there was a military motor car drawn up, into which we were ordered. A large crowd had collected out of curiosity, and a woman came pushing her way through the crowd; she seemed to be abusing them. She was a Mrs O'Brien, who kept a small shop on Richmond Road. She rushed over to me and shook my hand vigorously. I was afraid she would be arrested, but her action gave me a great cheer. She must have known she risked being arrested by what she did.

I was the first to be ordered into the car. Instead of getting in, I halted with one foot on the running board and said, 'I am making a last protest to you about this old lady, and wherever you take me I shall continue to protest against the outrage of arresting her.' I saw a sign of wavering in the officer's face, so I just stood, making no move to get into the car. With such a crowd around, I could see the soldiers were a bit nervy, and I sensed they feared hostility. The crowd far outnumbered them, and I took full advantage of that by not moving. I won; the officer agreed to let her go. He took her name and address, and then told her very rudely to clear off. I breathed a sigh of relief; my money was safe.

Sarah and I were then driven to the Clontarf Police Barracks, and locked in a freezingly cold cell. It interested me, as I had never been in one before; it was apparently a drunks' cell, as there was nothing movable in it. It had a window near the ceiling, a wooden bench built into the wall along one side, and a lavatory in one corner; I think the floor was concrete.

Poor Sarah, who had not long left the Aran Islands, was getting hysterical. What would her mother think of her being arrested and imprisoned, such a disgrace it was. She was moaning about what was going to happen to her. Poor girl, she did not know what it was all about. In my state of anxiety about my husband and brother, her condition was very trying. I did all I could to soothe her, but only made matters worse. She took to weeping. In sheer desperation, I told her that if she did not shut up she would be shot. It was brutal, but it calmed her, or perhaps petrified her. She stopped crying.

Then I told her I was going to try and get a cup of tea, and this cheered her up. I knocked at the door. In response a policeman opened it. I asked if we could have some tea, as we had had nothing to eat or drink since 8am that morning, and it was now after 3pm. I said I had some money and could pay for it. He said he would see, and in a short while he came back to say that as we were in military custody he was powerless to do anything without their consent. They refused to allow us to have anything to eat or drink. He was most apologetic. I thanked him for his efforts.

After an interval of perhaps an hour, we were taken to a motor car outside the police barrack, in which Arthur Griffith was seated, with two British officers. I was both surprised and overjoyed to see Griffith, my first thought being that he had been out in the Rising after all; 'Tom was right, and I have wronged Griffith.' It had been, I think, Ash Wednesday, when I had met Griffith in O'Connell Street and asked if he was ready for the route march on Sunday. From his reply, I had got the impression that he had no intention of being there. When I got to the shop, I had asked Tom whether Griffith knew about Sunday, and he replied, 'He does.' 'Well,' I said, 'he won't be there.' He had laughingly replied, 'Well, even if you don't like Griffith you should not be unjust to him. Of course he is going out. He has a Howth gun; why should he have that if he does not intend to use it?' I replied, 'I'll take a bet on it', but he did not bet.[5]

When I saw Griffith now in the car, and the Howth gun too, naturally I thought he had been out in the fight, and was full of regret for having misjudged him. I felt that all my doubts about him were unjustified. It was well that I did not remember what Tom had told me about Griffith helping McNeill in issuing the secret countermanding orders. I suppose I was too tired to think after the week I had been through, and the surprise of seeing him in the hands of the enemy put it out of my head. Had I remembered, I fear the car would not have held the two of us. Along with the Howth gun was a sack full of what the military called 'documentary evidence' from the Griffith home, and a similar sack from my home was added to it. The car moved off, to where we did not know, but it landed us in Dublin Castle.

As we turned into the South Quays, we passed a group of marching men, accompanied by British soldiers. Possibly through lack of sleep or other things I was a bit dull, and did not realise who they were, so I asked Griffith. 'Prisoners,' he replied. 'God Almighty,' I said, 'and we are passing them without a salute!' With that I jumped up in the car and waved to them as well as I could with my two hands; I had nothing else. Griffith caught a hold of me and pulled me down. 'My God,' he said, 'Are you mad? You will be shot before you know where you are.' 'I don't care,' I said, 'I am not going to pass our men without a salute.' When I had calmed down a bit, one of the officers in front said, 'Short shrift those fellows will get.' 'Well,' I said, 'they will die for their country, a thing you will never do with that coat on your back.' He was the son of a Dublin doctor I knew, and he was killed later in France.

By this time I had Griffith nearly in the jigs. I was lost to all sense of danger, and he feared for me. What I saw all around me keyed me up to the highest pitch. What must our men have gone through that the city had to be laid in ruins to compel their surrender? What agony must that surrender have been to them? Griffith was really in a state over me, and did what he could to restrain me, though I really was not acting wildly. I just wanted everyone to know I gloried in our men, and their stand against a mighty Empire.[6]

Arriving at the Castle without mishap, we were brought before a British officer and charged, with what I don't know, and I did not care, but I suppose it was being rebels. Griffith made no reply when charged. As he was moved off, he turned and insisted on leaving me his overcoat. It was very kind of him. I had only a light costume on and it was bitterly cold; I was very grateful to him. I was next charged, and the sack of 'documentary evidence' produced. Being near it, I gave it a kick, in a ladylike way of course, saying, 'As far as what is in that sack goes, there is not evidence in it to hang a cat on, but I have no hesitation in admitting that I and all belonging to me are in this thing, and proud of it.' The officer said very sternly, 'You are in this thing?' 'Yes,' I replied, 'up to that', putting my hand across my throat. 'Where are your men?' he asked. 'I do not know,' I answered. 'They are either dead or in your hands.' He nodded, and gave an order for me to be locked up.

Then Sarah was charged. I turned to the officer and said, 'Sir, this girl is perfectly innocent of any complicity in this thing. She knows nothing about it, she just has the misfortune to be earning her living in my home as a maid. I protested against her arrest, but this young man (pointing to the officer who had arrested us) would not listen to my protests. I would plead for her, sir, she is the innocent victim of circumstances.' He turned to the officer I had pointed out, and said in a very severe tone, 'Why did you arrest this innocent girl?' The young man got very confused, and stuttered, 'Ah, ah, well sir, I thought the evidence I got in the house was sufficient to remove every one and lock it up.' 'Yes,' I butted in, 'You left a poor dog, two cats and a dozen canaries to starve there.'

The officer at the desk said, 'You had no business to arrest this girl. Release her at once.' 'Sir,' I said, 'there is no use just releasing her. She does not know the city, and would get lost. If you would have her driven back to the house I would indeed thank you.' He said, 'Very well, I will have her driven back', and he ordered the young officer to have her driven back to the house she had been arrested in. ' I thank you very much,' I said. 'May I pass her the keys of the house?' He nodded consent. As I was passing the keys to Sarah, the young officer said, 'Oh, but sir, that will not do. It will open the house up again, and we don't want that.' I said, 'Why? You were over three hours searching it. What more do you want?' The officer at the desk here

Newspapers: *Irish Freedom*, December 1913 (with Tom Clarke's business stamp); *Irish Volunteer*, January 1916; *Irish War News*, April 1916. (*Courtesy E. Clarke*)

Daly family. *Standing from left*: Katherine O'Mara Daly, James, Ellen, Jim Jones, Eileen, Madge. *Seated from left*: Nora, Edward (aged 3), Agnes, Margaret Hayes Daly, Kathleen (aged 16), Laura Daly. *Seated on floor from left*: Carrie and Annie, 1894. (*Courtesy H. Litton*)

Below: Tom and Kathleen Clarke (composite photograph), 1901. (*Courtesy E Clarke*)

Thomas Clarke in 1881, aged 23. Artwork copy, Edmund Ross. (*Courtesy E. Clarke*)

Daly family before Kathleen's departure to the USA, 1901. *Standing from left*: Nora, Annie, Agnes, Carrie, Laura. *Seated from left*: Eileen (O'Toole), Kathleen, Madge, Edward. (*Courtesy E. Clarke*)

Left: Hanna Clarke, one of Tom's sisters, and Mrs Mary Clarke (née Palmer), date unkown. (*Courtesy E. Clarke*)

From left: Mrs O'Donovan Rossa, Fr Micheál O'Flanagan, Eileen O'Donovan Rossa, Tom Clarke, July 1915. (*Courtesy E. Clarke*)

Coat of arms designed for Kathleen Clarke as Lord Mayor of Dublin. (*Courtesy H. Litton*)

Below: Postcard montage of executed 1916 leaders. *Seated from left*: P.H. Pearse, J. MacBride, T. Clarke, E. Ceannt, J. Connolly, J.M. Plunkett.
Standing from left: W. Pearse, T. MacDonagh, S. Heuston, M Mallin, S. MacDermott, M. O'Hanrahan, E. Daly, C. Colbert. *Inset*: R. Casement, T. Kent.
Copyright Office of Public Works, Ireland.

ountess Markievicz with her daughter, Maeve, and stepson, Stanislaus,
rca 1904. (*Kilmainham Gaol Collection*)

Edward Daly in uniform. (KE 23, *Courtesy of the National Library of Ireland*)

intervened and told me to pass the keys to Sarah. Then he ordered the young officer to have Sarah conveyed back to the house safely.

I was marched off and locked up in a very dirty room, which I afterwards discovered was at the Ship Street end of Dublin Castle grounds. On entering, I saw a young girl sitting on a stool, and recognised her as a member of Cumann na mBan. While the soldiers who had conducted me to the room were present, we mutually avoided any display of recognition, but when they were gone she told me she had been held prisoner in Rathmines Police Station for some days, and had been removed to the Castle that day. All her brothers were out in the Rising, but she did not know where they were, or whether they were dead or alive.

Later that evening, Miss Marie Perolz and Miss B Foley were brought in. The girl and myself having previously decided we would not recognise anyone that might be brought in while the soldiers were present, we turned our backs on them until the soldiers who had brought them were gone. Then we learned that they had been arrested in different parts of the country, doing despatch work. We were talking, and exchanging experiences, when there was a commotion outside the door. It was banged open, and a woman with four soldiers tumbled in. She was holding them, two with each hand, and yelling, 'What did ye do with my dear, darling Doctor Lynn? Where is she?'

She was a big, powerful woman, and held the four soldiers apparently without much trouble; they were small and young. They were struggling to get free. In the struggle, her shawl fell off. To my horror her back was completely naked; the soldiers had torn every stitch of clothing off her in their struggles with her before they reached Ship Street. I picked up the shawl, put it around her, and whispered to her to let the soldiers go. In her surprise at my action, she let two of the soldiers go, but, looking at me very suspiciously, she retained her hold on the other two. Then Miss Perolz took a hand, and persuaded her to let the other two go.

She and Miss Perolz sat down in a corner and had a heart-to-heart talk. She told Miss Perolz that her brother had been out in the Rising, got wounded during the week and managed to get home. In the street where she lived were also many of those we called 'Separation Allowance women'. These women, whose men were serving in the British Army, were receiving weekly allowances from the British, and some of them informed on her brother. When the British soldiers came to arrest him he made an attempt to escape and was shot dead. She became abusive to the soldiers and they arrested her. That was how she had been in Ship Street with Dr Kathleen Lynn, and other women prisoners who were there. She had been released before Dr Lynn and the others were removed elsewhere.

That day, she told Miss Perolz, a British officer was passing down her street with a squad of soldiers and she recognised him as the man who had shot her brother. She caught up a brick and flung it at him, and that was how she came to be arrested a second time. While she was telling her story to Miss Perolz, she would look across at me every now and then, and whisper to Miss Perolz, 'Are you sure she is a Sinn Féiner? Are you sure she is not one of them wans in the pay of the British?' It took some time for Miss Perolz to convince her I was all right, and could be trusted. Then she announced that she would be out of there in an hour. She asked us to keep quiet.

She began by banging on the door and shouting, 'Sergeant, are you there?' Getting no answer, she continued banging on the door. Finally the answer came, 'Well, what do you want?' 'I want me babby to give him a drink, he'll die if I don't.' There was no reply, so she repeated her performance of banging and calling the Sergeant. After some time, the answer came again: 'What do you want?' 'I want me babby, he'll die if he doesn't get a drink.' She turned to us and said, 'He's weaned long ago.' Her acting was good, and for a time diverted my mind from my own troubles. We were all surprised when the Sergeant opened the door and said, 'Come out', and out she went, and all our sympathy went with her. The memory of her tragic story remained with us. The Sergeant returned later and said he had had to let her go; there would be no peace for anyone while she was there. She had kept it up all night when she had been there previously.

I asked the Sergeant if there was any possibility of getting us tea, and something to eat. I had not even had a drink of water since 8am that morning, and it was then about 8pm. He said he would try, and as it was beginning to get dark I asked if he could get us some candles too. I gave him ten shillings to pay for them. He returned about an hour later, when we had almost given up hope of seeing him. He brought a bedroom ewer of tea, without milk or sugar, a loaf of bread, a small tin of bully beef (which we could not open), and some candles. I could eat nothing; my anxiety was too great as to the fate of my husband and my brother. I drank the tea, which was hot and warmed me; the night was very cold.

After we had finished our repast, three or four young British soldiers came into the room. They started sneering at the folly of a few men attempting to attack a great Empire like the British Empire. The Cumann na mBan girl and I ignored them completely, but Miss Perolz and Miss Foley were unable to stand the taunts, and replied to them. The girl was sitting on a bench, reading, with her elbows on her knees, when one of the soldiers sat down beside her, flung his arms around her and attempted to kiss her.

She stood up without saying a word, boxed him thoroughly, resumed her seat and continued reading. I felt extremely proud of that girl; at the time I could have hugged her. From the way she tackled the young man I think she must have had boxing lessons. He was quite defeated, and made no further attempt to molest her. I only wish I could remember her name; she was a girl anyone would be proud of.

Some time after this episode I was sitting on a bench, completely absorbed in my thoughts and fears for my husband and brother, and in a dim way hearing Miss Perolz and Miss Foley arguing with the soldiers. Then Miss Perolz asked me something about my children, and the next thing I knew I was being chucked under the chin by one of the soldiers, saying, 'Surely this kid is not old enough to have children!' I was unable to box like the girl, though speechless with indignation, but under my gaze that man slunk away; there was murder in it. I sat for a few minutes to control my rage, then I got up and said, 'Gentlemen, I wish you would relieve us of your presence. We do not know what tomorrow may bring us and would like to get some rest, to enable us to meet whatever is in store for us.' They made some remark about wanting to cheer us up, and did not go for some time. On leaving, they said they would be in later to tuck us in. They did not return while I was there; I was removed between 12am and 1am.

When they were gone, we decided to try and get some rest. The floor was the only place to lie on, and the only coverings we could find were a couple of old blankets. Both blankets and floor were filthy. We laid one blanket on the floor and used the other to cover us, and by lying very close together it barely covered us. Before lying down I removed my costume and hung it up, so that it would not be soiled or wrinkled, even though I was shivering. I was thinking of the morrow, when in all probability I would be brought in front of some tribunal. I did not want to give the impression that the women of the Rising were slatterns, such as soiled or wrinkled clothes might give. Then I remembered Arthur Griffith's coat, and wrapped it around myself. It was a boon.

We were not long settled on the floor when we were again startled by a commotion outside the door. I feared it was the soldiers coming back, and possibly drunk. The door opened, and two women were flung in, shouting, 'We are not Sinn Féiners.' They seemed hysterical, and kept shouting until we asked them to shut up and let us get some sleep. We said we did not care what they were, but that we were Sinn Féiners. They would not believe us at first, but after some talk accepted our word, and then admitted that they were Sinn Féiners. We then agreed to let them share our blankets, and settled down, as we thought, until morning.

My mind was in too great a tension to sleep. I could think of nothing but my husband and brother. Were they blackened corpses in the smouldering city, or prisoners in the hands of our enemy, perhaps being tortured?

A knock on the door again startled us. This time it was the Sergeant. He entered and said, 'Which of you is Mrs Tom Clarke?'

I said I was, and he handed me a paper which read:

Detention Barracks, Kilmainham
Dear Madam,

I have to inform you that your husband is a prisoner here and wishes to see you. I am sending a motor car to bring you here.

I am, Madam, Your obedient servant,

W S Lennon, Major, Commandant.

Mrs T J Clarke, 10 Richmond Avenue, Dublin.

This had been sent to my home, now changed to 31 Richmond Avenue, and the maid had told the messenger that I was in Dublin Castle, a prisoner.

I had lit a candle when the Sergeant came in, and after reading the message I put on my costume. While I was doing this, Miss Perolz asked what was in the paper the Sergeant had given me, and I told her. 'I wonder what that means?' she said. 'It means death,' I told her. 'Oh God No, surely not that!' she exclaimed. 'Surely,' I said, 'you do not think the British are so good and kind as to send for me to say goodbye to my husband, if they were sending him any shorter journey than to the next world.' 'God, you are a stone,' she exclaimed. I felt like one. It seemed to me as if it was not I that was acting, but someone looking on. It was a queer feeling; my actions were more or less automatic. The predominating idea in my mind was to keep a brave front to the enemy, and not let them see me broken, no matter how I suffered.

I said goodbye to them all, and joined the Sergeant who was waiting outside. He had two soldiers with him. They had rifles with fixed bayonets. He handed me over to them. The order to march was given, and off we went into the open. It was pitch dark, and I did not know where we were going. The only thing I had to guide me was the tramp of the soldiers each side of me. The ground was level for some time, then we turned left and it became uphill. We went under what seemed to be an arch, then turned right and into a building which I afterwards found out was in the Upper Castle Yard. I was told to wait there until someone came, I thought they said the Provost Marshal. He came and looked me over, and gave an order for me to be driven to Kilmainham Jail. I was then put into an open car, with the same soldiers, and a third one who was driving. Snipers were still busy; we were stopped every now and then by British military, permits examined, torches flashed in our faces. Our journey to Kilmainham seemed endless; I began to wonder if we would ever get there.

When we did arrive there, it presented a scene of gloom and decay. It had been abandoned as a prison for many years. A damp smell pervaded the whole place, and the only light was candles in jamjars. The first person I saw was a brown-habited priest, who was standing in the hall as I entered. He approached me and said, 'I have been waiting for you, Mrs Clarke, to use your influence with your husband to see me.' I said, 'I am afraid you waited in vain, Father. I have never interfered with my husband in anything he thinks right, and I am not going to begin now. If he will not see you, he has his reasons.' He tried to reason and argue with me, but he left me unmoved. I did not know him, I had never seen him before. He then said something about Tom going before his Judge, to which I answered that the Judge he was going before would be more merciful than the human one he had been before, and as I knew what a pure soul Tom was, I was not afraid for him, or the Judgement of God for him. The strange thing was that no-one had told me that Tom had been tried and sentenced to death; I just knew.

After a short delay, I was taken up a stone staircase and along a narrow passage with doors on both sides. In the gloom it was hard to make out what kind of passage it was. The soldier who conducted me inserted a big key in the lock, and the door opened. There was Tom lying on the floor. He jumped up when he saw me. I rushed to him, saying, 'Why did you surrender? The last thing you said was no surrender.' I could not stop myself saying it when I saw the way he was treated; I thought any death would be preferable. He was very gentle with me, and said, 'I know, Katty, and I meant it. Had it rested with me there would have been no surrender. On a vote, I was outvoted. I had hoped to go down in the retreat from the GPO, but it was not to be. Perhaps it's all for the best.'

He asked me if I had got a note he and Seán MacDermott wrote to me, on the only piece of paper they could get; he had given a soldier his old watch for him to bring it to me. They were in Richmond Barracks at the time, and had thought they were going to be shot without trial. I said that so far I had not got it. I asked him what his trial had been like. 'It was a farce,' he said. Then I asked him what had happened between him and the priest who had been waiting for me. 'He asked me to use my influence with you to see him, and I refused.' He told me that the priest had wanted him to say he was sorry for what he had done; 'unless I did he could not give me absolution. I told him to clear out of my cell quickly. I was not sorry for what I had done, I gloried in it and the men who had been with me. To say I was sorry would be a lie, and I was not going to face my God with a lie on my tongue.'

'Never mind,' I said, 'God will understand.' When I heard his story, I did feel I could throttle that priest. Common humanity, common charity, would have dictated a different course on the part of a priest, a course which may have brought out a different result. Tom saw in the attitude of the priest the same old British official attitude he had met with in Portland, Chatham and other prisons, and quite possibly his old resentment against them flared up.

He said, 'I suppose you know I am to be shot in the morning. I am glad I am getting a soldier's death.' I said, 'I know, although so far no-one has told me; it has been left to you to do so.' He faced death with a clear and happy conscience, and knowing him to be one of the purest souls I had no fear. Then he told me my brother Ned would also be shot. 'Surely not Ned, he is so young,' I said. 'Yes,' he said. 'He is very young, but from the British point of view he has earned death. Tell John that he has every reason to be proud of Ned. He has proved himself a fine soldier and a hero.' Continuing, Tom said that all our men had been heroes, that he felt very proud of them, but that many would be shot. He knew MacDonagh and Pearse were to be shot with him that morning, and Ceannt, Plunkett, MacDermott, Connolly and many others would go too.

Then he said that there were two things he wanted me to do. 'It will be said that the Germans played with us, that they were false and did not carry out their promises of help. This I want you to refute; the Germans carried out their promise to us, to the last letter. They never promised men; we did not ask for men. They could promise only a small cargo of arms. What help they could give us would entirely depend on their progress in the war; they had promised that if they won out, they would free Ireland.'

The second thing is about MacNeill, he said. 'I want you to see to it that our people know of his treachery to us. He must never be allowed back into the National life of the country, for so sure as he is, so sure will he act treacherously in a crisis. He is a weak man, but I know every effort will be made to whitewash him.'

We then talked about our children. He begged me not to let his death shadow their lives. 'They have been so far such happy children, but train them to follow in my footsteps.' I said I would do my best to carry out his wishes, but his death would shadow their lives no matter what I did, and I thought it was a hard road he had picked for them, to follow in his footsteps; children did not always carry out their parents' wishes. I then said, 'I don't know how I am going to live without you. I wish the British would put a bullet in me too.' He said, 'It is not British policy to shoot women since the Nurse Cavell episode.[7] God will help you, and your own courage, also the children's need for you.'

We left the subject. It was too dangerous, and might break us. Then he told me to tell Uncle John that when they had arrived at the GPO from Liberty Hall on Easter Monday, he as President had shot the lock and ordered all those engaged inside to file out with their hands up. The other men who had accompanied him, four of them signatories to the Proclamation, MacDermott, Plunkett, Connolly and Pearse, fell back a step for him to do this. In this way, he was first into the GPO. He also told me to tell him that he had led the last charge out of the GPO. When it became impossible to remain in the burning building, orders were issued to evacuate. He was in a group going out the Henry Street exit when it had occurred to him that some prisoner may have been locked up and forgotten in the rush, so he turned back and made a tour of the building as far as he could.

Having assured himself that there was nobody trapped in the building, he returned to the Henry Street exit. Here some men were debating whether to go or stay. Either way seemed certain death; to cross to Moore Lane they would have to go through a crossfire of machineguns, but to remain was certain death by fire. He dashed across to Moore Lane, saying, 'Come on, boys, charge for Ireland!' They all followed, and to their amazement arrived in Moore Lane alive. He added that he had hoped to go down then, but that it was not to be. He had to go through the agony and horror of the surrender, and then the terrible indignities he was subjected to, with my brother, in the Rotunda Gardens, and finally to be treated like a mad dog or worse in Kilmainham Jail.[8]

When they reached Moore Lane, they got into some of the houses in Moore Street by the back doors. Here Tom was joined by MacDermott, Pearse and Plunkett. I'm not sure about Connolly, but presume he was there. The house they were in was owned by a man named Plunkett, no relation to Joseph. They remained the night there, debating what they should do, and it was there that the decision to surrender was taken. Tom was the only one against it, and though he did not agree with it, he said, perhaps it was all for the best. Pearse, as Commander-in-Chief, was the one to go to give the surrender.

All through our interview, I was conscious of the exalted, very exalted state of mind he was in. Looking into the future he saw suffering, but at the end freedom. 'He said, 'My comrades and I believe we have struck the first successful blow for freedom, and so sure as we are going out this morning, so sure will freedom come as a direct result of our action. It will not come today or tomorrow, and between this and freedom Ireland will go through Hell, but she will never lie down again until she has attained full freedom. With this belief, we die happy. I am happy and satisfied at what we have accomplished.' Then he said he would like me to make a short trip to New York, if it was possible, to tell John Devoy all I knew. 'Repeat to him all I am saying to you, particularly about MacNeill; I want him to have the right version.'

During the whole interview, my mind was concentrated on not breaking down. I knew that if I broke, it would break him, at least I feared it would, and perhaps leave him unfit to face the ordeal before him in the way he and I would like. Yet I did not miss a word he said. It is burned into my brain. It never fades, or never will. Looking back, I often wonder if he understood my seeming coldness. He told me that he had got the choice of a letter to me or an interview; he had first chosen the letter, then the longing to see me once again was so great that he asked for an interview. He gave our home address, not knowing that I had been arrested. A baby was coming to us, but he did not know. I had not told him before the Rising, fearing to add to his anxieties, and considered if I would tell him then, but left without doing so; I was not sure how it would affect him.

Throughout our interview a soldier had stood at the door of the cell, holding a candle. Our time together seemed so short when he said, 'Time up', and we had to part. I had to stand there at the cell door while the soldier locked the door of what seemed to me to be my husband's tomb. How I held myself together, with my head up, I do not know. I must have been turned to stone, as Miss Perolz had said, but the sound of that key in that lock has haunted me ever since.

6
After the Rising

1916

Release from prison – visiting brother Ned in jail –
trip to Limerick – illness – Cumann na mBan and the
Irish Volunteers Dependants Fund

While I followed the soldier down the stairs, it occurred to me
that they might not give me Tom's body for burial, and I
decided to ask for it. The same officer was in the hall as had
been as I went in, so I went up to him and said, 'You will please
notify me when death has taken place, so that I may send for
the body for burial.' He became quite confused and said, 'I am
not sure the body will be released for burial.' 'Surely,' I said,
'when you have wreaked your vengeance on him and taken his
life, the body becomes mine.' 'Oh well, madam,' he said, 'I am
sorry, but we have received no orders yet.' 'That being so,' I
said, 'will you make a note of my request?' He promised to do
so.

I was then taken back to the Castle by the same military guard.

Not a word passed between us on the way. On arrival there I was put into a guardroom on the right as you go in to the upper Castle yard, while my escort went to get instructions as to what was to be done with me. The only light in the room came from a huge fire, and a number of soldiers were sitting around drinking tea. One of them offered me a mugful; I took it and thanked him. It was hot, and I was stiff with cold. While I sat there the soldiers chatted amongst themselves; they knew where I had come from and all about me. From their talk, which I could not help hearing, I gathered they had great sympathy for me, but on such lines that it made me feel like killing them. I longed to tell them I wanted none of their sympathy, but feared to open my mouth lest I might break down; at all costs I must keep a stiff upper lip, at least in front of the enemy. So I had to sit and listen to talk that made me wild, though in a sense I knew they meant well.

Their talk was on the lines that it was all very well for those crazy lunatics to go out and start a rebellion, but what about all the suffering they brought on their women and children? Did they never think of that? What hope had they against England's might? Such madness, such foolishness; here was one of their women, and look what she had to go through, and so on. I wanted to dash the mug of tea in their faces, but I knew if I once let go of my self-control I would find it hard to regain it. It was a great relief when my escort returned and brought me to a small room on the ground floor, facing the guardroom I had left.

There I was left for a time in the charge of a military policeman. The man who had given orders for my journey to Kilmainham came in, looking very sleepy. He looked at me for some time and then said: 'You are free now, I will not keep you a prisoner any longer, but as curfew is on until 7am it is better for you to remain here.' Before leaving, he told the military policeman to make a fire, as it was very cold; he was very courteous. When the fire was lit a number of soldiers came in to warm themselves, and some of them lay down on the floor to sleep. One of them was a sergeant, and before lying down he let out a stream of the most foul language I ever heard. He said his parents were Hirish, though he was born in Hengland; his parents were always talking about Hireland, and he was delighted when his regiment was ordered to Hireland, but by this and by that he never wanted to see Hireland again —it was worse than Gallipoli.

He had just settled himself on the floor when a volley of shots rang out, followed by machinegun firing. He and all the other soldiers ran out, and returned in about ten minutes, exulting and rubbing their hands with apparent satisfaction. I gathered from their talk that a sniper had just been riddled; he had been sniping from a chimney commanding the Castle yard all the week. At dawn that morning, he was changing his position when the military spotted him, and fired from every quarter. They said he had been responsible for over one hundred casualties amongst military crossing the yard during the week, and there was intense satisfaction that they had at last finished him. Who he was I don't know, but I said a little prayer for him.

After that all was quiet, and I was left with my military police guard, who was an Englishman. He began talking to me, and said, 'I don't understand you Irish, why do you try to stab England in the back when she is at war? I come over here from England, where evidence of war is everywhere you turn, darkened streets, food rationing, wounded men everywhere, very little amusement. Here in Dublin I find your streets ablaze with light, picture houses, theatres, dance halls, every form of amusement going full blast, food in plenty, nothing to indicate war. Despite that, you start a revolution. Why?'

While he was speaking, I sent a little prayer to God to guide me in answering him, to help me make clear to him our point of view, and when he had finished I said, 'You, in your arrogance as an Englishman, would not admit that the Germans could win the war, but suppose, for the sake of argument, we say they did win. Then in conquering England and ruling her, they reduced her from a prosperous country, an educated people, to a poverty-stricken one; education ruthlessly stamped out, the German language substituted by law for the English; her population reduced to a third of what it had been; her people driven out to make room for the Germans; Germans planted in all the best positions in the country, all the best land confiscated and given to Germans; her people starved while the Germans were well-fed. Don't you think, as an Englishman, you would rebel?'

'I'm damn well sure I would,' he said. 'Well now,' I said, 'You have our point of view, in as few words as I can give it to you.' He thanked me for explaining things to him, and said he understood our point of view for the first time. He then asked me if I would shake hands with him. I hesitated. He said, 'Please do, I would appreciate it.' I shook hands with him, and I don't regret it. He was a decent Englishman.

At 6pm he said curfew would not be off until 7pm, but he would get a permit for me to go through the city. He took me to the Dublin Metropolitan Police office, just behind the City Hall, procured the permit for me and released me. He then walked with me as far as the *Evening Mail* offices, but before parting he said, 'Madam, I understand the Irish point of view now, as I did not before. I have the deepest respect for you. Goodbye. Will you shake hands with me again?' Strange as it may seem, I did.

The sun was shining as I faced down Dame Street. Dear God, I felt it cruel for the sun to be shining when so much sorrow and suffering was all around. I had often read of the sun seeming cruel to shine on individuals whose hope in life was gone and sorrow only their portion, but that morning it came to me as more than a figure of speech. As I walked through Dame Street, Westmoreland Street and O'Connell Street, and saw the destruction all around, I made up my mind that I would work to give England a very different reaction to their savagery than they had got after other risings and bids for freedom. Other risings left only despair, and efforts towards freedom left to the next generation. I would make every effort to keep the ball rolling, and in some way continue the fight for freedom, and not let it end with the Rising. I had a certain amount of money, entrusted to me by the IRB for the relief of dependants of men engaged in the fight, but the number of men arrested was so great the money I held would not be a bite. Looking after the dependants of men in jail was to be the same as looking after the dependants of men out fighting, and its object would be the same, to relieve the men's anxiety about their dependants. When talking to Tom in Kilmainham Jail, he had told me to use the money I held to relieve distress, but I am sure he had no idea of the thousands of men who would be arrested.

All the way home I was planning how I would act, and this despite the fact that my mind was in a state of agony that was indescribable. I pictured my husband as he faced the firing squad, arms pinioned, helpless to save himself from falling down after the volley was fired, but not dead, badly wounded, suffering tortures (he was very sensitive to pain), left there to die by degrees. There was nothing awful enough for my mind to conjure up, knowing the ferocity of the British towards us.

As I passed through Westmoreland Street, soldiers were lying asleep on the sidewalk rolled in blankets. There was no sign of life until I reached O'Connell Street. It was a terrible scene of desolation – houses down all around, some still smouldering; I had to walk along the middle of the road to avoid falling walls. The only living thing I could see in O'Connell Street was a policeman, standing at Nelson's Pillar. I asked him what was the best way to Fairview. It looked as if all streets were blocked, and he said, 'The best way would be down North Earl Street. The Parnell Street way is clear, but it is full of soldiers; it would be better not to go that way.' To go down North Earl Street, I had to climb over a mountain of bricks and mortar still hot, the debris of houses which had fallen on top of a tram that was there. Then down Talbot Street, along Amiens Street and the North Strand to Fairview. Along the way soldiers were lying on the ground, wrapped in blankets, asleep. There was no life until I reached Fairview, where I met the milkmen going their rounds.

The journey seemed endless; I thought I would never reach home. I had had no food since the previous morning, and had gone through such an agony of mind I felt it would leave me numb for the rest of my life. When I got home, Sarah had a good fire, hoping I would come. She had sat up all night waiting for me. The fire was very welcome, I was so cold. She got a meal ready for me in a short time, but I could not eat. I felt I must get forgetfulness for a time or go mad. I opened a bottle of wine, filled a tumbler full and drank it. Being a teetotaller, I thought it would at least give me twenty-four hours' sleep and enable me to face things. I lay down in bed and fell asleep, and woke as keenly alive to everything as I had been when I lay down. I looked at my watch to see how long I had slept; I had slept just one hour. After that, drink as a means of forgetfulness was taboo.

Later in the day two of my sisters, Madge and Laura, arrived from Limerick. I felt no surprise at their arrival; I felt nothing but the agony of parting with my husband, but I had to listen to their story. They told me they had got word of a train leaving Limerick for Dublin and rushed for it; they did not know what had happened in Dublin. No reliable news reached Limerick before they left. At Limerick Junction, they had seen prisoners being put on the train, and recognised one of them, Pierce McCann. I told them what had happened in Dublin - that Tom, MacDonagh and Pearse had been shot that morning, and many more would be shot, including our brother Ned; that in all probability the military would call for me that night to take me to see Ned. How I knew that, I cannot tell. They found what I told them hard to believe, and naturally were shocked and grief-stricken.[1]

I don't know how the day passed, but around eleven o'clock that night they started urging me to go to bed. I had not been to bed since the Rising started. I told them I was not going to bed, as I knew the military would come for me to take me to see Ned; I often wonder since why I was so sure of this. They decided to go to bed, and to avoid further argument I agreed to do so. I had no intention of doing so, but wanted to stop them worrying about me. We decided to sleep in a room with two beds. I pretended to undress, but only put my nightgown over my clothes; I was so convinced the military would come, I wanted to be ready.

I had the nightgown just on, and they were partly undressed, when I heard a military lorry. I stopped and listened for a while, then told them the military were coming, and that from the sounds I heard they were about at Summerhill, and that they would be here in a few minutes or less. I saw them looking at each other and could read their minds; they were wondering was my reason giving under the strain, as they could not hear a sound. I told them they need not worry, I was quite sane, and the sound I heard was I knew a military lorry; as it was curfew, no other lorry dared be out, and that it was now nearer than when I first heard it. I would say it was now at Bally-bough, that they had stopped for a few minutes, but were now on their way straight to this house. I could give them no reason, though I was certain of it. While I was speaking, I could hear the lorry turn into the avenue and come nearer, and in a few minutes there was a knock at the door.

When I opened, there was a policeman standing there. He asked if I was Mrs Tom Clarke. I said, 'Yes.' He then informed me that my brother, Edward Daly, was a prisoner in Kilmainham Jail, and that he wished to see me. There was a lorry waiting to take me to him. I asked him if my two sisters who had come up from Limerick that day would be permitted to come with me, that had my brother known they were in Dublin he would have asked for them too. He said he had no authority; he had been picked up in Ballybough to act as guide. He referred me to the soldier in the lorry. I walked out to the lorry and explained to the soldier about the unexpected arrival of my sisters, and asked if I could bring them with me. He said he would take any member of the family. It was only when I got back to the house I realised I still had my nightgown on.

I told them what I had done, and that they could come with me. Then I saw them signalling to each other that it would be better to leave me at home. I told them I saw their signalling, and reminded them that Ned had sent for me, and that I was going to see him. If they made any attempt to stop me I would go to the soldier I had been talking to and say I did not wish to bring anyone with me. I never asked them why they wanted to leave me behind; possibly they feared the strain after the previous day and night would be too much for me.

When we arrived at Kilmainham Jail, we were escorted to Ned's cell by five officers. It was a different part of the jail from the previous night. Candles were still the only light, and a soldier was holding the candle. Ned jumped up from the floor where he had been lying without covering. He was in his uniform, and looked about eighteen years of age, his figure was so slim and boyish. Madge and Laura entered the cell first. I stopped just inside the door, deliberately, to prevent the officers crowding in as they seemed inclined to do. This would give Ned an opportunity to say anything to Madge or Laura he would not wish the officers to hear. The officers remained outside the door; to get in they would have had to push me aside, or further into the cell.

To further increase the privacy for Ned, I engaged the soldier who was holding the candle in conversation. He remembered me being there the night before; he said he was the soldier who had held the candle there too. He knew all about Tom Clarke, knew his father's record in the British Army, and mentioned the name of the regiment he belonged to, which I had not known. I asked him if he could tell me if the man I had visited the night before was dead. 'Of course he is dead,' he said. 'Would you swear it?' I asked him. 'I would swear it,' he said, 'I was one of the firing party, and if it is any consolation to you, I can tell you I was in many a firing party, but I swear I never saw a braver man die.' I said, 'If you told me anything else I would not believe you, I knew him too well, but thank God he is dead and out of their hands. They can do no more to him, his sufferings are over.' The awful fear that was in my mind, of his being left to die a lingering death, was set at rest, at least for the time.

Only about fifteen minutes had passed when the officers outside said, 'Time up,' and so far I had not had a word with Ned. I protested, saying that I had got much longer with a prisoner the previous night. 'Indeed you did,' the soldier holding the candle said, 'you got nearly two hours.' My protest was unheeded; the officers insisted we must go. I had only time to kiss Ned goodbye. He whispered to me, 'Have you got Tom's body?' I said, 'No, but I have made a request for it, and have told Madge to make the same request for yours.' I thought it strange he should ask that question. He got no time to say more.

When we got back to the hall, Madge approached the officer at the desk and made the request for Ned's dead body for burial. He made no comment, but wrote down her request. Then I approached him to say I had not yet received my husband's body, though I had made a request for it the previous night. He told me he had no information on the matter; he had forwarded my request. Some weeks later, Madge received a letter which said as the body of her brother was already buried, they could not accede to her request. I got no answer to my request.

Before leaving the jail, I saw two sisters of Micheál O'Hanrahan. They were members of the Central Branch, Cumann na mBan. I spoke to them, and asked them why they were there. They said they had been sent for to say goodbye to Micheál. They had not the faintest idea he had been sentenced to death; they thought he had been sentenced to imprisonment, and perhaps was being sent to England. They thought that was the reason they had been sent for. 'Eileen,' I said, 'he is being sent into the next world. This is a final goodbye.' She screamed. I had given her an awful shock, but thought it better she should get it now than in Micheál's cell. 'For God's sake, Eileen,' I said, 'control your feelings before you see Micheál. Now you know the worst, pull yourself together before you see him or you will unnerve him.' She did; both sisters did, they were wonderful. They went through the interview with Micheál bravely, but Eileen went down in a dead faint as soon as she was outside the cell. I was so sorry for those girls, as Micheál's execution was a thing they never anticipated.

As we were being escorted to the lorry which had brought us to the jail, a young officer, who seemed to be in charge, said, 'I am sorry for you, ladies, and must say I admire your splendid courage, a pity it is not in a better cause.' With one voice we answered, 'It's our country's cause, and could not be better.' I have no recollection of what we did when we got home, but I remember feeling that if I could cry it would ease me. I could not.

Next morning after breakfast a number of British officers arrived and hammered at the hall door. I opened the door and asked them their business. They said they had orders to search the house. I said, 'That is very strange, as this house was searched for several hours on Tuesday by members of your army. You have already wreaked vengeance on the men belonging to this house. Where is your search-warrant?' For answer, they pushed past me and went up the stairs, into a back room where a few large trunks were stored. The trunks were full of old papers and letters I had received from my sisters when I was living in New York, all of which had Sinn Féin stamps on them (these stamps were a method of raising money used by Arthur Griffith for his paper, *Sinn Féin*). They removed all the envelopes that had these stamps; apparently they thought they had some connection with the Rising. I did not recognise any of them as the officers who had been in the house on Tuesday, but some of them must have been there, noticed the Sinn Féin stamps during the search, and come back to get them, as they did not go into any other room.

When they were gone, Madge, Laura and I set out for Richmond Barracks to visit the prisoners. We had been told we could see them through barbed wire. We walked down Ballybough Road hoping to pick up a cab there, as there were no trams running. We saw a cab and hailed it, but when the driver heard where we wanted to go, he made every excuse to get out of driving us. He only agreed to do so if we paid him beforehand, and did not expect him to drive us up to the barracks, but near it. We saw the prisoners; they were in a large field surrounded with barbed wire. We talked to them through the wire. There was a large number of visitors, many there in the hope of locating their men. All brought parcels of food, but we had not thought of doing so.

On our way home we got a copy of the English *Daily Mail*, with the announcement of the first executions as follows:

THREE REBELS TRIED AND SHOT.

OLD FENIAN, POET AND BARRISTER.

PENAL SERVITUDE FOR OTHERS.

MR BIRRELL RESIGNS.

'Mr Birrell has resigned his post as Chief Secretary for Ireland. 'Of the seven leaders of the rebellion, those who signed the "Republic" Proclamation, three were court-martialled, found guilty and shot yesterday morning, namely:

THOMAS J CLARKE, "President of the Republic"; old Fenian, convicted of dynamite outrages in the '80s, kept a tobacco and newspaper shop.

P H PEARSE, thirty-six, born in Dublin of English descent, "Commander in Chief", barrister; headmaster of St Enda's College for Boys outside Dublin, published poems in 1914.

THOMAS MACDONAGH, poet of the rebellion, M.A.; English tutor University College, St Stephen's Green; teacher at St Enda's.

'Three others were sentenced to three years' penal servitude. The remaining signatories of the Proclamation included:

SEAN MCDERMOTT or MACDIARMADA, ex-tramway driver.

EAMONN CEANNT, one of the founders of the Irish Volunteers in
1913.

JOSEPH PLUNKETT, who says he is a son of Count Plunkett. 'Apparently Jim Connolly, the organiser for Larkin and "General in Dublin", who was wounded last week, has not yet been tried. Sir Roger Casement is to be tried, said Mr Asquith yesterday, with the utmost expedition.'

That evening, I formed the first committee of the Irish Republican Prisoners Dependants Fund, and spent most of that evening and night distributing help and sympathy to those who called to the house for it. But so many called that I was ready to drop with exhaustion by 11pm. I was so dreadfully sorry for those women who came; many did not know the fate of their men, whether they were dead or alive. Some of them had made the rounds of the hospitals and even the morgue. Yet I did not hear one complaint. They were proud of their men, and they were women to be proud of.

All Commandants had been instructed to tell their men that in case of necessity, their women were to come to me for help, and each Commandant was to draw up a list of the families of men under his command who would be needing help. Tomás MacDonagh sent me his list by Maura Carron, a member of Cumann na mBan. I feared to keep it in the house, and sent it to Mrs Joseph McGuinness for safety, but after the surrender all the houses in the street were being raided, so she burned it lest it fall into enemy hands. That caused a lot of work, as we could only give temporary relief until we had the claim ratified.

On Saturday, Madge, Laura and I went to Limerick. I left money with Miss MacMahon, to relieve any case of distress during my absence. I wanted to see my children and give them their father's message, not to grieve for him, but to glory in what he had done, and to follow in his footsteps. When we got to Limerick the children were overjoyed to see me, and they were very sweet and comforting, but still I could not cry. Something hard would not break up. My mother's heart was broken over my brother's death; she had little sympathy for me, her own heart was too heavy. She adored Ned, but she thanked God for one thing, that he had died for Ireland, not like many other Irish mothers' sons who died fighting for England in France and elsewhere. She rarely smiled from 1916 to her death; the loss of Ned was ever present with her.

Uncle John was terribly grieved over Tom's death. His one wish was that he had been with him. I never saw such love or understanding between two men as between my uncle and husband. The joy it was to them to meet, the deep satisfaction they found in each other's company, was something one does not see every day. Sunday passed quietly; all the family, single, married and children, gathered together in the house in Barrington Street. Uncle John was very ill, but bursting with pride at what the men in Dublin had done, and though Ned and Tom's deaths were a great grief to him, he gloried in what they had done and how they had died. He broke down when I gave him Tom's message about Ned.

My sister Madge decided that if the British military came to raid the house, she would defend it. She would barricade the lower part of the house, and fire on them from the roof and upper windows. Her arms consisted of one Howth gun, one rifle and two revolvers. I told her she was mad, and asked her how long did she think her resistance would last, and what would be the net result. I said, 'You have an invalid uncle, an old mother and aunt, several sisters depending on you. How will they fare if you do this? As a result of your action this house may be burned down. The bakery, which is the means by which you are all able to live in comfort, may be laid in ruins as a reprisal. How will that help Ireland? It seems to me that all the sacrifices necessary have been made. Further sacrifices at the moment will not put us one foot further towards freedom. I am in total disagreement with you, but of course if you persist in going on, I shall stand in with you, even though I think it madness.' She was wild to get a blow at the British, but eventually my arguments prevailed.

On Monday morning, before anyone but the maid was up, the house was surrounded by a large force of British military. I looked out the window while dressing and saw it was a much larger force than had raided my home in Dublin, but arranged in the same semi-circular fashion, with rifles pointed to the roof. I made my way to the kitchen in the hope of getting a cup of tea, and found the rest of the family on the same quest. It was a huge old-fashioned kitchen, and the maid was serving tea to all who came. Seán O'Muirthile was there; he had stayed in the house the night before with the idea of protecting us, as the only man in the house was Uncle John, who was completely paralysed and very ill.

The military were all over the house, but had not yet reached the kitchen. When they did arrive, they immediately seized Seán O'Muirthile, searched him and arrested him.

When they went to the door of my uncle's room, Madge protested against their going in. She said he was dying (which was true), and not quite conscious, but they insisted the room must be searched. They agreed to let the policeman, who had led them to the house, do the searching. He did not like the task; Uncle John had the reputation of being very fierce when roused. He went into the room in fear, apparently, as the minute he got in he closed the door and dropped on his knees lest Uncle John would see him from the bed. He searched all around the room on his knees, and made an attempt to slip his hand under Uncle John's pillow. Uncle John, though quite unconscious of the policeman's presence, gave a moan and turned in the bed. The policeman dropped to the floor as if shot, crawled to the door, opened it and reported that there was nothing there and that the man was dying.

The soldiers were four or five hours searching the house, and the Fianna hall at the back of the house. The hall had been built by my uncle, and was used by the Irish Volunteers and the Fianna. The soldiers took a lorry-load of odds and ends from the house and the hall, and the rumour went around that they had taken a lorry full of German gold. England had, in various ways, with the help of the Irish Parliamentary Party, endeavoured to charge the revolutionaries with receiving gold from Germany to finance the Rising. It was utterly untrue; the only money received from outside Ireland came from our own people, the Clan na Gael in the USA and Irish people in England and Scotland. When the military left the Barrington Street house, they went to the home of my sister Eileen, and after raiding it arrested her husband, Ned O'Toole.

The day after the raid in Barrington Street I had an unusual experience. There was a knock at the hall door, and as I happened to be in the hall I opened it. There stood a British soldier. I asked him what he wanted, and he said he wanted to see John Daly. I said that was impossible, as he was dying. He begged me for God's sake to let him see him for one minute. I asked him what he wanted to see him for, as even if he was well he would not want to see anyone in that uniform. He said, 'I want to go down on my knees and beg his pardon for yesterday. I was one of the soldiers around this house, and I did not know whose house it was until afterwards. My father was a Fenian, and all belonging to me were Fenians. I wanted to see John Daly to beg his pardon, and swear before God that I will never obey an order to fire on my own people, even if it means I will be shot myself.'

I told him I was sorry, but that John Daly was too ill to be seen. He then asked me who I was, and I told him I was John Daly's niece. He dropped on his knees and asked me for God's sake would I shake hands with him. I did; I had not the heart to refuse him. His grief was so genuine I was sorry for him, and I realised it took some courage to come to the house in that uniform. When I told my mother and sisters about him, they were very angry with me for even listening to him. They said I should have kicked him out the door. Perhaps I should have done so, but still I'm glad I didn't.

Madge immediately started a branch of the Dependants Fund in

Limerick, and started the work of relief going. Though there had been no actual fighting in Limerick, men were being arrested every day. All the men who surrendered their arms were arrested and deported, and their women and children had to be looked after. I returned to Dublin on Tuesday evening, and Madge accompanied me. She stayed with me until the weekend, as I would be returning to Limerick to spend the few days with my children.

Before leaving Limerick, Madge received a letter from Miss Mary MacSwiney, saying that Terence had been arrested, and was being sent to Dublin. She and her sister Annie were going to Dublin, to be near him. I told Madge to write to Miss MacSwiney at once and tell her that it was quite possible hotels in Dublin would be reluctant to take her in, if they knew of her connection with the Rising, and that they would be very welcome to my home during their stay in Dublin; I would write and tell Sarah to make them comfortable if they arrived before me.

When Madge and I arrived at my home from Limerick, Mary and Annie MacSwiney were on the steps, just leaving for Richmond Barracks, where Terence was. I was surprised and shocked when Mary, without any preliminary, started to denounce the men who had been executed. She said they were nothing short of murderers. I said, 'Come back to the house and explain what you mean, Miss MacSwiney.' In the house, she repeated her accusation. She asserted that all the arms had been kept in Dublin, and that Cork was left unarmed, helpless to defend herself. I pointed out the erroneousness of her assertion, that I knew that Cork city and part of Kerry were well-armed in order to be able to cover adequately the landing of arms in which, with Limerick, they were to take part. Cork county and other counties were to be supplied with arms from the landing in Kerry, and with arms to be captured from British military and police barracks, which it was planned to raid. No matter what I said, she persisted in her accusation and her denunciation.

Finally I said to her, 'Miss MacSwiney, after all you have said, and the charges you have made against those who are dead and therefore cannot defend themselves, or refute your charges, I do not wish to have anything more to do with you. The old Irish hospitality which has been instilled into me prevents me saying what I would like to you while you are my guest, but I could not guarantee that I would always be able to exercise the self-control I am doing now, so we shall not meet again while you are my guest. My maid will look after your needs.' We did not meet again while she remained in my home, which she did until Terence was removed to England. I have never been able to understand her complete lack of sympathy with the sorrows of my family.

In August, she came to visit my sisters in Limerick. I was very ill at the time; she asked to see me, but my sisters said I was too ill and that the doctor would not allow visitors. She pleaded very hard to be allowed to see me for a few minutes, and promised faithfully she would say nothing to upset me. They agreed to let her see me for five minutes. When she came into the room, she immediately started to repeat the charges against the men who were dead. I got so excited that two of my sisters and the nurse had to push her out of the room. They were in a panic, fearing the result of the excitement on me. (I met Terence after his release from prison camp, and told him about Mary's charges. He said, 'You had the right version', and asked me to make allowances for her; she had been in such a terrible state of mind over his arrest.)

Well, to go back. Before I left Dublin that weekend, Miss

MacMahon, John R Reynolds and myself drew up an appeal for funds to carry on the work of caring for the dependants of the men in prison or dead. The decision to do this was mine. Reading of the thousands of men being arrested and deported every day, I saw that the amount left with me for the purpose would not be a bite to what would be needed. At that time, everything going into a newspaper had to be submitted to the Censor, and he refused to pass our appeal until we changed its name and its form. The name we had submitted was the Irish Republican Prisoners Dependants Fund, so we had to abandon that and change the whole appeal until it was to his liking. This took eleven days. By that time another group had started a fund for the same purpose. Reading the names of those who had started it, I could see it would be controlled by the Irish Parliamentary Party, and decided I would have to fight that.

When coming back to Dublin the following Monday, I brought my children and mother with me to let them see what the British had done to Dublin. While showing them around, I felt very ill, and consulted a doctor, who seemed very hostile to me when he discovered who I was. He said I should go to a nursing home or hospital at once, but I told him I could not, as I had to take my mother and children back to Limerick. 'If you do,' he said, 'you take your life in your hands.' I took my mother and children back to Limerick, and returned at once to Dublin.

I had a very busy time organising the work of the Fund with Miss MacMahon. She was wonderful; I don't know what I would have done without her, as I was feeling very ill. When it became known that we were helping the dependants, streams of women came to the house all day. John R Reynolds placed his office, 1 College Street, at our disposal, free of rent, and his daughter Molly helped in the work.

From then on the work was done in and from his office. It was a period of great strain; prisoners were being deported to an unknown destination every day. Women who could get no information about their men were in a state of distraction, and many came to me for consolation.

I cannot remember the sequence of events very well for the weeks immediately following the Rising, so much was happening, and so fast. I know I went down to Limerick every weekend to see my children, until I fell ill. I had not gone to the nursing home as the doctor had advised me, and I was quite indifferent about what was happening to me. One day, I got so ill in Reynolds' office that I had to go home and go to bed; I was in great pain. About five o'clock in the morning I could stand the pain no longer, so I called Sarah up and sent her to Mrs Seán McGarry to ask her to get a doctor for me. The doctor and Mrs McGarry arrived in a short time, and later a nurse. My baby was dead, and I hoped soon to be.

Then I had a strange experience. The doctor and nurse were busy with me, and while I was looking at them, suddenly everything went dark blue. 'This is the end,' I thought, and said, 'Goodbye, doctor, I'm off.' I heard him say, 'My God, nurse, she's gone.' I thought I was going to join Tom, and was very happy about it. I felt myself lifted up, through clouds which seemed to be arranged like feathers on a bird. As I passed through, they closed behind me. When I got up a certain distance I heard a great shout, like men's voices. They sounded joyous to me, and I recognised Ned's voice. Then what seemed a chorus of men were shouting joyfully, 'Here she comes.' Then there was silence.

I still kept going up, and through the clouds I saw Tom's face and then Seán MacDermott's. Seán said, 'She must go back, Tom, she must.' Tom said, 'God, Seán, we can't send her back, it is too cruel', and Seán said,' You know, Tom, she must go back. She has to do the work we left her to do.' On both their faces there was a look of intense sadness. I wanted to say I would not go back, but I was unable to speak. Their faces disappeared, and I felt myself being slowly but surely pushed down through the clouds of feathers. The next thing I heard was the doctor saying, in a very shocked voice, 'My God, nurse, she's coming back.' And back I was, and a more disgusted creature never arrived on this earth. But now I knew what I had to do, and gave up trying to take the easy way out. I just had to take up my burden and carry it as well as I could.

The doctor told me afterwards that for some minutes he had been sure I was dead; heart and everything had ceased for the moment. When my sisters arrived from Limerick later in the day and stooped over to kiss me, I cried for the first time since the executions, cried with sheer disappointment that I was not dead. A few days afterwards I was sitting up in bed, dealing with correspondence and the lists of those to be looked after by the Dependants Fund with the help of Miss MacMahon, who brought the letters up from the office every morning.

In my absence, Cumann na mBan had had Mass said in the church of St Mary of the Angels, Church Street, for the men who had died for Ireland. After Mass, they held a meeting of protest against the British action in executing and imprisoning men, and vigorous speeches were made. I came back on Monday, delighted with what the women had done. They repeated this every Sunday until the British military authorities sent word to the Church Street priests that if any other meetings were held after Mass, they would have machineguns trained on the meeting, and shoot down those participating.

Miss MacMahon came to me to know what they should do. The priests had advised them to abandon the meetings, but they would not consent until they knew what I thought about it. I told her to tell them I agreed with the priests; to be shot down now would not advance our objective one bit, although I doubted if the British would go so far when the meetings were held by women. I told her to point out to them that they had demonstrated to the British that they were solidly behind their men, and of greater importance, I believed, was that the reports of the meetings had helped to steady the country. The meetings were abandoned with reluctance. They were mostly Cumann na mBan, and were afraid of nothing. They were women any country would be proud of, and their courage and steadfastness were marvellous.

I am convinced that the action of Cumann na mBan in Dublin and all over the country, when they took up the care and mainte-nance of the dependants of those dead or imprisoned, and the corre-spondence between His Lordship, the Bishop of Limerick, and General Sir John Maxwell were the two things at that time that did more to steady the country than anything else. It shut down on the rumours afloat that the Rising was a Bolshevist one, a rumour which in all probability was deliberately set afloat. This action on the part of the Bishop of Limerick was a great surprise to me as a Limerick woman, but coming at the time it did I could have kissed his feet for it. In his young days, he was very hostile to the Fenians.[2]

Some weeks after the Rising I received the following letter, or rather note, from Tom and Seán MacDermott. It had been written in Richmond Barracks, before Tom's trial, on the only bit of paper they could get, torn out of a small notebook. When I was with Tom in Kilmainham Jail, he had asked if I had got it; he said when they had written it, they had thought they would be shot at once, without trial. He had given the watch he had with him, a silver one (he had left his good one at home) to a soldier who had promised to get it to me. Tom wrote on one side, Seán on the other:

> 'Dear K.
> I am in *better health* and more satisfied than for many a day – all will be well eventually, but this is my good bye and now you are ever before me to cheer me – God bless you and the boys, let them be proud to follow same path – Seán is with me and McG[arry], all well – they are all heroes – I'm full of pride my love,
> Yours,
> Tom.
> Love to John and Madge.'

On the other side was Seán MacDermott's note:

> 'Dear Cáit,
> I never felt so proud of the boys. Tis worth a life of suffering to be with them for one hour.
> God bless you all,
> Seán.'

It had been sent to me by a Mrs O'Toole, 32 Kings Inn Street. I could imagine Seán's grin of mischief when he wrote 'Dear Cáit', as he had never dared to address me as other than 'Mrs Clarke' in all our years of friendship and comradeship.

As I said, before our appeal for funds for the dependants was released, another party conceived the idea of starting a relief fund. When I read the list of names I knew I was right, that it had been instigated by the Irish Parliamentary Party. When the Censor released our appeal for funds, with John R Reynolds' name as Honorary Secretary, John immediately got an order from the British military authorities to deport himself to Coventry, England. He asked me what I would advise him to do, and after thinking it over for some time I advised him to go, otherwise he might be landed in jail. There were enough men in jail, and he might be of some use to the Irish in Coventry. If he went without a fuss they might forget him, and he would be able to slip home. He went reluctantly, but was not able to come back as I had hoped; he was not allowed back until the general releases. Reynolds had been with all those who had surrendered from the GPO, but when brought before a tribunal had been clever enough to convince them that he was a victim, not a participant. He was then released and came to see me at once to help, and was a great help until his deportation.

I got the idea of holding a series of flag days for the Fund, to be held on Sundays. The first was to be Wolfe Tone flag day, and those to follow were to be named after the executed men, starting with the signatories to the Proclamation in the order in which their names appeared on it, for seventeen Sundays. I was stopped in my gallop by the British Commander in Chief of the Forces in Ireland, who wrote:

'Whereas I am informed that you, the committee of the Irish Volunteer Dependants Fund, having temporary offices at 1 College Street, Dublin, propose to hold a public flag day collection in Dublin and elsewhere in Ireland on Sunday 25th June, 1916, and subsequent dates;

'And whereas it is proposed that the said Flags shall contain portraits of persons who have been in rebellion against His

Majesty the King;

'And whereas there is good reason to believe that the said public collection and distribution of the said flags are likely to cause disaffection to His Majesty the King, and prejudice recruiting of His Majesty's Forces...and also cause disaffection amongst the civilian population...

'Now I, General Right Hon Sir John Maxwell KCB, KCMG, GVO, DSO, Commander-in-Chief of His Majesty's Forces in Ireland, Competent Military Authority for Ireland, do hereby warn you and each of you that all persons organising or taking part in such public collections, or public sales, shall be liable to arrest and prosecution under the Defence of the Realm (Consolidated) Regulations.'

This was delivered to me while I was still ill, and was alone in the house except for Sarah - my sister and the nurse had just gone out. A man asked to see me, and Sarah said I was ill in bed and could see no-one. She asked if she could bring a message to me, but he said no, he wanted to see me, but he would not tell her who he was. I told her to tell him to wait until my sister returned, that she would not be long, and that I was not well enough to see anyone. He said he would wait.

After a while, I felt a creepy, uneasy feeling as if something evil was waiting there to pounce on me. I tried to reason with myself, that it was an overactive imagination due possibly to my illness, but it was no use. The feeling grew into suspense, horror – would my sister never come? I could stand it no longer; I rang for Sarah and told her to tell the man I would see him. When he came in, I recognised him at once as a G-man I had often seen near our shop in Parnell Street.

He seemed shocked at seeing how ill I was. He apologised for coming, and explained haltingly that he had to carry out orders. He handed me the above document.

I tried to read it, but the print danced before my eyes, and the paper was enlarging and contracting. The feeling of faintness was dreadful, but I fought it – at all costs I must not faint, I must not give him the impression I feared him. I did not, but I was so weak. Eventually I mastered the contents of the paper, and asked if his master knew that the flag days were for a charitable purpose. 'Yes,' he said, 'but he also knew they had a propaganda purpose too.' I said, 'Well, you can report to your master how ill I am, and you can tell him that were I able to get up and out, I would challenge the authority of his order by going out and selling the flags. Since I am unable to do so, there is nothing left to me but to call off the whole thing; I will not allow Cumann na mBan girls to challenge his authority unless I can be with them in doing so.' He said nothing, but tiptoed out of the room. No wonder I felt the slime of his presence.

When it became known that there were two Funds, apparently for the same purpose, I was approached from many quarters to amalgamate with the other Fund, called the National Aid Fund. I refused; I said unless the British soldiers, the MPs and Mr Sherlock, whom I looked on as a nominee of John Redmond, were dropped from it, I would not amalgamate. I looked on these men as enemies of the executed men. I explained that the Irish Volunteer Dependants Fund had been operating since the week of the first executions, but that owing to the hold-up of the Censor we had been unable to reach the public earlier. We were going to continue our work.

I went down to Limerick to consult with my sister Madge about it, and she did not quite agree with me. She thought that the men who composed the committee of the National Aid were well-known and influential, and would be able to collect more money than our committee. Her chief concern was for the people who needed help. My answer was that the National Aid were using the names of our dead to collect, not their own influential names, that we were the direct representatives of the dead men and had the influence of their names behind us, and that I would not work with men whom I considered their enemies.

Madge said that she would talk it over with Uncle John and see what he had to say – she was the only one who could understand what he said, as he was suffering from paralysis. I had already made up my mind – it did not matter what anyone said, I would not amalgamate unless the conditions I laid down were agreed to. When Madge put the case to Uncle John, he asked her to give him the night to think it over. In the morning, he told her to tell me I was right, and to go ahead. Madge made no further kick. Indeed, I knew her heart was not in the kick, but she considered it desirable to put before me the possibility of failure.

I returned to Dublin, and went on with the work of the Fund. Miss MacMahon was chief organiser, secretary, everything; I never knew a more competent girl in my life. Cumann na mBan took up the work of collecting, distributing the Fund in Dublin and all over the country. We had Dublin city divided into areas, and each worker collected and distributed in their own area. In addition, they had to make a thorough investigation of each case, since the lists of the dependants of the men in Dublin had been burned. Many subscribers could give only a small subscription every week, but big or small, every subscriber was welcomed. Each one was a friend. It meant a lot of work for the collectors, but they made no complaint. After their day's work they collected every night and distributed once a week. They certainly were wonderful women.

All over the country, Cumann na mBan did the same. The Dublin lists of married men or men with dependants were to be followed by lists of men with dependants outside Dublin. I had been left a certain amount of money to use for the start (£3000), and it was expected that as the fighting continued money would be sent to me as needed; they had expected to last out about six months, counting on the landing of arms from Germany. This was the reason for my not being allowed anywhere in the actual fighting; the care and maintenance of the dependants of the men out fighting was considered too important to be left to chance. After the surrender, the British soldiers who were raiding did not know friend from foe, and raided the most unlikely places, except when accompanied by G-men, who gave them all the information they wanted.

Planning and organising the Fund was tough work, but Miss MacMahon was equal to it. She did marvellous work. She had had a well-paid position which she gave up to devote all her time and energy to the work. She spent money she had saved to keep herself, and would not accept one penny from the Fund; she also postponed her marriage until after the amalgamation of the two Funds. My sister Madge undertook the organising of the Fund in Limerick, helped by Cumann na mBan and my other sisters. Miss Mary MacSwiney did the same for Cork.

To restart the Central Branch, Cumann na mBan, Miss MacMahon and I called a meeting of the members, held in 25 Parnell Square. It was a very stormy meeting. 'Where were you? Were you out? If not, why not?' were the questions bandied about. A motion was proposed that those who were not out in the Rising should be expelled; some members showed intense bitterness towards those who had not been out. I was in the chair, and instead of dealing with the motion I pointed out that the failure in most cases was due to the treacherous action of John MacNeill and his countermanding notice, which caused confusion and upset all plans. I said that the Rising was only the first blow, that the fight for freedom had to be carried on, and that our duty to Ireland and to our executed leaders was to close our ranks, forget our failures and get to work.

'There is plenty of work to be done. Why waste your energies fighting each other while all that work is waiting for you? Our men are nearly all in prison, some are dead, and it is up to us to carry on their work, as well as caring for their dependants. The Irish Volunteer Dependants Fund needs the help of every member to make a success of it. Let us show our enemy what we women can do.'

Most of those present saw the sense of what I had said, put aside their rancour towards each other and went to work with a right good will on the Fund, the success of which was much greater than we had anticipated. I often think of these women of Cumann na mBan and the trojan work they did all over the country. It was surely a labour of love, labour and self-sacrifice. This was not confined to Dublin, it was the spirit throughout the land.

7
Continuing the Fight

1916-1917

Irish Volunteers Dependants Fund – Amnesty
Association – Cathal Brugha – prisoners released –
de Valera and MacNeill

Early in June 1916 I was convalescent, and sitting in my room wondering who I could get to do the work I wanted done throughout the
country. All the men I knew and could trust were in prison, and a
woman would not suit the particular work I had in mind. A man
came to the front door and asked for me; Sarah came to my door, but
before she could say a word the man rushed in. He looked like a
sailor, and it took me some time to recognise him. When I did, I felt
God had answered my prayer for help; I had needed a man who
would not be known to the G-men, one I could trust.

This man's name was Liam Clarke (no relation). He was a Volunteer and a member of the IRB who had been badly wounded at the
GPO on Easter Monday and been sent to hospital. He had just come
out of hospital, and came to see me to ask if there was any work he

could do. As all the men whose names I had been given to call upon were either in prison or on the run, I had to break new ground and trust to my own judgement in my selection of helpers. I decided to trust Liam; he was the only available man, was prepared to do anything and was full of enthusiasm. Being young and unknown, he could do a lot without arousing enemy suspicion. I was followed everywhere at the time, and thought it marvellous to get someone who could move around freely, without being watched.

He agreed to start work at once, so I gave him instructions as to what I wanted done. It had nothing to do with the Dependants Fund, but if the police or G-men questioned him he could pretend it had. I pledged him to secrecy as to who was directing him, fearing that those I told him to get in touch with in various parts of the country, in order to get the IRB and Irish Volunteers restarted, might hesitate if they knew it was a woman who was directing. The message I gave him was very simple: the Rising was only the first blow, and they were to keep on drilling and arming and preparing for the next blow. I knew that the message would be sufficient; our people have quick intelligence and imagination and would not need details, at least for a start.

My idea was to get the thought travelling through the country that the fight for freedom had only begun with the Rising. Though thousands of men had been arrested, there were many thousands ready to join in with the Rising who had not been, and it was to these my message was going, as well as to the younger generation who were full of admiration for the revolutionaries of 1916. I told Liam that if he was asked whose authority he was acting under, he was to be vague, and give the impression that it was a headquarters he was not free to divulge. If he whispered that he had been in the Rising, and did not want it known because he did not want the G-men to get on his trail, it would help. Since Liam had to live, I paid him a small salary, with travelling expenses; I had received money from Clan na Gael, to use for any purpose I liked. He went all over the country and back to Dublin at intervals for consultations, and money to carry on. I sent him to Dr Pat McCartan in Co Tyrone to acquaint him with what I was doing, and ask him to get out and give a helping hand. His report back was that McCartan was in the *Hue and Cry*, a police paper, and could do nothing, as the police were watching for him.

My sister Nora, who had been staying with me from the time I fell ill, prevailed on me to let the house and go down to Limerick. She said I could stay in Limerick for the weekends, and in some hotel in Dublin for the rest of the week to carry on the work of the Fund, and I would not have the bother of the house. Though I had no intention of settling in Limerick, I thought it the best thing for the time being. I had just decided this when word came from Limerick that Uncle John was dying, and to come at once. I arrived on 30th June in time to see him alive, but unconscious; he died that night. At his funeral, men marched in military formation for the first time since the Rising, even though they all knew they were likely to be arrested for doing so. The country had already rallied. I kept going up and down between Dublin and Limerick until I left Limerick for good in 1917.[1]

I continued to work for the Dependants Fund. I knew that there were many members of the National Aid Committee who had no motive in being on it different from those who had suffered through the Rising, but I believed the move to start it came from the Irish Parliamentary Party. In my belief, it would have been used as a means of doing what they aimed at in their Manifesto, published in May 1916:

THE ONLY ALTERNATIVE

On the morrow of this tragedy (the Rising) we feel called upon to make solemn appeal to the people of Ireland to draw the conclusions which these events force upon them. We must leave no misunderstanding in their minds as to our convictions and resolves. Either Ireland is to be given over to unsuccessful revolution and anarchy, or the Constitutional movement is to have the full support of the Irish people, and go on until it has completed its work.

We lay before the people of Ireland these alternatives, not for the first time. Indeed, except in certain small sections of the people, this alternative of Constitutional movement was chosen and adhered to for nearly half a century.

After the revolutionary movement of the sixties, Isaac Butt proclaimed to the Irish people that the Constitutional movement was the only sure and certain method of obtaining their rights. Parnell renewed that policy and that hope. The people of Ireland accepted that policy, and that policy has never been seriously questioned by the Irish people.

I was down in Limerick when I heard that a Clan na Gael man named John Archdeacon Murphy had arrived in Dublin from the USA. I decided to go at once to see him, but was taken suddenly ill on the way to the train and had to turn back. An immediate operation had to be performed on me, so Mr Murphy had to come to see me. He told me he had been sent over by Clan na Gael when they had heard of the two Funds, to get the reason for it and to try to bring about an amalgamation. I outlined my conditions for that, gave him my reasons, and listened to his arguments, which were that I should agree to the amalgamation, as the people I mentioned would not agree to withdraw from the National Aid.

I was not even able to sit up in bed to speak to him; nevertheless, my mind did not weaken. He got very angry with me, saying, 'My dear Mrs Clarke, this is a very stupid attitude to take. In America, we fight like anything when there is an election on, the opposing parties saying everything they can think of about each other. When the election is over, they forget all about it until the next election, and keep the best of friends all the time.' 'My dear Mr Archdeacon Murphy,' I said, 'I know how things are done in America, I have lived there, but you are trying to do an impossible thing in expecting things in an unfree country like Ireland, and a free country like America, to be similar. Our differences here are fundamental, vital; there is no analogy, and can be none, between how you in a free country may act in a given case, and how we in an unfree country may.'

Weak as I was, he left my bedside without having accomplished his mission. He was very angry with me, and when he returned to Dublin he said I was 'the goddamndest, most stubborn human being he ever met'. Later, he sent Mrs Ceannt and Mrs Pearse down to try and influence me, and I explained my reasons to them. I could see his arguments had influenced them, so I told them that if every member of the Dependants Fund reneged on me, I would still carry on with it. I had no fear such would happen, but wanted to impress them, and show them I could not be moved.

Mr John A Murphy knew very well, as I did, that if he went back to America and said that he had succeeded in bringing about an amalgamation between the two Funds, but that I would have nothing to do with it, and was carrying on the Irish Volunteers Dependants Fund, he would have been seen as having failed in his mission, and someone else would have been sent over to find out the exact position. John Devoy, having received instructions before the Rising to communicate directly with me if anything happened, would know there was something wrong if I held out. In forming the IVDF I had especially selected women relatives of the executed men, knowing John Redmond and his party dared not say boo to us. They had shown very hostile feelings towards the Rising in the House of Commons, except for one member, Laurence Ginnell. All the women I selected were Cumann na mBan, except for Mrs Pearse; she had never been in anything outside her home before, and at times I think she was bewildered. But we all had one thing in common, we were standing behind our men no matter what the consequences.

Mr Murphy eventually succeeded in bringing about an amalgamation, and on my terms. He called all the parties together. I sent Madge to Dublin to represent me, as I was still unable to travel; she would have been there anyhow, as a member of the IVDF Executive. I heard that it was a very stormy meeting, and many hard things were said at it. When the Funds were amalgamated, the IVDF had its accounts audited, and our lists and money were handed over to the joint Board. I continued my work with the National Aid and Volunteers Dependants Fund (NAVDF), as it was now called, until 1929. At the first meeting of the amalgamated Funds which I attended, every member stood up when I entered and remained standing until I was seated. I took it as a mark of respect to my dead husband, but felt greatly embarrassed. From that time I worked in the greatest harmony with all the members.

Joseph McGrath was the first secretary of the National Aid. He had been in the Rising under Commandant MacDonagh in Jacobs' Factory, but managed to escape arrest. Fred Allen, who had been a member of the IRB and secretary to the Electricity Supply Committee of Dublin Corporation, had been nominated as Secretary to National Aid, but they needed a full-time secretary, so Fred had nominated Joseph McGrath to take it on, in the interests of the participants in the Rising. In that way I gathered that Fred Allen had had the same suspicions as myself as to the ultimate object of the National Aid. On those terms McGrath took it on, but when men were being released from prison he decided to resign. When he had taken it on, he had not known of the existence of the Irish Volunteer Dependants Fund.

Michael Collins and another ex-political prisoner applied for the position of Secretary, and Collins called to ask me to support him. He was only just back from prison camp in England. After talking to him for a while, I decided he was just the man I had been hoping for. He was IRB and Irish Volunteer, and also reminded me in many ways of Seán MacDermott. He also agreed with my idea that the fight for freedom must be continued, the Rising to count as the first blow. As Secretary to the NAVDF, he would be free to move about the country without molestation. Everyone would be free to go into the office of the Fund without arousing suspicion, as so many people were seeking help, and there contacts of every kind could be made. With the information I had been able to give him, he was not long in getting into a leading position. With his forceful personality, his wonderful magnetism and his organising ability, he had little trouble in becoming a leader.

An Irish-American, who was over here on a visit, suggested that the shop in Parnell Street should be bought and converted into a memorial hall or something of that kind in memory of Tom Clarke.[2] He deputised Mrs Séamus O'Doherty to ascertain my views on the matter; if I agreed, he would have the money to do it collected in the USA. I told her that so long as there was a human sufferer remaining as a result of the Rising, I would not consent to money being put into bricks and mortar or any form of memorial to Tom, as I knew he would not wish it. Since then I have sometimes felt regret, that I may have been wrong in taking that attitude, as so far [1940s] not even a lane, much less a street, has been named after him in Dublin.[3] All the men alive who worked with him will admit freely, when talking privately, that he made the Rising possible; in public they are silent, with a few exceptions.

After the Rising the press, alluding to it, called it a Sinn Féin Rising. This was not correct; the organisation then called Sinn Féin was not a revolutionary one, and had been very nearly defunct. It had very little to do with the Rising. Arthur Griffith, its President, had been one of those who had decided, with MacNeill and others, to send out the countermanding orders to stop the Rising, which had been planned and was carried through by the IRB, with the Irish Volunteers, Cumann na mBan and the Citizen Army. I resented it being referred to as a Sinn Féin Rising, but considered it unwise to challenge this, fearing to raise any question which would in any way result in delaying our organisation. Other questions I had to let go, too, at the time, which would have been controversial.

I suspected that the Irish Parliamentary Party were responsible for calling the Rising a Sinn Féin Rising, since the name Sinn Féin was to some extent associated with the idea of failure in the minds of the people. They were out to try and prove to the people the foolishness and uselessness of the Rising, especially when Home Rule had been promised for the end of the First World War; if England won the war, she would be so grateful for Ireland's help, she might give us more. History could have told them that the thing called gratitude was unknown to England so far as Ireland was concerned.

When they were defeated in their plans for the National Aid, I felt sure that the IPP would move in another direction to wean the people from the revolutionary idea. I told Miss MacMahon I was sure that their next move would be an Amnesty Association, and if she got a hint of it to let me know at once, to wire me wherever I was. I attended a weekly meeting of the National Aid and Volunteer Fund one Monday in September; my train from Limerick was late, and the meeting was well advanced when I arrived. Alderman Corrigan was on his feet talking, and I sat and listened. He was saying that after a meeting of Dublin Corporation that day, a group of them had got together and decided to start an Amnesty Association, that something had to be done, and done quickly, to get the prisoners released. He drew a very pathetic picture of the sufferings the prisoners were undergoing, and ended by asking for the help of the NAVDF.

When he was finished, I got up and said that I had the greatest sympathy with the Alderman, for whom it was hard to know that his son was one of those enduring so much, but that I would like to ask him if he had the consent of his son and the other prisoners to plead for an amnesty. 'No, Mrs Clarke,' he said, 'I have not.' 'Well,' I said, 'I think even a father has no right to ask for amnesty for these men without their consent. The definition of amnesty being a Royal Pardon, I feel there is not one of these prisoners who would consent to that. They are all very proud of what they have done, and asking for amnesty is in a sense putting them on their knees, looking for pardon from the nation against which they took up arms to free their country. And I certainly would oppose any move which would put them in such a humiliating position.

'I am old enough to have grown up with the last Amnesty movement, and I am well aware of its complete failure from the point of view of getting Irish political prisoners out of prison before their time. Most of the Irish political prisoners of that period were only released when broken in health physically. When broken in health mentally, they were not released but transferred to criminal lunatic asylums in England. Only one came out not broken mentally or physically, and he had served his full time; that was Tom Clarke. Not one of them was released as a result of the work of the Amnesty Association, though it worked very hard. But I have a very distinct recollection of hearing it said that the Irish Parliamentary Party were using it for their own ends.'

When I had sat down, a vote was taken without further discussion, 'That the National Aid and Volunteer Dependants Fund would give no assistance to any Amnesty movement.' I was very gratified at the decision, and heard no more about amnesty. I was sure the move had come from the Irish Parliamentary Party.

Late in September, I was lying up in a nursing home with a severe attack of neuritis when Liam Clarke came to see me, to report on the work he was doing, and to receive further advice and instructions, as well as money to carry on. I assumed he was acting on my instructions, and had no reason to assume otherwise, so I was very surprised when a day or two after his visit a sailor called to the home and asked to see me. I did not know him, but he told me he had come from Clan na Gael in New York with money for the IRB.

He had been instructed to leave the money at Séamus O'Doherty's for Liam Clarke, but when he got to O'Dohertys' there was no-one home. He had found out where I was, and came to ask me to take charge of the money, as he did not want to take it back with him and he had to be back in Liverpool in time to join his ship. I agreed to do so. When Liam next called to see me I asked for an explanation, but got none. I was glad then that I had not given him any information, only instructions. My association with him ended then, though I was sorry for him. I knew he was suffering a good deal with his wounds, and was in and out of hospital constantly for treatment. I was satisfied with the work he had done under my instructions, when few men were available.

As prisoners were now being released and taking over, things were easing for me. After Batt O'Connor's release from prison camp, I was again a guest in his home, and one evening he told me he was going to a meeting summoned by George Gavan Duffy, who had come over from England to start a new National organisation. He asked me what I thought of the idea. I said we already had a number of organisations, which had participated in the Rising, and that I thought these should be maintained, and all our energies bent on strengthening and consolidating them. If Gavan Duffy desired to participate in the continuation of the fight for freedom, he could join any of these organisations and give them the benefit of his ability and experience. I thought a new party was neither needed nor desirable. Batt agreed with me and said, in his simple outspoken way, that it was a sound outlook. He went to the meeting determined to push through this idea. Apparently he did, as I heard no more of the new party. Batt O'Connor was one of the very fine characters of the period; he was simple and straightforward, intensely National in his outlook and one of the kindest and most generous of men. His wife and family were just like him; I never met a more hospitable or more Nationalist family. They kept open house for all with the right Nationalist outlook, and during the Black and Tan war housed many of the republican leaders.

When Cathal Brugha was released from the military hospital where he had been a prisoner since the Rising, I got in touch with him immediately. I had only met him once before, and we had clashed over his arrogant attitude on the question of the Irish language. I had had no desire to meet him again, but his participation in the Rising had changed my feelings towards him. He invited me to a Sunday dinner at his house, where we could discuss matters, and I gave him an outline of the steps I had taken to maintain the national spirit and generally keep the ball rolling.

Cathal Brugha paid very little attention to what I had to tell him; he was full of himself. He started off by saying that divided counsels had caused the failure of the Rising, therefore there would be no more divided counsels. In future there would be only one organisation, the Irish Volunteers. I told him that that had not been Tom Clarke's view, when speaking to me only hours before his execution; he had said the failure was due to the unexpected arrival of Roger Casement, and to MacNeill's action in sending out the countermanding orders, a thing which no group or organisation could protect itself against.

I told him that when the IRB had started to plan for the Rising, it was decided that members should join every Nationalist organisation, such as the Gaelic League, and secure leading positions in them with the object of spreading the revolutionary idea and directing the people's minds towards a fight for freedom. As a result of this deliberate policy, decisions of the Supreme Council of the IRB were carried into effect in other organisations, so that there were no divided counsels or conflicts. I said he would be undoing much that the Rising had done to bring the various groups together, and to break down any unfriendly spirit that might have existed. If he wanted the IRB to die, let it die a natural death, as it would if all felt it was the failure that he seemed to think it was. If he desired to attain and maintain unity, he would not achieve it by going out to denounce the IRB and proclaim his intention of smashing it.

'You say the IRB failed!' I exclaimed. 'I cannot see how you have come to that conclusion. In point of numbers, more members of the IRB participated in the Rising than any other body, and of the executed men the majority were IRB men. If you persist in this, which seems to me a mad idea, instead of the unity you say you desire every member of the IRB, if for no other reason than loyalty to the dead leaders, will do his utmost to oppose you. You will not only cause a split, but you will destroy that wonderful unity that is now there, a unity that is essential to carry on the fight for freedom. There is another danger that I see; through your action the IRB may fall into the hands of those who would use it for their own ends.'

I put every argument I could think of before him. I felt so strongly that the result of his action might be tragic, but I failed to make an impression on him. About 9pm, he got up and banged the table, saying, 'I have decided, the IRB must go!' I stood up and said that he was a very small man to make such a big decision, and that I hoped for Ireland's sake he would not be forced to regret it. I think I banged the table too, for I was really exasperated with him. I did not meet Cathal Brugha again until the Treaty was under discussion, but I did hear that he went all out to smash the IRB. I also heard that he soon saw the error of his action, and abandoned it. Judging by later events, the mischief that I had feared had already been done.

By December 1916, all the prisoners who had been in camp prisons in England had been released. This was, of course, hailed with great delight all over the country, but it was a great strain on the resources of the NAVDF, at least until men were able to resume their work. In many cases, men had lost their jobs as a result of their participation in the Rising, but the spirit of all was very fine. That concluded my direction of affairs along one line; the released men were ready to take up the work. I felt I had been true to the trust imposed on me, reorganising so that when the prisoners returned to Ireland they found a spirit of national pride and enthusiasm, and not the slough of despond which had followed other risings.

I went down to Limerick for Christmas, and in January 1917 I took a furnished house in Dundrum, Co Dublin, bringing my three children from Limerick. I had been feeling the strain of going up and down, and I could not leave Dublin. Early in 1917 some hundreds of prisoners were arrested; many of them had only been released the previous December. They were deported to England, and instead of being put into a prison or camp they were placed in small groups in towns, under what was termed open arrest. They were given maintenance allowances, and allowed to move around the district, within limits.

I had a communication from New York, and desiring to consult Seán T O'Kelly and other IRB men about it I went over to England to see them, at a place called Leominster. I arrived there on a Saturday night, dead tired; I had been travelling all day. Travelling in England then was a dreadful experience; troop trains took precedence of all other trains, and the result for the ordinary traveller was long waiting on platforms and sidings. I was five hours on one platform, Shrewsbury, I think, not allowed off because it was a military zone, and I could not get a bite or even a cup of tea.

My arrival was a great surprise to the prisoners. There were only four there, as I recall, Pádraig O Máille, Herbert Pim, Seoirse Nicholls of Galway and Dr Pat McCartan. They told me that Seán T O'Kelly was in or near Fairfold, with many others, and we decided to visit them the next day. The four prisoners decided to take French leave and accompany me, intending to be back that night. It was about twenty miles away, but we took hours to get there, as the only car we could hire was decrepit, with its tyres worn out. We had punctures on the way, and limped into Fairfold on the rim of one wheel.

We got an enthusiastic reception from the prisoners there. As the car would not be ready to take us back that night, we had to remain, and spent the night talking very happily about Ireland. The group resided in a small hotel, and a large hall was placed at their disposal as a diningroom and general sittingroom. It had a huge fireplace, big enough to heat it well, and after supper we all sat around the fire. I was being asked endless questions about home, and the things happening there. Someone asked me what the people at home were thinking of doing about the prisoners. I said that so far as I knew they were not thinking about doing anything; 'They are waiting for a lead from you. Each of you in a way is a leader in your district. That being so, the people at home would not attempt to give you a lead, or suggest what you should do. They will follow any lead you give them.'

Another asked what I thought they should do. 'Well,' I replied, 'I can tell you what I would do if I had been placed in your position. Do you want me to tell you that?' They all said Yes. 'It is this,' I answered. 'I would not stay twenty-four hours under open arrest; I'd take French leave as we did, and make tracks for home.' Someone said that I would be arrested before I got very far, and would be put in prison. I replied, 'I know that, but I would be forcibly held. I would not be like a good child, doing what I was told.' I felt that some of them were annoyed with me, and indeed I sympathised with them. Most of them had already been in prison, and did not relish a return to it. But they had asked for my opinion, and had got it; I would not have volunteered it. I parted with them next day, and went home; the other four went back to Leominster.

When I arrived, the Longford by-election was on. Joseph McGuinness, one of the sentenced men still in prison, had been selected to contest it against a member of the Irish Parliamentary Party (IPP). Remembering what Tom had said to Seán MacDermott about elections to the British parliament, I decided to take no part in it. I went to Limerick, and there found a letter begging me to help in Longford to get McGuinness elected, as it was going to be fought very bitterly by the Irish Parliamentary Party. I could not ignore the appeal, as McGuinness was an imprisoned 1916 man. I sent a note to Mrs Ceannt, Mrs Pearse and some others to meet me at Broadstone Station and accompany me. There was a great crowd waiting for me at the station, including Father Micheál O'Flanagan, and down we went to Longford. McGuinness was elected, with a bare majority.

Before polling day Seán T O'Kelly, Pádraig O Máille and Dr Patrick McCartan arrived in Longford. Apparently they had thought my idea about taking French leave was a good one, and had arrived home safely. Some others followed, but the rest were locked up before they could make a move, and released later in the year. It was a thrill to me to read, in Piaras Béaslaí's memoirs, that the prisoners in Portland after the Rising had a strong feeling against elections to the British parliament, and that Joseph McGuinness had refused to be nominated.

The IPP did fight the election very bitterly, and the Separation Allowance women who were supporting them gave us a hot time.

One Sunday we held a meeting in a town some distance from Longford, and returning to our HQ that evening we were met by an organised gang who attacked us with stones, bottles and other missiles. I was in the first car to enter the town, with Count and Countess Plunkett and Laurence Ginnell, MP, so we got the heaviest part of it. The Countess had her nose cut with a bottle; I got a big stone on the head, which certainly would have split it only for a hard hat I was wearing, off which it bounced. The only injury done was to my feelings; I was mad enough to want to throw stones back at them. There was one lane in Longford that we had to pass going from our hotel to headquarters; we called it the Dardanelles, because every time we passed it stones and bottles came flying out at us.

I was still living in Dundrum when the release of the sentenced men was announced (June 1917). It created a great thrill and a sense of victory, and I decided to go to Westland Row Station to meet them the morning they were due to be in. Two of my sisters came up from Limerick for the same purpose. Admittance to the platform was controlled by the Irish Volunteers, so we were able to be on the platform through their courtesy, even though we had no man of our own to greet. They were due to arrive on an early morning train, so I had to make a very early start from Dundrum. My sisters stayed in Dublin for the night, and we met on the platform.

It seemed as if all Dublin was at Westland Row to meet them, and when the train was coming into the platform the excitement was fierce. The ex-prisoners were jumping out of the train before it stopped; everyone was embracing someone, wives, mothers, children were being hugged and crying and laughing with joy. Seán McGarry was the first I recognised; his wife and family were standing with me. When his welcome to them was over he turned to me and said, 'Who the hell made Pearse President?' I said, 'I was waiting for you and the others to come home and explain that to me. I presumed you would know if anything had happened during the week in the GPO to change the order of things they had started with, though Tom had no knowledge of a change when I was speaking to him in Kilmainham Jail.' Seán said, 'Nothing happened to change things. Tom was President.' He said no more, as friends were crowding round him, but he gave me to understand he would not leave the matter there.

When the excitement over the releases died down, I was as determined as ever that the fight should continue. My one desire was to see Tom's great faith in our people justified. I knew a younger generation, full of fight and admiration for the 1916 men, had come into things since the Rising, and were ready to continue; I was not so sure that all who had had a taste of prison life would feel that way. In the wholesale release of the men taken in armed rebellion and tried by courts martial, some sentenced originally to death and some to different terms of imprisonment, we had a new situation. Why the releases? England had never shown any leniency to those who had opposed her rule in Ireland before. Did she hope that by acting thus, it would end for this generation further attempts towards freedom? We must show her that the reaction which she expected or hoped for would not be forthcoming.

I looked around for something to keep the ball rolling. The Clare election campaign was taking place, and I feared the demoralising influence of elections. When I heard that de Valera had insisted on MacNeill accompanying him to Clare, it confirmed my fears. I knew there were many thinking like me about MacNeill; if men like him were to be the new leaders, we might say goodbye to any more fighting. All my fears may have been unnecessary, but I was taking no chances.

I came to the conclusion that a public meeting, to demand that the bodies buried in Arbour Hill barracks yard should be handed over to us, would be a good start. I approached the Executive of Cumann na mBan to ask them to inaugurate the campaign, starting with a meeting in the Mansion House, but they refused and suggested I do it myself. I was very disappointed, as doing it myself would look like a personal thing, but I was determined to go on with it somehow. I approached William O'Brien, of the Irish Transport and General Workers' Union, and asked for his help. I got it readily, and we started work for the meeting, though he did most of the work.

The night of the meeting, the Round Room of the Mansion House was packed with a very enthusiastic audience, and an overflow one outside. We had invited de Valera to speak, and he had agreed to come up from Co Clare. He came by the evening train and was late in arriving, so I had no time to outline the purpose of the meeting before he went on the platform. He was received with tremendous enthusiasm, and the meeting went wild when he said that he was in perfect agreement with the demand for the bodies, but could not agree to make the demand unless or until he could back it up with the force of arms.

Immediately on his statement I saw the campaign finished. There would be no hope of getting the other meetings we had planned after that statement. I was very angry with him, and tackled him the minute he came off the platform, pointing out how he had destroyed the campaign. He said that he had only said what he felt, but I said, 'My hope of succeeding in this demand was not through the force of arms, but through the force of public opinion, which we women had been able to arouse when you men were in prison.'

I really had planned those meetings with no great hope of success, or that the demand would be acceded to, but to maintain the atmosphere of rebellion. I had been in communication with Cork and Belfast about organising meetings to follow the Dublin one, but as I had feared I found they were not inclined to go on with the project after de Valera's statement. However, though disappointed in one way, in another I was more than satisfied at the result of the meeting. When I sat down to think it over, de Valera's statement had set the headline for a continuance of the fight, even if he had not meant it to be interpreted in that way.

I was amazed when I heard that de Valera, despite all opposition, insisted on John MacNeill accompanying him to Co Clare. I thought that he must not know of MacNeill's action in sending out the countermanding order, so I decided I would tell him what Tom had thought of MacNeill and his treacherous action in attempting to stop the Rising. While de Valera was in prison, I had been told, he was looked on as a leader there, being the only Commandant in Dublin who had participated in the Rising and had not been executed.[4] Because of this position, which he retained on release, I felt it was important that he should hear Tom's opinion of MacNeill, an opinion shared by all the signatories of the Proclamation. I invited both de Valera and MacNeill to my home in Dundrum, telling them the reason for the invitation, and de Valera accepted for both.

They arrived at the house on 28 July 1917, and I told them the story about MacNeill as Tom had given it to me on Easter Sunday, in the presence of Seán McGarry and Tommy O'Connor, and repeated to me in Kilmainham Jail an hour or two before his execution. Tom had told me either that MacNeill had signed, or had agreed to sign, the Proclamation, but I had forgotten which. I had also brought a message from Pearse to Limerick on Holy Thursday, which was that

MacNeill had signed, or agreed to sign, the Proclamation, and that he had been quite enthusiastic.

MacNeill's answer to that was that he had not signed the Proclamation. I said that if he had not actually signed it, but had agreed to do so, to an honourable man that was as good as signing, and that his action in sending out countermanding orders secretly all over the country, and his orders to the Irish Volunteers through the *Sunday Independent*, were dishonourable. MacNeill answered that the only reply he could give was that Tom Clarke had been given wrong information. To that I heatedly replied that he was adding insult to injury; he was suggesting that those whom Tom Clarke worked with and trusted, and who were dead and could not defend themselves, were guilty of treachery to him. His suggestion was most despicable. He said he had no further explanation to offer.

I told him of the instructions I had received from Tom in Kilmainham Jail, that MacNeill must not be permitted to come back into the National life of the country again, for if he was he would in a crisis again act treacherously. I had promised to carry out these instructions if I could, but I was faced with a situation Tom had not visualised, MacNeill in an English prison as an Irish rebel. That fact tied my hands, and while he remained so I could do nothing. He was an Irishman, and to my mind a bad one, in the hands of our enemy England. I continued that circumstances might still tie my hands, and I might not be able to carry out my promise to my husband, but the story of his treachery would not die with me, that I would write it and leave it as documentary proof against him.

That ended our interview. De Valera listened throughout, but said nothing, and both left the house. Soon after, I left the house also, to go into Dublin. When I got to the railway station I found de

Valera walking up and down waiting for a train, and I joined him. We walked up and down chatting; he reverted to MacNeill, and said he was sure that MacNeill had not signed the Proclamation. I said that I had had Tom's word for it, given when he was facing death, that MacNeill had either signed it or had agreed to sign it, and I said, 'That is good enough for me.' 'Well,' he said, 'I was very intimate with Tommy MacDonagh, who often tried to get me to join the IRB. I'm sure if that had happened, Tommy would have told me.'

I replied that the Proclamation had not been signed until Tuesday night in Holy Week, that Thomas would not have had much time to tell him then, even if he was free to do so, and I did not think he had been. No matter what his friendship might have been, there were things MacDonagh would not have been free to tell him; he was a very honourable man. From the time the Rising started, de Valera had not been in touch with him and later, when the question arose, MacDonagh was dead. De Valera replied that he still thought I was wrong. I could have argued further, but our train came in and put an end to it.

Now, I had got the story on Easter Sunday from Tom on his return from Liberty Hall, and again about 2am on the morning of May 3rd, in Kilmainham Jail. He was facing death; the dawn would see his stay on earth finished. He was a man who in everyday life never prevaricated, much less lied. Why should he lie then, and do what to him would be an unworthy and dishonourable act, to tell a story of the treachery of another man that was not true? I knew him well enough to know he was incapable of doing such a thing. If the treachery had been directed against himself, he would have died without saying a word, but treachery that affected his country was a different matter, and the man who committed it would continue to be a danger to the country. I do not know whether de Valera, in saying he thought I was wrong, meant to convey to me that Tom was lying or that, as MacNeill suggested, he had been misinformed by his comrades.

The fact that the Rising was now being called a Sinn Féin rising gave Arthur Griffith his chance, one he was quick to seize. When he was released from prison camp in England [1917], he started Sinn Féin as his organisation, though the Sinn Féin which grew out of the Rising was a totally different one from that which had been in existence before the Rising. The new Sinn Féin was a continuance of the aims and objects of the IRB, a free, separate, independent Irish republic. I am not sure if Griffith intended this, but the trend in that direction was too strong for him or anyone else to resist. Griffith also brought out as his own the paper called *Nationality*, which had been the property of the IRB and of which he had been the paid Editor.

After the releases in June 1917, a Sinn Féin Ard Fheis [convention] was held in the Round Room of the Mansion House. Madame Markievicz had come to my house in Dundrum some days before to discuss the question of attacking MacNeill, who would be present. She thought he would be nominated for a position on the Executive, and that I knew so much about it that I would be the proper person to make the attack. I told her that members of the Irish Volunteers had come to me and advised me against it, and that I had agreed to act on their advice. 'Well,' she said, 'if you won't do it, I will.' I tried to reason with her, but it was no use; she was determined on attacking him. I told her I would not support her.

At the Ard Fheis, de Valera was elected President, and John MacNeill was proposed for a position on the Executive. Madame Markievicz stood up and attacked him on the question of the secret countermanding orders. Her attack got such a bitterly hostile reception that despite my decision not to support her, I got up and did so. It seemed to me that the meeting was so hostile to her for attacking MacNeill that if there had been rotten eggs or anything else handy they would have been flung at her. This amazed me; here was a woman who had come out and risked her life, had been sentenced to death and imprisoned for her participation in the Rising, and Irishmen were ready to do violence to her for attacking a man whose action had caused the failure of the Rising, and who had not participated in it. The thing was hard to understand, and under the circumstances I felt bound to stand by her.

On thinking it over afterwards, I was not so surprised. I remembered that de Valera had championed MacNeill in prison, insisted, I was told, on all prisoners in jail with him honouring him, on the grounds that MacNeill was a very much wronged man and had been made a fool of by the IRB, an accusation utterly without foundation. MacNeill knew the position very well indeed, and he certainly could not deny that he had sent out the countermands and issued the call-off. I came to the conclusion that the demonstration was not so much against Madame as anger at her ignoring the wishes of the Irish Volunteers; they had reasons for not wanting MacNeill attacked at that meeting.

Late in the autumn of 1917 I left Dundrum and returned to my old home in Richmond Avenue. I went down to Limerick for Christmas with the children; Ernest Blythe and Séamus O'Sullivan had been invited and were also there.[5] It was a sad, quiet Christmas.

8

In Prison

1917-1919

Arrest – in Holloway Prison – Countess Markievicz
– Maud Gonne MacBride – release

At this time, activities in the political field were increasing. Under the title of Sinn Féin Clubs, the revolutionary elements were organising and educating public opinion. This caused uneasiness to our enemy, so in 1918 they discovered a German plot, possibly with the hope of putting an end to such activities. They started arresting hundreds of men and transporting them to prisons in England, on the assumption, seemingly, that they were involved in the German plot.

A meeting of the Sinn Féin Executive was to be held in Jones' Road (now Croke Park), as members who were on the run could not go to the Harcourt Street office. At that meeting, Mick Collins told me that I was on the list for arrest, and advised me to go on the run, but I doubted I was, and would find it difficult to go on the run with three young children. I decided against it; I was neither temperamentally nor physically fit for such a life. Besides, I would feel like a fool if it was discovered I was not on the list. However, the decision was taken out of my hands.

I was followed home from that meeting by two G-men; I saw them, but it was such an everyday thing that I did not pay much attention to it. Next morning, before I was up, my maid came up to tell me there were two men downstairs to see me; I got up, dressed, went down and recognised them as the two G-men who had followed me home the night before. I asked them their business; they hummed and hawed a bit, then they told me they had instructions to arrest me. I said I had had no breakfast yet, and they agreed to wait until I had eaten. They told me to pack a bag, and that they would carry it. I told them that if they took me away immediately then there would be no-one to look after the children, as I had no relatives in Dublin and the maid I had was too young to do so; could they give me time to make arrangements with relatives to care for them? They said they were sorry, but that I must go with them. When I was leaving the room one of them started to follow me, but was stopped by the other.

While I was eating my breakfast, I told the children that I was being arrested by the British who had murdered their father and uncle, and that I did not expect to be back with them until the end of the war. I told my eldest son, Daly, to telegraph to his aunts in Limerick to come up at once. He was a frail, delicate boy, and I felt heartbroken leaving him, he needed such care. 'Now,' I said to the three boys, 'when I say goodbye to you in the presence of these men who are arresting me, there must be no tears. Remember, these men are our country's enemy, and you are the sons of a patriot and martyr. I will write and let you know where I am as soon as I am allowed.' When it came to saying goodbye the youngest, Emmet, was sneaking his handkerchief to wipe away a few tears that had escaped. I pretended not to see, and was nearer tears myself than they knew. When I was going down the steps between the two detectives, they waved to me. I was just heartbroken at having to leave them.

When we got to Ballybough Bridge the detectives hailed a butcher's cart that was passing, commandeered it, bundled me into it and drove me to the Bridewell. There, I was put into an office and left for some time. One of the detectives who had arrested me came in and told me that he had heard that a detachment of military was being sent to my home to search it. He asked if there was anything there I would like to have removed before they got there, and gave me to understand that if there was, he would have it removed.

I told him that I would like to have my children removed. He replied that he did not mean that; he had been thinking of firearms, incriminating papers and things of that sort. 'Why, sir,' I said, 'you do not take me for a fool, I hope. If I had any incriminating papers and other things as you have suggested, I surely would not be foolish enough to keep them in a house likely to be raided any minute, as mine is.' He flushed, and said that his intention had been to be kind, and perhaps relieve me of anxiety. I replied that my only anxiety was for my children, that it was possible that he had meant to be kind but that I did not forget, and neither should he, that he was in the pay of my country's enemy. He left me then.

Within an hour I was removed to Arbour Hill Military Barracks in a Black Maria, or prison car, which was a funny contraption. It seemed to consist of three compartments; the one I was put into had a seat fastened along the side, so narrow I had to sit sideways. It was most uncomfortable. At Arbour Hill, I was put into a guardroom first. The sergeant on duty came over to me after a few minutes and said, 'Lady, I am an Englishman, and proud of my country, proud to fight for her. I never thought until today that my country could do anything I would be ashamed of, but today I am ashamed to the ground at seeing a lady like you brought in here, a military detention barracks. Will you accept an Englishman's apology for that act?' I answered that I was glad to meet an Englishman who could feel shame for his country's treatment of my country.

Before he or I could say another word, a soldier came to take me to a cell where I was locked up. The cell was much better than an ordinary jail cell; it had a board floor, a small stretcher bed, a small chair, a table and a fair-sized window, low enough to look out of. I was given pen, ink and paper to write to my relatives. I asked for information as to my destination, to convey to my relatives, and was told it was not known.

I sat down at the table facing the window, with my back turned to the door, and started to write my letter. Suddenly I heard a voice saying, 'Lidy, what youse in for?' I looked around, but there was no-one but myself in the cell. The voice came again: 'Lidy, what youse in for?' Startled, I looked everywhere to see where the voice was coming from; I looked hard at the door, as it seemed to be coming from there, then I saw the eye. It made me jump; it looked horrible. I remembered hearing that prison cells had spy holes in the doors, and was satisfied to have located the voice. I presumed it was one of the military prisoners, and I wanted no talk with him, so I turned my back to the door and shrugged my shoulders. I heard the voice saying, 'Oh, she don't kire.'

I had just finished my letter when the sergeant came in with a small tin of what was then called bully beef, and four large biscuits which looked like dog biscuits; he said they were my day's ration. I asked if I might have a cup of tea, but he said he was sorry, that I was leaving there immediately. He took me out to a yard where there was a lorry full of soldiers with rifles and fixed bayonets. Three or four men were being hustled into the lorry, and in front of it was a motor car with officers in it. The sergeant said he thought I would be going with them, and made no attempt to put me in the lorry. One of the officers came up and bawled at him to know the cause of the delay, and the sergeant said he thought the lady would be going in the motor; he seemed to think the lorry was no place for a lady. The officer, a very haughty individual, said, Certainly not, I was to go in the lorry.

The sergeant said he did not see how I was to get in, it was so high from the ground. 'Get a ladder,' the officer said, but no ladder was to be found. A table was brought out, but that was not high enough, so a chair was put on top of the table. Another chair was brought for me to climb up to the table, and so between tables and chairs I finally reached the safe quarters of the lorry. I could see the sergeant was upset at me having to go in it; the officer was fuming at the delay. There was no seat for me in the lorry, and I found it hard to keep standing when it turned a corner or swerved. The men prisoners, one of whom was Seán Etchingham, seeing this, took off their overcoats, dropped them on the floor and made me sit on them. When we arrived in Dun Laoghaire, it was cheerful to hear children in the streets shout 'Up the Republic!' as we passed, knowing their shouting was defiance at the British military.

When we got aboard the mailboat, the other prisoners were separated from me, and I was taken to what seemed to me to be the bottom of the boat. I was put into a cabin with several berths made of wood, but with no furniture, or covering of any kind. Two soldiers were put outside, and one of them brought in a lifebelt for me to put on. I told him to take it out, that I did not want it, but he said it would be better to put it on, as submarines were knocking around. He urged me to put it on for safety; he had one on himself. I said that if I had been born to be drowned, I would not be hanged. He flushed, seeming to think I was sneering at him for having one on, and explained it was army regulations. Poor boy, he was only a youngster, and seemed bewildered; he did not know, of course, that I was in a fighting mood, ready to fight anything.

When he went out, I lay on the bunk. It was mighty hard, and I rolled up my coat for a pillow. Some time later, apparently, someone, thinking I was asleep, tiptoed in and put a rug over me. It was a kind act, and done very, very gently. It was only when I had been some time in Holloway Jail that I learned that the rug had been sent by my sister Agnes; she had arrived from Limerick before the boat left, but had not been allowed to see me.

When the boat neared Holyhead, I was told to get ready for landing. I asked to be allowed to wash. The soldier accompanied me to the bathroom, and ordered the stewardess to go in with me. She refused, saying it was not her duty and that he could do his own dirty work. While they were disputing I slipped into the bathroom and locked the door, leaving them to fight it out.

At Holyhead, I was put in the charge of four soldiers and one officer. He and I were put in a first-class carriage, and the soldiers in a third-class one near us. From the time we left Holyhead until we reached Euston Station in London, the officer and I did not exchange one word. He was a young Irishman, and I scorned him and made him feel it. There was a terrific storm as we were coming into Crewe Station. The officer seemed asleep; I debated with myself whether I would give him a good fright by slipping out at Crewe while he slept. The thought of doing it gave me amusement for a time, but I was too tired to indulge in the prank.

While we were waiting in the Station Master's office at Euston for a conveyance to Holloway Jail, the officer asked if I would like some tea, and I replied that I would. When the waitress brought it in, I noticed that the officer was paying for it; I had not understood that when I said Yes, so I took money out of my bag and laid it on the tray. He understood my action, I knew, by the way he flushed up.

An ambulance arrived in about an hour, driven by a girl, and the officer sat in front with her. I was put in the back with the four soldiers, all English by their accents. Listening to their talk, I gathered they were very hungry and had little money to buy food; their rations did not fill them. I gave them the contents of my purse, saying that I would not need it where I was going, and they might as well have a good meal with it. I thought, they are only boys, and their mothers like myself were worrying about them. They were very surprised, and thanked me very nicely, but they were not more surprised than I was myself at my action. Looking back, I am not sorry I did it.

Holloway Jail depressed me, it was so gaunt and gloomy-looking. When we got inside, I was taken to the Matron of the prison. After she said 'How do you do' to me, I heard her giving instructions to a wardress to have me searched. I protested, saying that I had been in custody since the previous morning and could not see the necessity of the search. She said that it was the rule, but that if I would give her my word that I had nothing on me, she would accept that. I assured her that I had nothing more on than when I had been arrested, and that was only my clothes. Having given my word, I escaped a very unpleasant experience.

She then asked if I would have my meals sent in, that Madame Markievicz was having her meals sent in and was paying for them. I said that of course that was Madame's business, but that I certainly was not going to pay for my meals; 'The people who sent me here are responsible for my well-being, and for everything I need to keep me alive in good health.' She said that was all right; she had only wanted to know if I wished to do the same as Madame.

I was then marched off to a cell in the top storey of the building, and locked in. I wonder if there is anything in this world more horrible than being locked up; it gives one such a feeling of rage and helplessness, you feel you would like to batter the doors down. The only thing which stays your hand from attempting it is your common sense and reason, which makes you realise the uselessness of the endeavour. The sound of the key in the lock brought Kilmainham Jail back to me, and the night when I listened to the sound of the same type of key turning in the lock of the door of the cell where my husband was. The agony I then endured came back in full force, and every time the key turned in the lock of my cell the same thing happened. I could not get used to the sound. I sat down on the bed and asked myself how in God's name did my husband live through nearly sixteen years of prison of the worst kind, when I, just being interned, was feeling so dreadful?

I was let out of the cell later in the day for one hour of exercise, and met Madame Markievicz and Madame MacBride. I asked Madame Markievicz if she was getting in meals and paying for them, and she said Yes, she was; when she had been arrested she had just been recovering from an attack of measles and was very run down, and she feared she would not get well on the prison diet. She did look very ill, and I felt very sorry for her. Madame MacBride said she was taking the prison diet, as she was in perfect health. The hour for exercise, spent just outside the cells, passed very rapidly, and we were locked up again for the next twenty-three hours.

When the officials had received orders to prepare for the reception of rebel Irish women, they must have thought it was wild animals they would have to deal with. All one side of what was called the 'Hard Nails Wing' of the jail was cleared of all other prisoners, and between each of our cells there were three empty ones. The cells were furnished with a camp bed without springs, just iron slats with hills and hollows, and a mattress that seemed made of hay. After a short time lying on it, the hills worked their way up, and poor sleepers like myself spent the night trying to dodge those hills. The pillow was another sort of torment; I don't know what it was filled with, but it was so hard the head made no impression on it. Then the blankets were so hard and stiff that all efforts to snuggle into them for warmth or comfort were unavailing, and the sheets were thick, coarse and hard. These things, which were such a source of discomfort to me, had no effect on Madame Markievicz. She said she could sleep on stones, and Madame MacBride made no complaint.

The first month in prison I lost nine pounds in weight. At the time I could not afford to lose one pound, I was so light. I had no news of my children, where they were or what had happened to them after I had left them in Richmond Avenue, and for six weeks I was kept in this state of suspense, as up to then we were not allowed to write or receive letters. If I had been told that the rug the soldier put over me in the boat had come from my sister, I would have known their aunts had arrived in Dublin and that the children would be all right, and I would have been spared the awful weeks of suspense.

The Governor became alarmed at my loss of weight, and came to my cell with the Matron to talk to me about it. I told him about my children and my anxiety about them, not knowing what had happened to them. He asked if it would relieve my mind if he could find out from the Dublin Metropolitan Police where my children were; if so, he would telegraph to them. I thanked him, and said I would indeed be relieved. That evening, long after we had been locked up for the night, the Governor and Matron came to my cell with a telegram he had just received from the DMP in answer to his enquiry about my children. The telegram said that their aunt, Miss Daly, had taken them to Limerick on the evening of the day I had been arrested, and that they were still in Limerick. I thanked him again for his kindness.

The anxiety caused by not knowing what had happened to my children had killed all desire for food. Even it had been good, I could not have eaten it. That anxiety being eased, desire for food returned, but the prison diet was so repulsive I could not eat it – cocoa, margarine and a thing they called 'skilly' which I abhorred. So my breakfast consisted of dry bread and cold water. The dinner was also uneatable. I was eating so little the wardress noticed it, and one day asked me if I was on ' 'unger-strike'. I said that I was not, but that no-one could eat the food we were getting. She told me to put myself down to see the doctor, and to tell him; he was the only one who could change the diet. I asked why she had not told me that before; since it was my first time in prison I did not know the rules. I told her to put me down for the doctor.

The doctor came and put me on what he called hospital diet. Instead of cocoa, I got tea and a rice pudding with a glass of milk for dinner, and then he very kindly put Madame MacBride on the same diet. Madame Markievicz was still getting her meals in.

I had one great trouble all through my imprisonment, I could not sleep. Hour after hour went by each night, but no sleep. The doctor offered to give me things to make me sleep, but I was afraid of them, and refused. My imagination worked overtime during those long, dark, sleepless nights; I pictured countless dangers for my children, and went from that to my husband, and all he had suffered during those terrible years in prison. Memories of Kilmainham came alive, and from that my mind went to the prison yard where I pictured him shot, not dead, but wounded to death and left to die slowly, in agony, or else finished off by an officer with a pistol. A story had circulated after the Rising that one of the executed men had met with that fate, and I always feared it had been he. Lying awake in the dark, from 8pm until seven o'clock in the morning, there was nothing too awful for me to imagine. During the day, I could find occupation for my mind, and keep these thoughts at bay, but it was always a maddening thought that no matter what happened to my children, I could not go to them.[1]

At first we were only allowed out of our cells for one hour out of the twenty-four. I told my fellow-prisoners that I would fight for better conditions. I put down for the doctor, and told him that if I did not get more fresh air than I was getting, my health would suffer. As a result, we got two hours' exercise. This did not satisfy me, and I put down for the doctor again and asked for more. He said it was impossible, as there was a shortage of wardresses, but I said we could do without a wardress. He was shocked; that would be against all prison rules. Still I kept on, and eventually my persistence was rewarded, and we were allowed out for most of the day. This made a great change in Madame Markievicz's health; she got well enough to stop her meals being sent in, and went on hospital diet, the same as

Madame MacBride and myself.

When I had got all I needed in the way of fresh air, I turned my attention to the diet. I kept constantly putting down for the doctor and asking for improvement in the diet, and succeeded in being allowed an egg a day, which the doctor told me cost one shilling each. Everything I succeeded in getting the other ladies got too. I asked them to stand in with me in looking for those things; I said it looked bad for only me to be doing the fussing about food and conditions. Madame Markievicz said that if they started giving trouble they would be looked on as a nuisance, they were both so big and strong. It might end in our being sent out of London, and she wanted to be near her sister Eva, the one person in the world she loved. She considered that I was so frail that my demands would seem reasonable.

I did not bother after that, I went my own way. I cared nothing about food, it was just something to occupy myself with. My loss of weight continued, and it worried the doctor; prisoners are weighed every week. He suggested I should go into the hospital, where I would have a better bed, and perhaps get some sleep, and I said I would be glad to go if my friends could go too. He said there was no room for them there. Then I said that I would stay where I was, that I did not want to be separated from my friends. He said I could sleep in the hospital and come back to my friends in the morning. No, I said, I would have no privileges that they did not have.

My weight kept going down, despite the improved diet. My two friends, as well as the doctor, began to worry about me. Madame Markievicz became a nuisance to me over it; she fussed, which I hate, so I told her one day that if she wanted an occupation to look elsewhere, that I was in no humour to provide her with an occupation or thrills, but that did not choke her off. The doctor came to me one day and said that he did not know what to do with me, that he was getting the best food he could for me yet I kept losing weight. 'As you know, the food is rationed here.' I asked if I would be allowed to get food from home; there was plenty of food in Ireland. He was afraid that would not be permitted, he replied, but he would see what could be done. In a few days he was back to tell me that he had got permission for me to get one parcel of food from Ireland every week. It was almost impossible to get the food I needed in England, he said.

This was great news to all of us, and from that until our release a large parcel came from my sisters every week, with every conceivable delicacy, and a box of eggs from Miss Barton [unidentified] for Madame Markievicz. Still the doctor kept urging me to go to hospital, but it was no use, I would not go without my friends. Then one day he came into my cell, beaming; 'You are getting your own way at last,' he said, 'I have got room for you and your friends in the hospital.' I thanked him, and said I would be very glad to go there now.

When we were settled in the hospital, Madame MacBride wrote out that we were all in hospital, and that I was terribly ill, which was not quite the position. I was not very well, but I was not terribly ill. I did not know that she had written like this until I saw a report of it in the *Irish Independent*, which we got every day. It made me furious, knowing the anxiety it would cause my mother and sisters, especially when she knew and I knew the circumstances under which all of us had been moved to the hospital. I had a really serious row with her over it. I wrote home as soon as possible, to let my mother know I was not very ill.

We had been some time in hospital when we were informed that we could have visitors, either relatives or friends. Naturally, we were all overjoyed. The Governor undertook the job of acquainting our relatives, and I gave him my sisters' address in Limerick. The other two ladies had relatives in London. Madame Markievicz was the first to receive a visitor, her sister, Miss Eva Gore-Booth. Madame came back from her sister's visit in a wild state of excitement, bringing a large basket of fruit and flowers. Madame MacBride was the next; she had a visit from her son and daughter, who were able to come at once as they were living in London. I had to wait until my sisters received their notification, and made arrangements for the journey from Limerick.

A few mornings after these visits, I was reading the *Irish Independent* in bed, and was surprised to read a report of the visits from the visitors and the conditions under which they had seen the prisoners. They were not the usual conditions, and, it seemed to me, were designed to humiliate us and our visitors. I notified the Governor immediately to cancel my request to see my sisters, and to inform them of my decision not to see them under those conditions. My two friends were out at exercise, and when they came in I informed them of what I had done as a result of the report. Madame MacBride did not agree with me; she said she would see her children no matter what the conditions were, and told me I was cutting off my nose to spite my face. We agreed to differ. Madame Markievicz said that when she saw her sister she had been so excited she had not noticed the conditions, but she agreed with me that if they were as stated in the *Irish Independent*, I was quite right. She would notify the Governor that she would not see any more visitors unless the conditions were changed.

In the early days of our imprisonment, when we were out for exercise, Madame Markievicz and Madame MacBride walked up and down the exercise yard together, discussing their mutual friends and acquaintances, and disputing as to which of them had the highest social status. Madame Markievicz claimed that she was far above Madame MacBride; she belonged to the inner circle of the Vice-Regal Lodge set, while Madame MacBride was only on the fringe of it. I sometimes listened to them, quite amused; I was outside their social circle, and had nothing in common with them socially. Madame Markievicz took pains to make me aware of the social gulf between us; it didn't worry me. I walked up and down alone, reading the Irish newspaper, eager for news from Ireland. The Governor and Matron usually walked through the yard on their morning rounds while we were there, and they had a few words with us in passing. The Governor always asked how was little Mrs Clarke; I suppose I did look small beside the other two ladies, who were both very tall.

When Madame Markievicz did talk to me in those early days, I sensed a certain amount of patronage in her tone and manner, and that I was not prepared to take from anybody. It appeared to worry her that such an insignificant little person as myself was put in prison with her. Again and again she said to me, 'Why on earth did they arrest such a quiet, insignificant person as you are?' I told her the only information I could give her was what was on my charge sheet, which was exactly the same as hers. If she wanted some information on the matter, she could send her query to the British government.[2] That did not stop her. She kept on referring to it constantly, until one day, my patience being exhausted, I said that she seemed to forget that when important people like her were in prison, somebody had to carry on, even insignificant nobodies like myself, and that anyhow I was not here as a result of going on platforms and making speeches asking for arrest. She asked if I meant that she had done that, and I replied that if I was to take what she had been telling Matron was true, then she had done just that. She never questioned after that about the absurdity, as she looked on it, of my arrest, but her attitude was that the British were a blundering lot of fools to arrest someone like me. That is how we stood to each other at the beginning of our lives together in prison.

Madame Markievicz never questioned Madame MacBride's arrest, or thought the British fools for arresting *her*, even though she had been in France nearly all through the war until her arrival in Ireland, either just before or about the time of the German plot, and the wholesale arrests over it. When we were put into the hospital and our cells left unlocked all day, I used to stay in bed until dinnertime. Both ladies would come in to my cell and unload their grievances on me separately. They were not on such good terms with each other as at first; Maeve [Maud] was this and that, Connie was that and this. When one came in, the other went out. I had to listen and sympathise with each of them; it became quite a strain.

We had a little excitement when Mrs Sheehy Skeffington was brought into us. She had been arrested in Ireland, and immediately went on hunger-strike against her arrest. She explained to us that she was bound, as a suffragette, to do that. We were charmed to see her, though naturally deploring the fact that she was a prisoner like ourselves. She was a very highly-gifted woman, and one of the straightest I ever met, and I had a great admiration for her. She remained on hunger-strike until her release, which came a few days later.

We talked all the time she was with us. She was able to give us all the latest news from home, things the newspapers did not give. Though delighted with her company, we were all glad when she was released, as we knew she would keep on the hunger-strike until the bitter end. Her visit was a great break in the monotony of our lives.

We could not join her in the hunger-strike, as the policy of Sinn Féin was against hunger-striking at that time, unless we were refused political treatment.

It was a great thrill one day when we read in the *Irish Independent* that three Irish prisoners had escaped from Lincoln Prison, Eamon de Valera, Seán McGarry and Seán Milroy. Micheál Staines, who had helped in the escape, told me afterwards that they had examined Holloway Prison to see if by any chance they could engineer our escape, but decided it would be impossible.

Madame and I were very glad when Madame MacBride was released [October 1918]. Imprisonment had a very depressing effect on her, and was undermining her health. All through her imprisonment she was kind, gentle and very courteous; she had very charming manners. I missed her, but was glad she was out of it. When she had gone some days, the doctor came to me and asked me to make an appeal for release on the grounds of health, as I was a good subject for release on such grounds, much better than Madame MacBride. He said that if I would appeal, he would have me released in a week. I refused, saying that I would never appeal to the British government for anything; when I left the prison, it would not be as the result of an appeal from me. He looked at me as if he could not understand me, and walked off without another word. I think I bewildered him many times.

With Madame MacBride's release, my troubles began with Madame Markievicz. She had the belief that she could, as she put it herself, 'kick anyone to heel'. She tried it on with me. She wanted to impress the prison officials, and show them how she could dominate me. This was rather foolish, as prison officials are very observant. I had no desire to quarrel with her, but I certainly would not allow her to 'kick me to heel'. I wanted to live in peace, but for my own protection I had to quarrel. She was very persistent in her efforts, but when she found she was not successful I became 'dear Kathleen' to her, instead of 'Mrs Clarke'. She then made efforts to get me to call her Connie, but Madame Markievicz she has always remained to me.

Prison is a very trying place, even under the best of conditions. To be deprived of one's liberty galls, and people are inclined to be irritable over trifles not worth bothering about normally, but I could not forget her attitude to me in the beginning, being just as faulty as any other human being.

All through our imprisonment, the prison officials, from the Governor down, were very decent to us. After giving me permission to get food from home, and establishing us in hospital, the Governor ordered a gas-ring to be put in one of the bathrooms for our use. He sent us a kettle, teapot, frying-pan, saucepan, cups, saucers, plates, knives, forks and spoons, so that we could cook rashers, eggs and many other things that we got in our food parcel every week from my sisters. He allowed us a quarter pound of tea and our sugar ration, so we could make tea any time we liked. I was head cook, but Madame Markievicz took to making stews of the meat we were allowed for dinner, as it was always tough. She was always looking for flavouring, and one day I brought her something on a plate saying, 'Madame, this might flavour your stew.' 'Oh thank you, darling Kathleen, you are an angel.' She was very shortsighted, and she was just about to put the thing in the stew when I remarked that it might make it a bit soapy. She looked closer, to discover that I had given her a bit of soap! Then she told me I was a little divil.

The doctor, in his daily round of visits, had one day said I needed a stimulant, and suggested whiskey, but I said I was a teetotaller. He said it would be used as medicine, and he would send up some every day. I said no, that I did not want it; I thanked him for his kindness, but I wanted no stimulant of that kind. When I told the others, they were exasperated with me; they said I should have taken it. Madame Markievicz said that if I would not take it, she would; she would enjoy a drop of whiskey. I said that it had never occurred to me that either of them would care for it, but if they liked I would tell the doctor in the morning that I had changed my mind, and would take the whiskey. He began sending up an ounce bottle of whiskey every day, which Madame Markievicz enjoyed; it was a real stimulant to her. I don't know what they would have said if I had told them the doctor had offered to send me champagne from his own house, when I refused the whiskey![3]

The winter was very cold, and acting on the doctor's advice (when it suited me to do so) I stayed in bed part of the day. I had got permission to get in materials for crochet, knitting and embroidery, as well as materials for making Limerick lace, and was occupied with one or another of them all day, with an odd spell of reading. Madame Markievicz said that watching me, always so busy, made her feel like working too, so she asked for permission to get in water-painting materials, also materials for black and white sketching. She had studied oil painting in Paris, but had never done water colours, so it was a great novelty to her. She worked very hard at it, and produced a number of small pictures and a good many in black and white. Amongst them was a caricature of myself, trying to thread a needle, with my face all puckered up. It really was very funny, and very clever.

When I stayed in bed she would come into my room smoking, painting and chatting. Knowing I was very particular about order in my cell, she would be very careful for a while, then she would begin to get careless, throwing her cigarette ashes around and flicking the paint and water off her brush. I told her that if she continued creating disorder in my cell, she would have to stay out. She promised to be more careful, and was for a day or two, then forgot. I ordered her out. She was a picture of dismay at the order; she promised to clean up and not forget again, but out she had to go. Her untidiness distracted me. She had to sit in the passage outside our cells, all alone. Every now and then I would hear a deep sigh coming from the passage.

We had a gate instead of a door to our cells in the hospital, and next morning she came to my gate and asked very meekly if she could come in. I said, 'No, I have had enough of you.' She went away and after a while came back and said, 'May I come in, Kathleen?' I said, 'No, you may not.' 'Why?' 'You are too disorderly.' 'But Kathleen, I won't be, I'll bring a plate for my cigarette ash, and a jar to flick my paint brushes into, and I won't throw my stubs on the floor.' I said, 'No, I don't want you, I'm fed up with you.' She went away, and after some time she came back and said, 'But Kathleen, I'm lonely.' I could not resist that plea, so I yielded, saying, 'Come in so, but remember the conditions, out you go if you don't keep them.'

These quarrels, if one could call them such, were only occasional. We tried to make life as pleasant as possible for each other. We were very curious about a report book the wardress was always writing up, which she kept in a cell at the end of a passage. Madame Markievicz stole it one evening, and we had great fun reading it. Every move we made was recorded, from the time our cells were opened in the morning until we were locked up at night. According to her report, I ate nothing, Madame ate everything, and ate all day.

We spent many hours reading. Madame Markievicz loved poetry, especially Browning. I did not care much for it, but she would read it aloud. I preferred history, and strange to say I got a history of Ireland by D'Arcy Magee in the prison library. She ordered a lot of books on economics, labour, socialism and other topics. She never had patience to read through a book, she would skim through it, trying in her quick way to get the sense of it. I could not do that; I had to go right through a book to get any pleasure out of it. She spent a lot of money on those books, and told me she intended to give them to [the] Labour [Party], as the nucleus of a Connolly Library, when she was released. She was devoted to James Connolly.

One Sunday morning in December we had a visit from the Governor and Matron; as a rule they did not visit on Sunday. They had come to inform Madame Markievicz that she had been elected a Member of Parliament. I was delighted to hear it; at last, I thought, women are going to get recognition. Madame got so excited she went yelling and dancing all over the place. Before leaving us the Governor said, 'And what about little Mrs Clarke?' He made the remark to me, but Madame heard it; she rushed over and flung her arms around me and said, 'Never mind, Kathleen, I'll see you get elected when I get out.' Her air of patronage made me feel like hitting her, but with the Governor and Matron present I had to control my rage. I was genuinely glad of her election, but her air of patronage was the one thing I could not stand.

When I came out of prison, I heard the reason why I had not been selected or elected. I had been nominated by the North City, Dublin Comhairle Ceanntar [constituency council] for that area. When my name had been sent to Sinn Féin HQ for ratification, Harry Boland and Dick Mulcahy called on John R Reynolds, Chairman of the Comhairle. They asked him to have my name withdrawn in favour of

Dick Mulcahy, as I had been ratified as a candidate for Limerick City and I was sure of election there. John R Reynolds told them that he had no power to do so, but that if the matter stood as they said he would summon a meeting of the Comhairle, and place the matter before them. The meeting was called and the matter put before it, and the members said they did not wish to change. According to Reynolds, Harry Boland told the meeting that literature was already out for my election in Limerick, and that I was sure of being elected there. The meeting very reluctantly agreed to the change.

Harry Boland was one of the Honorary Secretaries of the Sinn Féin Executive and must have known the exact position at the time, which was that Micheál Colivet had been ratified by headquarters as the candidate for Limerick City, and his election literature was already out. I was very angry when I heard all this, but was glad to know it was not the fault of the people. My sisters knew all about it, and were also very angry. Dick Mulcahy was not then the well-known figure he became afterwards.

At Christmas time, the weather was very severe, and I suffered very much from the cold. Madame Markievicz did not seem to mind it. The prison officials gave us all the hot water jars we wanted, so bed was the most comfortable place and I stayed there most of the day. I got up for my dinner on Christmas Day; I had been out to Mass early. My sisters sent everything they could think of to make a lovely Christmas dinner, and Madame Markievicz decorated the small table we had in the passage outside our cells with the lovely flowers her sister had sent, together with a bottle of champagne. We had a grand dinner. Madame had the champagne all to herself, though she tried very hard to make me take some.

After Christmas, my heart started giving me trouble. I said

nothing to Madame Markievicz or the doctor about it. I got attacks in which I became rigid and speechless, but not unconscious; they did not last long, and came without warning. When Madame Markievicz did see me in one, she said I turned quite blue.

Then we read of the terrible epidemic of 'flu raging all over England and Ireland. The newspapers were full of it. In a letter from home I got news that some members of the family were down with it, and for weeks after that there was no letter. I was sick with anxiety. What was wrong that I had no letters from home? Were they all dead? At the end of five weeks I got a big bunch of letters; they had been held up in the Censor's Office. I wondered if that Censor knew what suffering he had caused me, holding my letters up at such a time. However, the news was good. The family were neither dying nor dead, though some of them had had the 'flu. I think the anxiety made whatever was wrong with my heart worse, as the attacks became more frequent, accompanied by sharp pain. Still I would not consult the doctor.

One day, going his rounds, he came into my cell to ask how I was. I said,'Just as usual, doctor.' As he was leaving the cell he made some remark. I was not sure what it was, and said, 'I beg your pardon, doctor, I did not hear what you said.' He turned back and said, 'I said you were sheer grit.' As he was looking at me, an attack came on. He rushed over to me, asking all sorts of questions, but I was unable to speak until the attack passed. He seemed quite alarmed, and ordered my gate to be unlocked day and night, so that the wardress could come to me if I wanted her. A specialist was brought in to examine me, but I told him I would only allow the examination on one condition, that he would tell me exactly what he found wrong. He agreed. When the examination was over, he said the trouble was my heart. I said that was strange, as it had never given me any trouble before I came to Holloway. However, within a week I was released; whether the diagnosis was right or wrong, the result of it was good for me.

A few days before my release, the Matron came into my cell and sat down beside my bed. She started talking about my release, and after a while said, 'You know, the Governor, the doctor and myself often discuss you ladies, and you are the only one we cannot understand. We have done everything in our power within the prison rules to make things easy for you. The other two ladies responded, and seemed to appreciate what we did, but you have not. You have kept us all at arm's length.' 'I hope, Matron, you are not accusing me of discourtesy,' I said. 'Certainly not,' she said. 'Indeed, you have been courtesy itself, but you have never allowed us to draw near. No matter what we did you remained hostile, when the other ladies were so friendly. Can you explain it?'

I said, 'I can only explain it in one way, Matron. I am Irish, purely Irish, and as such, knowing my country's history, how can I be other than hostile to my country's only enemy, England? You, the Governor, the doctor and all the officials here represent that enemy, and no matter how kind you may be, and I admit your kindness, I cannot forget what you represent. The other two ladies are different in this way, that they are of English descent, born in Ireland, and they belong to what we call there the Ascendancy, or English element. They have many English relatives and friends, whom they think highly of. They have identified themselves with our struggle for freedom from the conviction that our cause is a just cause, and they have worked and suffered with us in that cause, but naturally they cannot feel the same hostility to England as I do.' 'Well,' she said, 'I belong to the North of Ireland, but I have lived most of my life in England,

and a nicer or kinder people one could not live amongst.' 'I have no doubt, Matron,' I said, 'that that has been your experience. I have no knowledge of the English in their own country. I only know the history of the English in my country, and if there is anything worse in the world than that, I do not know it.' She said, 'In every word you have spoken, there is the same unbreakable hostility you have shown since you came in here.' 'Matron,' I said, 'the thing is there in my blood. How could it be otherwise, with generations of oppression by the English of my people?' She stood up and left the cell without another word.

I was released on 18 February 1919, and felt sad at leaving Madame Markievicz there alone, but I had no option in the matter. Miss Eva Gore-Booth invited me to stay with her until my sister Madge and Micheál Staines, who were on their way to escort me home, arrived. She was the essence of kindness to me, though I was a perfect stranger to her, but as a friend of her sister that she loved she thought she could never do enough for me.

Unfortunately, on my way home I contracted the 'flu, which was still raging, and by the time I reached Dublin I was utterly unable for the wonderful reception Dublin gave me. Cumann na mBan gave a dinner in the Gresham Hotel to celebrate my homecoming, and the crowd outside the hotel wanted me to speak to them from the hotel window, but I was unable to do so; I don't know how I got through the dinner.[4] Next morning I was removed to a nursing home, where I had to remain seven weeks, during which time death and myself had a big tussle. When I was convalescent I went down to Limerick, where my children were. It was some time before I was fully recovered. Madame Markievicz was released three weeks after me, as well as all the other prisoners. It was a great pleasure to hear of her release, as even three weeks alone must have been very bad; she loved company and people to talk to.[5] The war had been over since November, and why we were kept prisoners for so long after I don't know.

9
Raids and Committees

Markievicz released from prison — Dublin Corporation
— the Black and Tans — de Valera — Sinn Féin Courts
— raids on Kathleen's home

When Madame Markievicz arrived in Dublin from Holloway Prison
(March 1919), she came to see me in the nursing home. She told me
she had gone to live in my home in Richmond Avenue, as she felt at
home there, having four rooms in my house filled with her furniture.
At the time of her arrest she and Mrs Ginnell had been living
together, but Mrs Ginnell had decided she would not keep on the
house and had written to Madame Markievicz to know what she
should do with her furniture. Madame was distracted; she had some
very valuable pictures, and she could not think of anyone who had a
house large enough to take them in. I told her she could have them
put in my house until I returned home, and she told me I was a darling. She engaged a maid for me, and lived in my home until my
return from Limerick. Then she told me she would like to stay on

221

with me, and I agreed.

Some time later, I met de Valera outside the GPO. He seemed pleased to meet me, and was for him rather gushing. He said he was very glad to meet me, as he was thinking of going to France to seek aid for Ireland, and what did I think of the idea? I said France had no interest in Ireland now, and that the place to go for help was the USA, where so many of our people were. He said perhaps I was right, but before going there he would like to talk to me, as I would know many of the people he would be meeting and could give him a line on them, which would be very helpful. I said I would be quite happy to do so any time he wanted. The next thing I heard was that he had gone to the USA and had not come to see me. I was sorry, as I knew the people he would be meeting so well, and this would have helped him in his dealings with them. I went home and told Madame about meeting de Valera, and what he had said. She was surprised.

That night we were all in bed when a messenger arrived from Michael Collins, saying that the house was going to be raided and that Madame had better clear out.[1] Madame got into a wild state of excitement, rushing here and there and asking what she would do. I suggested she should first get dressed, and while she was dressing I would think of what was best to do. Curfew was on, which would make a difficulty in moving around the streets. I got Tom and Emmet up and dressed, and told them to go around to Miss Skinnider in Waverley Avenue, near the back of the house, to knock gently on the hall door so as not to attract the notice of the neighbours, to hide in the hedges if they saw a curfew car coming, and to tell Miss Skinnider that Madame Markievicz would be around shortly as we were expecting a raid, and to leave the door open for her. Then I told Madame of the arrangements. Off she went to

Waverley Avenue, but owing to her short sight she could not see the number of the house, and I heard later that she kept wandering up and down and whispering, 'Margaret, Margaret,' until Miss Skinnider heard her and brought her in. She was safely in Miss Skinnider's, and the boys were back and in bed asleep, when the raiders reached my house.

I often look back and think what a very hard life my children had after the Rising. That night, they were taken out of a sound sleep, and told to dress and go around to Miss Skinnider during curfew hours; most adults would not have liked to go out during curfew hours. Later that night, they were pulled out of bed for the British soldiers to search their beds. I think we had more raids than other people, but those lads never showed the slightest sign of fear, though naturally they must have felt the strain of it.

That night, they were so sound asleep when the military arrived, at about 2am, that I could not wake them. I said to the officer who had ordered them to be removed from the beds, 'Could you not search the beds without removing them? You see how sound asleep they are.' 'I have my orders, ma'am,' he said. 'Oh yes,' I said, 'I know you have your orders, but even military orders may be carried out with a little humanity.' But he insisted, out of the bed they should come. I had to drag them out of bed because I could not wake them, but they woke when they were put standing on the cold floor. Daly, in another room, was awake like myself. He was never sleepy, and was very frail. No woman ever had better sons.

Madame stayed with Miss Skinnider for some months. While there she endeavoured to disguise herself, but she was not so easily disguised, she was so tall and big in every way. I am sure any who knew her could easily penetrate the disguise. She was quite happy, though, believing that her knowledge of theatrical make-up enabled her to make a perfect disguise. One day, however, she forgot she was acting the part of a decrepit old lady, and in a hurry to catch a tram picked up her long skirt and ran for it. She was horrified when she arrived on the tram and remembered her role. She later left Miss Skinnider and came back to live with me.

She brought an Australian officer home to tea one day. He had been through the war, and before returning to Australia had decided to take a medical degree in Trinity College. I don't know where she met him, but he expressed a desire to meet as many of those who had participated in the Rising as he could, so she brought him to see me. He was a very courteous man, and was interested in everything connected with the Rising. After tea we walked around the garden, and while doing so he said, 'Mrs Clarke, there is one thing I am puzzled about. Your husband was first signatory to the 1916 Proclamation.' I said, 'Yes, he was.' 'Well,' he said, 'taking all precedents as a guide, he would then be President. How is it some people call Mr Pearse President?' I said, 'That is as much a mystery to me as to you. When they entered the GPO on Easter Sunday, my husband was President of the Provisional Government. He told me so when I was speaking to him in Kilmainham Jail a few hours before his execution. He made no mention of a change taking place during the week.' 'It is very strange, very,' he said.

Later in the year [June] Madame Markievicz went to Cork for some meeting, and was arrested and imprisoned there. She wrote me continuously from that prison, and came back to live with me when she was released. Though we quarrelled occasionally, I was fond of her; she had some very fine qualities. One day she wanted to make a bet with me that she would scrub my kitchen floor, which was a tiled

Cumann na mBan, 1916.
(*Kilmainham Gaol Collection*)

ight: Maud Gonne MacBride
*v*ith children, Seán and Iseult.

Seán Mac Diarmada. (KE53, *Courtesy of the National Library of Ireland*)

Tom Clarke. (KE235, *Courtesy of the National Library of Ireland*)

Eamon de Valera in uniform. (KE26, *Courtesy of the National Library of Ireland*)

State funeral for Kathleen Clarke: the cortege pauses before the GPO, *The Irish Times*, 4 October 1972.

Below: Kilmainham Jail, Dublin. Copyright the Office of Public Works, Ireland.

1858—Commemorating Thomas Clarke—1916

POBLACHT NA H EIREANN
THE PROVISIONAL GOVERNMENT
IRISH REPUBLIC
TO THE PEOPLE OF IRELAND

Lá a Chéad Eisiúna
First Day of Issue

LUIMNEACH
28 VII
58

Miss Helen Bulleean.
71 Mutgrove Park.
Cronskeagh
Co Dublin

First Signatory of Proclamation of Irish Republic.

First day cover, Tom Clarke commemorative stamp, 28 July 1958. *(Courtesy H. Litton)*

Kathleen Clarke, after Easter Rising, 1916. *(Courtesy H. Litton)*

Kathleen Clarke at the wedding of her son Tom, in 1939.
Photo: Vincent H. Corcoran, Glenageary, County Dublin.
(Courtesy H. Litton)

Teddy and Maria Fleming (née Clarke), Tom's elder sister, date unknown.
(Courtesy H. Litton)

From left: Dr Emmet Clarke, Kathleen Clarke, John Daly Clarke and Tom Clarke Junior, after Mrs Clarke was presented with an honorary doctorate of law by the National University of Ireland, 14 April 1966.
(*Courtesy of E. Clarke*)

Lord Mayor of Dublin,
Kathleen Clarke
(*Courtesy of E. Clarke*).

one, much better and quicker than the maid. She said she had learned to scrub floors in Aylesbury Jail, where she had been sent after the Rising, and where she had had a very hard time. I told her I would take her word for it, that I had no desire to see her scrub my kitchen floor, but she insisted on doing it just to prove to me that she could.

She came into the garden one day, where I was planting some vegetables, to tell me she would not be back to lunch. While she was speaking to me I coughed a little, and some blood came up on my handkerchief. She screamed at the sight of it, and said I was to come in at once and go to bed, and she would get a doctor. I told her I was not going to bed, it was nothing, I had to finish my planting, and to please mind her own business. I got a bit cross with her. I suppose I was a bit worried, as the blood had been coming all the morning. I wondered when she did not try to bully me as usual, but turned and walked out of the garden without a word. Then I was sorry I had been cross with her; I feared I had offended her, and I knew she meant to be kind, but to call her back would mean an argument for which I did not feel able, so I let her go.

Hours later I was still planting, when I heard someone coming down the garden. I looked up, and was surprised to see Dr Kathleen Lynn and Miss ffrench-Mullen. I went to welcome them, though not too pleased at my planting being interrupted. They caught me by the arms, marched me into the house and up to my bedroom, undressed me and put me to bed, completely ignoring my protests. They then put packs of ice on my chest and left me that way, warning me not to move hand or foot until they came again. I was kept that way for days. I asked for an explanation of their action in swooping down on me they way they did. They told me that when Madame had left the garden that morning without arguing with me, she had gone straight to Dr Lynn and asked her to come out and see me at once, as she thought I looked very ill.

While I was still under orders not to move, and the ice was still on my chest, I heard a tramp, tramp, which sounded like military, coming up the avenue at about 8 o'clock. Forgetting all the warnings, I jumped out of bed, sending the ice packs in all directions. The tramp, tramp proved to be a number of the Dublin Metropolitan Police, and I called to Madame as they were knocking at the door. She called out the window to them to know what they wanted, and they said they had orders to search the house. She dressed while the maid let them in, went down to meet them and accompanied them in their search through the house. When they came to my room, she tried to prevent them entering, saying I was very ill, but they insisted, saying they had to carry out their orders. However, they were decent about it; they just looked in, and agreed with Madame that I was very ill indeed. I did not agree; I thought Madame was making a fuss about nothing. Madame was arrested that evening; I forget what prison she went to then.

When Madame Markievicz was made Minister for Labour she came rushing home to tell me.[2] I asked her how she had managed it, as I had noticed that the present leaders were not over-eager to put women into places of honour or power, even though they had earned the right to both as well as the men had, having responded to every call made upon them throughout the struggle for freedom. She told me she had had to bully them; she claimed she had earned the right to be a minister as well as any of the men, and was equally as well fitted for it, educationally and every other way, and if she was not made a minister she would go over to the Labour Party. With all the sacrifices women have made for freedom in this country, only one woman other than Madame Markievicz has been selected for honours by the Government. That was Mrs James MacNeill, who had been a member of Cumann na mBan.

There was a municipal election late in 1919, and I was nominated for two wards by Sinn Féin – Wood Quay and Mountjoy wards – and was elected Alderman for both. W T Cosgrave was also elected Alderman. He was Minister for Local Government in the Provisional Government of the Republic, Dáil Eireann. At the first meeting of the Council after the election the Town Clerk, Henry Campbell, called the roll, as was the usual procedure. When he came to Mrs Wyse Power's name he stopped, and said she must leave the council chamber as she had not been legally elected. Her name was on the register in Irish, and English was the legal language of the country, therefore she was disqualified. This was a bombshell, but Mrs Wyse Power was equal to it. She refused to leave, and said that Irish was the natural and national language of the country; she dared him to prove that she was not properly elected. The battle was left between them, but she knew we were all ready to stand by her; we knew she was an extremely clever woman, and well able to defend herself. She made a gallant fight and won; the Town Clerk could not prove his claim. I never admired any woman as I did her that day.

On 3 May 1920, Dublin Corporation acknowledged the authority of the Government of the Republic of Ireland, Dáil Eireann, as the duly elected Government of Ireland, and undertook to give effect to all decrees promulgated by the same Dáil Eireann. It was not a unanimous vote, but the Republicans had the majority vote in the Corporation and on the various committees, and so had their own way in most things. Not so with the various Boards on which we represented Dublin Corporation. Meetings were held every day, nearly every hour, all having the one purpose, doing the work of the Corporation and upholding the Republic.

Things went smoothly in the Council until the Black and Tan war started, with one exception, an incident of some interest, I think.[3] The auditor for the British Local Government demanded the books of the Corporation for audit, and the Town Clerk was ordered by the Council not to submit them to him. He refused to carry out the order, so the Council then appointed another Clerk, Mr Walshe, to carry out the duties of Town Clerk. This he did faithfully and well all through the Tan war, until the Treaty.

One day we had a raid by the Black and Tans during a meeting of the Council. They came into the chamber, took hold of the roll book and proceeded to call the roll. One of them called the roll, while the others watched the faces of the members. I called out, 'Let no-one answer.' No-one did, even the Aldermen and councillors opposed to us, which I thought was rather fine of them. Despite that, the Tans' plan was partially successful; not everyone has a poker face, and the slightest flicker in the face of a member whose name was called and he was noted, pounced upon and arrested. The Tans adopted this method, I think, to get men whose names they had for arrest; they did not know them, and no-one would inform them.

Later, the British Government demanded the surrender of the Public Health Offices, and the matter came before the Public Health Committee. The demand was refused, on my motion, on the grounds that the offices were absolutely essential to us for the public health business of the city. One of the opposition members asked what was the use of refusing; the Government wanted them, and would take them without our consent. I said that that was quite possible, but that then we would not have yielded to an outrageous demand. They did take the offices by force, and then demanded City Hall. This demand went before the council and was refused, and City Hall was taken by force, so the Council had to meet in the Oak Room of the Mansion House, and the public health business was scattered all over the city.

One thing that made the work of the Council very difficult during this time was the stopping of all payments, or part payments, by the British Local Government on schemes such as tuberculosis, school meals, and others. This left us entirely dependent on the rates. The school teachers had been getting a bonus for superintending the preparation and serving of the school meals. I was Chairman of the School Meals Committee at the time, and I found we could not continue the bonus under the circumstances. The Committee asked me to approach the teachers of the schools where the meals were served, and explain the matter to them. With the Secretary of the Committee, I waited on the teachers of the schools and put the position before them, and asked if they would be willing to carry on without the bonus. In every case, the teachers agreed to do so willingly. It was a sacrifice on their part, and I thought it rather wonderful of them. I thanked them in the name of the Committee, and said how much we would appreciate their services.

Some of the Boards on which I was a Corporation representative had the reputation of being hostile to Sinn Féin members. One such was the Harcourt Street Children's Hospital Board, and the first meeting I attended I went prepared for hostility, with my colours up. To my surprise, when I entered the room Lord Powerscourt, who was in the Chair, stood up and welcomed me as a new member, and all the other members followed his lead. When the meeting was over Lord Powerscourt conducted me all over the hospital, and was the essence of courtesy. The hospital was full of wounded British soldiers at the time.

I was wondering all through the meeting where I had seen the Chairman before, and it was only when I got home that I remembered. When I had been a prisoner in Dublin Castle in 1916, he was the man who was called up to sign the order for my removal to Kilmainham Jail to see my husband on the night of May 2nd. Later, on the morning of May 3rd on my return from Kilmainham, he had again been roused to decide what was to be done with me. He was certainly very courteous to me then.

Alderman Laurence O'Neill was Lord Mayor of Dublin all through the Black and Tan period. He did not belong to Sinn Féin or any other party, but he was very sympathetic to Sinn Féin, and very helpful. He never refused to do anything Sinn Féin asked him to do. As I was the only Sinn Féin Alderman always available, he appointed me his *locum tenens* whenever he left the city. At de Valera's request, he started the Irish White Cross, and sent me the following invitation to act on it:

> Mansion House, Dublin
> 19 January, 1920
> Dear Mrs Clarke,
>
> It has been suggested to me to take in hands the forming of a 'White Cross', to act in co-operation with the 'White Cross' already formed in America for the relief of our suffering people.
>
> With that object an Executive Committee will be required to work out the scheme, and I would feel deeply complimented if you would act on that Committee, as of course it will not be

narrowed in its construction by any sectional considerations.

The duty of the Committee will be to act in conjunction with the smaller committees that will be set up throughout the country, for the consideration and distribution of the Funds.

I am, Yours faithfully,
L O'Neill, Lord Mayor.

There was a large body called the Council [of the White Cross], composed of representative men and women from all parts of the country. There was a certain amount of risk in grouping together so many of varied outlook and ideals, especially when most of the Sinn Féin members would not be available, either through being in prison or on the run. But on coming to work it out, I found all to be working with one ideal, that of relieving the suffering of the people. The nature of the war being what it was, the savagery of the Black and Tans fell heavily on the civilian population as well as on the IRA. I worked in the greatest harmony with all the members, and I must say that when the winding-up of the Irish White Cross came, it left me with sincere admiration of those who had worked in it with me, yet differed with me in many things.

One thing done by the Irish White Cross I shall feel proud of, and that was the setting up of the Orphans' Care Committee. The idea originated with John O'Neill of the Lucania Works, and he asked me what I thought of it. I told him I was in entire agreement with him. He said he was going to propose it at the Council meeting, and asked if I would second it. I said I would be very glad to do so, but thought it would be better if someone not so involved in things would do it. I would support him, and get others to do so. On thinking it over, he agreed that was a better way. As far as I can remember, he got Mr Webb to second it.

When the Council met he proposed that a large sum of money be set aside for the orphans of the war and used only for them, and that a Committee be formed to administer it. The Council agreed, and a Committee was set up forthwith, composed of six members: Mr John O'Neill, Mr J H Webb, Miss Barton, Madame O'Rahilly, Mr David Robinson and myself. When we held our first meeting Mr John O'Neill was made Chairman, Madame O'Rahilly and Mr J H Webb Honorary Treasurers, and myself Honorary Secretary. At a later meeting we appointed Mrs Eamonn Ceannt as General Secretary, a position she held until the work of the Committee came to an end. As it was a whole-time job, she was of course paid for doing it.

We had over six hundred children on our books at one time. When the Military Service Pensions were introduced, many of these came off our books until the age of sixteen, when we took them on again to help to establish them in some form of work that would give them a living until they reached the age of twenty-one. We were enabled to do this through the shrewd and careful investment of the money entrusted to us, on the advice of Mr John O'Neill and Mr J H Webb. Mrs Ceannt was an ideal secretary for the work, and took as much interest in it as if the children were her own. She has written a detailed account of the work done by the Committee in a little book, which was published when our work was finished.

Dr Pat McCartan has written a book entitled *With de Valera in America* [Dublin 1932], which is a history of the events as he knew them there.[4] At this side of the Atlantic, very little was known of the things he has written about, but while he was in America a Clan na Gael man who was on a visit to Ireland called to see me. What he had to tell me about things among the Irish in America was very disturbing. He asked me if I could have de Valera recalled; he said he had made a tour of the USA as President of the Irish Republic, and had been treated like a prince everywhere. His reception was the biggest any man from Ireland ever got, but under the surface there was trouble. A split between John Devoy and de Valera was imminent, and it would be well if de Valera left before it came to the surface. If it did, the results would be disastrous. I told him I would see what could be done, but I had little hope of being able to do anything. He seemed very sad about it.

Harry Boland came home for a short trip at about the same time, from New York. He also called on me, and I told him what the old Clan na Gael man had said. He got very angry, and said, 'De Valera is not coming home.' 'Well,' I said, 'if what the old Clan man said is true, I think he should come home. He has had a triumphal march through the USA and Ireland is now his place, at least I think so, or he could seek help in some of the South American republics.' At that Harry got wildly angry with me, and said, 'He is not leaving the USA until he finishes the row, no matter how long it takes.' 'Well, Harry,' I said, 'if that is the case, may God help us. I know Devoy and the men who stand by him. They are men who have worked all their lives for Ireland, men who love Ireland, and many of them have suffered for it in British and Irish prisons. If this row, as you call it, becomes public, neither you nor I or de Valera will live to see the end of it.'

The split did come to the surface, and to my mind was disastrous, and its effects are to be seen to this day.

With the start of the Black and Tan war, things became very difficult. They were an undisciplined force, and were drunk more often than they were sober. They raided homes indiscriminately, and from the time they entered your home until they left, one could not be sure of what would happen – it depended entirely on their mood or whim. For instance, they entered a small cottage on the outskirts of Limerick and told the woman of the house they wanted her husband; she asked them to let him finish his tea, and they told her not to worry, that they would be finished with him in a few minutes. They took him outside the door, and the next thing she heard was shots. She rushed out the door, to find her husband dead. Some of them were demobilised soldiers; others, it was believed, were recruited from the criminal classes in prison in England, and certainly their conduct seemed to bear that out.

The great need of the IRA was arms and ammunition, but to get these they had to have gold. They had to be purchased outside Ireland, and only gold would be accepted by those who were selling them, so people all over the country were collecting gold. It was very scarce, as the British Government had called in all the gold on the outbreak of war. From the moment war was declared, in 1914, Uncle John had given my sister Madge orders to hold all gold coming into the business and store it, as it would be needed in the fight. She did this, but as the Rising was of such short duration, no call was made for any of it. Still she kept on storing, and when it was needed by the IRA they got it.

I was on a visit to Limerick with my children, but before leaving Dublin I had arranged with Mick Collins to bring as much gold as I could get from Madge back with me. Something happened before I left Limerick, I forget what it was, but it resulted in the British stopping all trains in and out of Limerick from Nenagh and Limerick Junction. Under these circumstances it was a risk to bring gold out of Limerick, but knowing the great need for it I decided to take the risk.

I hired a taxi to take me to Limerick Junction, and filled it with strawberry canes, gooseberry bushes and various odds and ends for a garden, to make it look like just a family party, then with my three children I started for the junction. I had two packets of gold. One I put on my chest, and a heavy poultice it was, but my black furs covered the slight bulge. I put the other in my muff, which was black too, and large. To my horror, we were stopped by a group of soldiers about a mile from the Junction, ordered out of the taxi, and it was searched very minutely. The package in my muff was so heavy that I thought I would drop it getting out of the taxi, so I acted as if I were ill to cover my awkward movements.

I think the garden things did the trick which they were intended to, of proving we were a simple family party, and we were allowed to return to the taxi and resume our journey. Another thing helped; I was in mourning, and women in mourning for their men killed in France were plentiful in Ireland.

I got the train to Dublin at the Junction, but I had not an easy moment until I got the gold safely to Mick Collins; the sum was £2,000. It was a hair-raising experience, but everyone engaged in the work for freedom at that time had scares every day of the week. We learned to take chances without turning a hair; we never knew when walking along the street but that we might run into an ambush, or be held up by British military. The tram one was in might be held up by British military and everyone searched. They were trying and stirring times, but the spirit of the people was so wonderful, one felt so proud.

When it was decided to start Republican Courts, I was recalled from Glendalough, Co Wicklow, where I was on holiday with my children, to help to start the Courts in the North City, Dublin.[5] The

Courts were to be under the control of the Department of Home Affairs; Austin Stack was the Minister for Home Affairs. We were told to go and start the Courts, and that they must be self-supporting; there would be no money to help us. We tackled it as we did everything at that time, with enthusiasm, and the result was success. Three Courts were set up, Circuit, County and Parish. The Circuit Court judges were all legal men and were paid by the Department. In that Court, it was the rule that when the case to be tried involved a woman, a woman judge must sit with the Court Judge. I acted with Judge Creed Meredith on these cases, as there was no woman Circuit Court judge.

I was elected one of the County Court judges, and Chairman of the North City, Dublin, judges. In the County Court, three judges sat for a hearing, according to the rule laid down for them, but in the Parish Court only one judge presided. The North City judges met once a month for the purpose of discussing the working of the Courts, recording their experiences and seeking ways of improving the working of the Courts. Many of the suggested improvements were forwarded to the Minister for Home Affairs, and in most cases adopted by him.

Running the Courts was not easy. We had no special place to hold them in, and we were likely to be raided by British military or Black and Tans, and that made it difficult to rent places to hold the Court in. Great credit is due to a girl named Sheila Bowen who acted as typist, and a young man named Fitzgerald, who acted as Clerk to the Courts, for the way they searched and found places to hold the Courts in. Their job was a whole-time one, so they were paid, they had to live. Really nothing would pay them for the work they did and the way they did it.

At the last meeting of the Dáil before the plenipotentiaries went to London after the Truce [August 1921] Austin Stack, in giving a report on the work of his department, said that the North City Courts were the only ones which functioned without a break from the time they started, with the exception of a small country place, the name of which I forget, and that the North City success was due entirely to the enthusiasm of Mrs Tom Clarke and the work she put into it. This was to some extent true, but I could not have succeeded without the wonderful help I got from other women as enthusiastic as myself. Those women were Mrs Wyse Power (later Senator), Mrs O'Shea Leamy, Mrs Buckley and Mrs McKean. Any time of the day a Court could be held, they were ready. Even though they all had their own business to attend to, they never allowed it to prevent them holding a Court when it was necessary. Some men helped, but until the Truce few men were available, as they were wanted for other work. With all our enthusiasm, we would not have been so successful without the help of Sheila Bowen and the young man Fitzgerald. Austin Stack also said that the suggestions forwarded to him from the North City, Dublin, judges for improving the working of the Courts were invaluable.

I shall never forget the brutal murder of Peadar Clancy, Dick McKee and Conor Clune.[6] I did not know Clune, but I did know Peadar Clancy and Dick McKee. Both men were of an outstanding type, and their death was a terrible loss to us. They were men who would have been outstanding anywhere. The British were very discriminating in the men they sought to destroy. The bodies of the three men were handed over to their relatives and lay in the mortuary chapel of the Pro-Cathedral, Marlborough Street. I went in to see them and say a few prayers for them.

While I was there Mick Collins came in; when he looked in the coffin of Peadar Clancy, tears rushed from his eyes and fell on Peadar. I did not wonder; all three men were horribly mutilated. One had a large hole in his forehead; it looked as if an explosive bullet had been used. All the faces had the look of tortured men, which even death had not washed away the memory of. What I saw in those coffins would bring tears to the most stony-hearted; Mick Collins had no need to be ashamed of those tears. He took great risks of being captured in coming to see them. We are asked to forgive and forget. How can we forget those things? Forgiveness can only be considered when the power behind the perpetrators of such deeds earn it by their complete removal from our thirty-two counties, leaving us in complete freedom.

Peadar Clancy told me once that he would never forget how the British officer treated my husband and brother in the Rotunda Gardens after the surrender in 1916, and at the time he made a vow that if he ever got the chance, the officer responsible would pay for it with his life. I had only got a hint of what happened at the time, just that they had been singled out for shocking treatment by an officer, and I asked Peadar to tell me what had happened. He said, 'No, it is better not, better you should not know.' Apparently it was bad enough to implant in a young man like Peadar such a desire for vengeance. That officer's action was avenged; he was shot dead some years later in Wexford.

During the Black and Tan war my home was continually raided, sometimes by military, sometimes by Black and Tans. The first one occurred one morning at about 2am; there was a loud knocking at the hall door, and I opened my bedroom window and asked who was there. 'Military,' was the reply. 'Open the door in the name of His

Majesty the King. We want to search your house.' I asked 'Have you got a licence or search warrant?' and the answer was Yes. I said, 'Put it in the letterbox until I see it.' 'You had better be quick, or we will break down the door,' I was told. I dressed and came down the stairs, crawling by the wall, as the stairs faced the front door, and I feared they might shoot the lock. I got to the letterbox and took out the order. It was an official one all right, and I let them in. There were only myself and the three children in the house, and they were fast asleep, but I had to wake them and get them up for the military to search their beds. That was the only time I looked for an official order to search the house; as time went on I learned that the only law was the law of force, and the sooner I opened the door when they knocked the better for all concerned.

Another night, I knew real fear for the first and only time. It was a military raid, as usual after midnight, and we were all in bed. When they came into my eldest son's room (he was sixteen years of age and in very bad health), they asked his age and examined his face to see if he was shaving, and they started debating whether they would take him. It was then I knew fear, a fear that congealed the blood in my veins. I made up my mind they would only get him over my dead body; however, they decided against taking him. It took me some time to get over the horror of it. I had reason for the fear, as several lads had been taken from their homes by the military at that time, and their corpses found by the roadside in the morning. In one case, two lads were put sitting up by a wall, dead, with biscuit tins on their heads.

When the IRA started bombing military lorries passing through the streets of Dublin, their bombs were very faulty. I did not know this until a clerical student came and told me that the bombs they were using were more a danger to themselves than those they were fired at. He said he had studied the manufacture of bombs, and he would give me a safe formula, if I would pass it on to the proper quarter. As I had known this young man from childhood, I trusted him, and undertook to do what he asked. He brought it to me, and I had it to Peadar Clancy in a few hours' time. Peadar was delighted. There was also enclosed a list of firms where the materials could be purchased safely.

A week or so later the student brought me another one. It was late in the evening when he called, so I had to keep it until next day. That night I had a military raid, and I was scared lest they come on the formula. I did not dare go into the room where I had it concealed, fearing the force of the anxiety in my mind would direct them to it. The search lasted three hours. They measured every wardrobe outside and inside, and examined every drawer and cupboard minutely, and every bit of furniture in the house. From minute to minute I feared to hear they had found it, and for some time after they left I did not dare go into the room where it was concealed, as sometimes they would turn back when one would think they were gone, but at last I found my bit of paper safe. After that I put my young friend and Peadar Clancy in touch with each other; the risk of being captured by bringing them to me was too great.

I had a Black and Tan raid soon after, and at the time my greenhouse was full of unripe grapes. The raiders cut them all down, and when the neighbours opened their hall doors next morning, they found their knockers decorated with my unripe grapes. They also ate all the food I had in the house that night, and I had to go out next morning to buy food for breakfast.

I had another Black and Tan raid shortly after this. After searching the house, they went into the garden and killed a Kerry Blue pup of mine, who apparently had the impudence to bark at them. They just bashed it to bits. I found the poor little mangled body in the garden in the morning, and for some time could find no trace of the mother and the two other puppies. I feared they must be dead somewhere, but I kept searching and calling them for some time. Then I thought I heard a sound from an empty lime barrel, and there I found them crouched up in the end of it, whimpering and trembling. It took me some time to coax them out, for they were terrified. Looking at the poor little dogs, and at the dead one, I thought human beings would get the same treatment from those devils.

Another night, after searching the house and being as insulting as possible, they went into the garden, a portion of which I had railed off for fowl. They opened the fowl-house door and chased the fowl into the garden, then they turned the hen-coops and the dog kennel upside down. I only knew what had happened in the morning, when I found the fowl having a great time in the garden. It all seemed so senseless. After the death of the puppy, I kept my dogs in the house at night.

When coming to the house the military would draw up their lorries at the end of the avenue and come up to the house in rubber-soled shoes, hoping, I suppose, to take me by surprise. Usually they arrived between midnight and 2am. There was never the same tension when it was a military raid; they were a disciplined force, and were always under the command of their officer. Not so the Black and Tans. At one Black and Tan raid I asked one of them who was their officer: 'Oh, madam,' he said, 'we are all officers.' 'What a wonderful army,' I said. Sometimes, when the military left my house they would go to McGarrys' house in Philipsburgh Avenue, and I would go to McGarrys' in the morning to exchange condolences.

After a long series of raids, I was feeling the strain. Though in writing about them they may not seem much, from the time they entered one's house possible tragedy also entered. I decided to go down to my mother and sisters in Limerick for a rest. I arrived on a Saturday, and that night there was a raid on my mother's house, a military raid. On Monday night there was a Black and Tan raid, and raids also on Tuesday and Friday night. It looked as if I was not going to get the rest I had hoped for. On Saturday I went down to Kilkee, Co Clare, to my sister Eileen, where she was on holiday with her family, and that night there was a raid on her house. I gave up trying to dodge raids after that.

One night, when I was staying at my mother's house, we were all at supper. It was 10pm, and curfew was on. There was a low tapping at the door, and one of my sisters went to open it. It was an IRA man looking for somewhere to sleep, and he was made welcome. It was a common occurrence. We all sat down to resume our supper; he was congratulating himself on having got a bed to sleep in, and a supper all ready for him. We were all laughing and joking when there was a loud knock at the door. There was consternation; we all knew what that meant – a raid. God, what were we to do? Where could we hide the man? If they caught him they would in all probability shoot him. One had to think quickly in those days.

Madge said to me, 'You go to the door and parley with them, while I find somewhere to hide him.' I went to the door and asked who was there. The answer was, 'Military. Open the door at once.' 'All right,' I said, 'I am trying to open it, but the lock is very stiff.' 'Open the door at once,' they shouted, 'or we will break it down.' I said, 'I am only a visitor here, and don't know how this lock works. If you wait one minute, I'll get one of the family to come and open it.' Then I got a whisper from the back of the hall, 'It's all right, let them come in.' All was dark; when curfew was on, no light dare be shown. I opened the door and in they rushed, upstairs, downstairs, into every room in the house, and looked rather foolish when they found only women and children. They must have traced the man, given him time to get in and then pounced, sure of their prey. The puzzle to them was, Where was he? They had left men outside, so he could not have got out, as they would have caught him. I was as puzzled as they were.

When the Auxiliaries did not get their man, they endeavoured to take it out on the family. They went into the diningroom where my sisters and children were pretending to continue their supper, and they gave them a bad half-hour sitting at the table, questioning them, smoking, and puffing smoke in their faces. Then they got up and went through the house again, in and out of my mother's room where she was in bed, looking very frail and ill. She was ill with fright, poor woman. They questioned her, and searched her room, then they left, and in a short time returned and searched every inch of it again. Then they went downstairs and out. The raid was over, but one could not be sure. I asked Madge where he was. 'Hush,' she said, 'they may come back again, wait a while.' I was kept in suspense for what seemed hours before I was told where he was hidden.

When I did hear, I did not wonder my mother looked so ill. She had been in bed when the raiders knocked. All her life she had been accustomed to sleep on a feather bed, and when hair and spring mattresses came into fashion she got one, but would not be parted from her feather bed. She insisted on having it on top of the hair and spring mattress. Between the hair mattress and the feather bed, the man was stretched out. All the feathers were drawn to one side of the bed, and my mother lay on top of them. The bedclothes were drawn over all, and it looked just like an old lady in bed. Poor mother, what she must have suffered while the raiders were searching the room, not knowing but that any minute they might order her out of the bed to search it, find the man, and perhaps kill him before her. When we finally thought it safe to uncover him, he was nearly suffocated.

A Limerick man had been sentenced to death, and was to be shot in the military barracks. On the morning of his execution, all the members of Cumann na mBan went to the barracks and knelt outside the gate to pray for the man who was to die. While they were kneeling there, the barracks gate was opened and a military lorry full of Black and Tans drove out. The thing was so unexpected that some of the women, thinking the lorry was going to run over them, got up and ran. The Black and Tans jumped out of the lorry and started beating up the women with the butts of their rifles. My mother and sisters, Mrs O'Callaghan and her sister, and some other women who had remained on their knees were all beaten severely. My mother's hands were all cut and bleeding from the efforts of one of the Tans to get her beads from her. My sister Laura was confined to bed for several days, black and bruised all over from the beating she got. All the women present were injured.

I experienced a Black and Tan raid during one of my visits to my mother. It was a small one, about seven men, all drunk, but it was rather a terrifying one, as one never knew what drunken men would do. I had just sent the children to bed when I heard the raiders, and mother-like I rushed up to their rooms to be near them. I bustled them all into one room and stayed with them. One of the raiders came into the room. He was armed with a rifle, and was quite drunk.

He put the muzzle of the rifle resting on my chest, saying, 'I'll teach you not to bring men down from Dublin to shoot us.' He was so drunk, it seemed as if he was keeping himself standing by holding on to the rifle resting on my chest. Fearing it might go off, I moved it quietly from its resting-place on my chest, and then said in my coolest voice, 'My dear man, I don't know what you are talking about', but he kept on saying, 'I'll teach you', over and over, holding on to his rifle and reeling about, until there was a call for him from downstairs.

During this time, things were happening downstairs. One of the raiders lifted his rifle to smash a large picture of my brother and my mother tried to stop him. He turned on her, and with the butt of his rifle came down on her shoulder with all the force he had intended for the picture. That night cost her many years of life, and great suffering. The doctor was called in next day, when the pain got bad, but he thought the pain was neuritis, and though she suffered pain from the time she got the blow the cause was not discovered for a long time. The shoulder bone had been cracked, and bone disease had set in. For five years, before her death, she suffered severely, and died in great agony.

In another raid on my mother's house, a rather funny incident occurred; it was carried out by military, and caused us great merriment. The officer in charge was a young man, full of his own importance and very eager to show his efficiency at his job. He placed men in each room and gave orders what they were to do. In the drawing room, he directed that the carpet be taken up and the floor boards lifted to look for hidden arms. He was doing a thoroughly systematic job, going from room to room directing. Coming back to the drawingroom, he found that his men had lifted the carpet, but were unable to lift the floor boards. He was very scornful of their efforts, and said, 'Give me that axe!' He would show them. He made a swipe at the floor with the axe, and it flew out of his hands, hit him and knocked him over. My sisters and I were looking on, and we burst out laughing and laughed and laughed. It was so funny we could not stop. He did not enjoy his discomfiture, but we did. He was so upset he blew his whistle, assembled all his men and marched them out, and so the raid ended.

When we were putting back the carpet after they had gone, we discovered a few rifles, which were behind an armchair and had been covered by the carpet which the soldiers had thrown over them. In the excitement of the raid we had forgotten all about them. They had only been a short time in the house, on their way elsewhere. Had the military found them, I don't know what would have happened; I suppose it would have been a case of the Lord have mercy on us. The military raids were not so bad, as they were a disciplined force, but a good deal depended on the officer in charge.

My sister Madge was staying with me in Dublin for a few days in September 1920. When we came down to breakfast one morning, I took up the paper to have a look at the news, and dear God, what did I read but that the previous night my sister Agnes had been dragged out of the house in Limerick by the hair, her hair cut off and her hand cut almost in two by a razor. I could never faint, but if I had had any weakness in that direction I would certainly have fainted then. Madge asked, 'What is wrong with you?' but I could not answer her, I just handed her the paper. She was just as shocked as I was, and we took the first train to Limerick we could get. We found the house swarming with policemen, the officer in charge, inquiring into the outrage. He was told by my sister Agnes that it had been one of his

Black and Tans who had committed the outrage upon her. She had recognised one of them, and was prepared to identify him, but she got no chance to do so. The police were not paraded for her to pick him out. He must have been removed from Limerick, as she never saw him again.

I heard the details of what had happened when the police had left the house. Curfew was on, and everyone had gone to bed. Agnes thought she heard a tapping at the hall door; her bedroom was at the front of the house. She opened the window and asked who was there. A voice whispered, 'It's me, Miss Daly, let me in.' Naturally, she thought it was an IRA man looking for shelter, and dressed quickly and went down to the door with only one thought in her mind, to let the man in quickly before the curfew force came round and caught him. When she opened the door, a group of masked men faced her. They grabbed her, threw her on the ground and pulled her to the gate on her face, by the hair. Then one of them put his foot on her back and stooping over, cut off her hair with a razor. While he was stooping over her, she made a grab at his mask and pulled it off. It was a moonlit night, but clouds were moving rapidly, sometimes covering the moon, then leaving brilliant moonlight. As she pulled the mask off, the moon shone out brilliantly. 'Now,' she said, 'I can identify you, you murderer.' With that he took her hand, with which she had pulled the mask off, and cut it in two between the two middle fingers, right to the wrist, with the razor.

Meanwhile another sister, Carrie, thought she heard a noise, got up and came down to the hall. She was immediately seized, and told if she made a sound she would have her brains blown out. My mother in her room also thought she heard a noise, and also came down to the hall. She was immediately seized too, and the same threat made to

247

her. With the shock she became hysterical and started screaming, and could not stop no matter how they threatened her. She was over seventy years of age at the time. They shook her, but she only got worse, so they left. When they had gone Agnes called to my mother and Carrie, and between them they got her back to the house, blood streaming from her.

Carrie had first aid training and tried to stop the bleeding, but she found it hard to stop it as an artery had been cut. It took an hour to stop it completely. They could not get a doctor, as the Tans paraded up and down outside the house all night, some of them playing a mouth organ. When the doctor did get to her in the morning, he had to tie the artery and put several stitches in her hand. It took her a long time to recover from the loss of blood, the shock, and the bodily injuries from being dragged such a distance by the hair.[7]

Some months after this, she began going into the bakery for a short time each day, although she was not quite recovered. One day a number of Black and Tans came in, handed her a poster and ordered her to paste it up in the window. It was a proclamation of some kind. She refused to do so, and one of them walked inside the counter, got into the window and stuck the poster up there. A crowd had collected outside to see what was happening. When he came out of the window, she said, 'I'll take that down when you are gone.' 'You will do so at your peril,' he answered. As they left the bakery she heard a voice say, 'Ah, the Dalys are bet at last.' When she was sure they were gone, she stepped into the window and pulled off the poster. The crowd outside held their breaths for a second, then awed and scared disappeared like rabbits, fearful of what the result of her action might be. To her surprise, the Tans did not return.

At the beginning of the 1914 war the British had needed horses, and horses were commandeered from all over Ireland. A demand was made for the bakery horses, but on the instructions of Uncle John Madge refused to surrender them. She told the British officer who made the demand that the orders from her uncle, the owner, were that rather than let the British have them, she was to have them shot, and she was quite prepared to carry out the order if any attempt was made to take them. He left the premises, saying they must have the horses, but he never came back, and no attempt was made to take them.

Those raids I have mentioned were only the bad ones, that is why I remember them so well. From 1916 until my eldest son reached manhood, there was no man either in my mother's house or in mine, yet the raids were continuous. Several attempts were made by the Black and Tans to burn down the bakery, but they failed, owing to the fact that it had been built as a bakery and there was nothing to burn but the mixing troughs. Failing to burn it, they defaced the walls with obscenities. One night they set fire to the stables at the back of the bakery, leaving the horses locked in. They were saved by a man going home late who noticed smoke coming from the stables. He got out the horses, wild with terror. They raced all over the city, and some of them were not recovered until the next day. The man had the fire out before much damage was done.

After Kevin Barry's arrest, I have a very vivid recollection of how horror-struck the people were when it was announced that he was to be hanged.[9] He was only a boy in years, but one with pride and courage who resisted all efforts to get him to betray his comrades. He was a soldier of Ireland, a hero. His mother, though heartbroken, was very proud of him, proud of the calm courageous way he faced death, and he was certainly one to be proud of.

Shortly before the Truce, curfew was again imposed on Limerick, and without warning, as a reprisal it was thought for some ambush, but no-one seemed clear about it. It was on Saturday, the day people come in from the country to do their shopping. A proclamation was issued by the British military, ordering all business premises to be closed by 2pm, curfew to start at 4pm, and cancelling all fairs and markets, advising people to leave their windows open. During the day the police beat the people off the street with sticks, then turned their attention to pony, horse and donkey carts. They beat the poor animals, and sent them wild around the streets. My sisters' bakery was entered several times by them during the morning, and customers beaten out of it. They closed the bakery at the hour ordered, and went home.

Between three and four o'clock that evening, about two hundred British military arrived at the Daly home on the Ennis Road, and the roads back and front of the house were held by a large force. My mother and sisters thought it was the usual raid, but wondered at the numbers. The officer in charge told them that he had orders to burn the house and its contents, and he would give them fifteen minutes to clear out. They would be allowed to take family portraits, but nothing else, no clothes but what they had on.

My aunt Lollie was over eighty years old, and with the shock of hearing that the house was to be burned down, she seemed to get paralysed. It took some time to get her down from her room, and the fifteen minutes were up when they got her to the hall. The officer looked at his watch and said he would give them two minutes more to be out of the house. His attitude seemed to be that if they were not out in the time allowed, they would be burned with the house.

They were ordered into the back garden, and the military, with the aid of the Black and Tans, entered on their work of destruction. For some reason unknown to us, they did not burn the house, as they had said they had orders to do, but everything that would burn was removed to the road, and there petrol was thrown on them and a match put to it. It was a huge bonfire. Then with sledgehammers and other implements they set to work on the destruction of the house. Gas, water and electric wires, pipes and fittings were torn out, the windows and doors were smashed, and everything that could make a wreck of the house was done.

While this destruction was in progress, two officers went down the garden to where my mother, aunt and sisters were. One of them asked for Miss Madge Daly, and they told him she was in Dublin. He took a paper from which he read that, as the said Miss Madge Daly did not give notice to the military authorities of the ambush which had taken place in John's Street the previous night, all the contents of the house were to be destroyed, by order of the military. In the destruction by fire, a unique collection of souvenirs of dead patriots was lost.

There they were, a group of five women, left homeless. They would not be allowed back to the house, even though it was only a shell. My mother and aunt were old, and a lot of the furniture was old and had sentimental associations for them. They were sad to see it all going up in flames; nevertheless, they showed a proud front to the enemy, and we were very proud of them.

Where would they go for shelter? They did not wish to go to any of the married sisters, lest they bring vengeance on them and their young families. They went to a hotel in the city, whose management showed such symptoms of nervousness at having them that they decided to leave after a few days. As the married sisters' homes had been raided in the meantime, they decided to divide up between them until they could get another house. At the time this occurred, Madge was with me in Dublin, but she rushed home when she heard what had happened.

10

The Treaty Debates

1920-1924

Truce – Treaty – Civil War – executions – arrest

On 6 February 1920, Eamon de Valera gave an interview to the *Westminster Gazette*, in the course of which he said: 'The United States, by the Monroe Doctrine, made provision for its security without depriving the Latin republics of the South of their independence and their life. The United States safeguarded itself from the possible use of the island of Cuba as a base for attack by a foreign power by stipulating "That the Government of Cuba shall never enter into any treaty or other compact with any foreign power or powers which shall impair or tend to impair the independence of Cuba, nor in any manner authorise or permit any foreign power or powers to obtain, by colonisation or for military or naval purposes or otherwise lodgment or control over any part of the said island."

'Why doesn't Britain make a stipulation like this to safeguard herself against foreign attack as the United States did with Cuba? Why doesn't Britain declare a Monroe Doctrine for the neighbouring islands? The people of Ireland, so far from objecting, would co-operate with their whole souls.'

When I read this statement, I could scarcely believe it. Surely de Valera must have known very little about the Cuban question to make such a statement. I was living in New York during the Cuban War, and knew many who took part in it. When it was over, many Americans cried shame on their government for its attitude towards Cuba, and one noted American writer wrote a pamphlet on the subject.

At this time I was President of the Children's Court and the Court of Conscience. The Courts were held in the South William Street courthouse. I had a Court that particular morning, and when it was over and the policemen who attended it had gone, I went down to the basement where some of the Dáil clerks used to work to talk over the matter of de Valera's statement with them. There were four young men there. I asked if they had seen the interview in the *Westminster Gazette*, and told them what I thought of it. I was never so surprised in my life when the four of them stood up and glared at me. They were blazing with indignation at my daring to criticise their chief, and looked ready to do violence to me. They showed their anger in every way. I had gone down in the friendliest way to discuss a thing which I thought they knew little about, intending to tell them all I knew about it.

Well, it looked as if I had a genius for walking into trouble. I left, feeling that those men were angry enough to throw me out if I did not go. It made me sad. I had worked and suffered for my country at least as much as de Valera or any other man alive, and thought I had as much right to have an opinion and to air it as de Valera or any other man on things which affected my country. Yet these young men were ready to rend me for daring to have an opinion different from their chief. Strange to say, two of these young men took sides against de Valera on the question of the Treaty. My opinion of that interview in the *Westminster Gazette* was that it was the first sign of weakness the British had seen since the Rising, and they seized upon it; here was a man ready for compromise. The Truce followed.

A long discussion took place in the Dáil on the question of sending plenipotentiaries to London to meet Lloyd George and other British ministers, for the purpose of coming to an understanding on the question of our freedom. It was decided to do so, a decision which de Valera favoured and pushed, but he refused to be one of the group to go. He gave his reasons, but they were not very clear, at least to me. He wraps the explanations of his reasons in so many words that, like a badly-developed negative, one has a suspicion of what they are, but it is too cloudy to be sure. One of his reasons, I thought, was that if the plenipotentiaries made a mistake, or agreed to do something of which he did not approve, he would not be involved, but would be there as head of the nation to correct their mistake, or repudiate their action. If that was what he meant, I was inclined to agree with it. Many members thought he should go, but he persisted in his refusal.

Griffith and de Valera were then instructed by the Dáil to make a selection of those they thought most suitable to send. De Valera said he thought Mick Collins should be one of them. Collins was most reluctant, but after a good deal of argument de Valera prevailed on him to consent. It was suggested by some member that there should be one woman selected, and Griffith and de Valera promised to consider it, but did not act upon it. This seemed strange to me, knowing that only for the work done by the women after the Rising, they and their comrades might still be in prison.

The Dáil adjourned to give Griffith and de Valera time to make their selections. The meeting had been held in the Oak Room in the Mansion House. I happened to be the last out, as I had business with a Corporation clerk, one of those working in the Mansion House since the British had taken over the Corporation offices. Everyone had gone when I reached the hall, except Griffith and de Valera. They were just turning into the drawingroom, and were talking. De Valera raised his voice and said, 'You know, Griffith, we must have scapegoats.' All through the adjournment my mind kept going over what I had heard de Valera say. What did he mean? Did he mean that he had no hope for a settlement and that the people, being disappointed in their hopes for peace, would blame the plenipotentiaries for the failure? In that sense, those selected would be scapegoats. I thought of many explanations but none satisfied me, and to this day I do not know what he meant. At the time I was afraid to mention it to anyone, lest I start trouble. When the Dáil met again, it ratified the selections made; from remarks I heard, they did not get unanimous approval, even though none voted against them.

When I was in Holloway Jail and de Valera was in Lincoln Jail, Limerick Corporation decided to bestow the Freedom of the City on John MacNeill, de Valera and myself. After the escape of de Valera, Seán McGarry and Seán Milroy from Lincoln Jail, and the release of all the German plot prisoners soon after, de Valera went to the USA, and the question of when it would be conferred on him had to be postponed. John MacNeill received the honour alone. While the plenipotentiaries were in London, de Valera decided to arrange a date for receiving the honour, and I received a letter from the Mayor of Limerick, informing me that they wished to honour me on the same day, 6 December 1921. I accepted with pleasure, and went down to Limerick the day before, as I was not invited to join the President's party. He travelled to Limerick in great state, with a large retinue in several first-class carriages.

Limerick gave us a great reception. After we received the Freedom of the City in the City Hall, there was a big parade to the Theatre Royal, where we were both to speak. I could never speak from notes, but I had a speech outlined in my mind, which I thought was good, but was not sparing our enemy. Just before I was called on to speak, de Valera turned to me and said, 'Be very careful what you say. The times are very critical.' This made me nervous, and fearful of saying something which might hurt what the men in London were trying to do. I dropped my speech and confined myself to thanking the people for the honour conferred on me, and for their reception. Had de Valera spoken to me earlier, I would have thought out a speech on different lines. Since I was not very familiar with public speaking at the time, it was easy to confuse me.

I was returning to Dublin the next day, and arriving at the railway station I found de Valera and his retinue were returning by the same train. I met Cathal Brugha on the platform, and he insisted on my joining de Valera's party, of which he was a member. I told him I did not wish to do so; I really did not, as I had not travelled down with them and had only a third-class ticket, but he waved all my objections aside. At Ballybrophy station we got the Dublin evening papers, which gave the first news of the agreement being signed in London by the plenipotentiaries. Cathal Brugha handed the papers to de Valera. When he had read them he said to Cathal, 'If they have signed, they must have got all we demanded.' When we arrived at Kingsbridge Station, there was a large number of motorcars to meet the party. As I did not consider myself one of them, I slipped away and got a bus home.

When the 'Articles of Agreement for a Treaty' were published, they caused a howl of indignation from one section of the people, and approval from another. De Valera issued a statement to the press saying that he was summoning a meeting of the Dáil to discuss the proposed Treaty, and that he saw a way of settling our differences. As the wording seemed ambiguous to me, I felt I must ask him to clarify it before the meeting of the Dáil, and I went to the Mansion House, which was then his headquarters, to see him. I met Miss MacSwiney at the door, and she told me she was there for the same purpose. He said he was very glad we had come, and handed each of us a document to read which he said he was going to propose at the meeting. He said he believed he could get unanimity on it, and thereby have the proposed Treaty rejected. He would like our opinion on it.

Miss MacSwiney said she would like to study it before giving an opinion, and that if he could give her a copy to take away with her she would do so. He then turned to me and asked what I thought of it. 'Well,' I said, 'on a first reading I see little difference between this and the proposed Treaty. There is scarcely the toss of a sixpence between them. Like Miss MacSwiney, I would like a copy to take away with me. Perhaps on a second reading I may think better of it.' He assured me there was a vast difference between the two documents, and gave each of us a copy. The document he handed to us was afterwards called *Document No. 2*.

In reading it again very carefully, I saw no reason to change the opinion I had first formed, and decided to vote against it, if it came to a vote. Before the debate on the proposed Treaty began, Cathal Brugha, hearing that I was not going to vote for de Valera's document, came to me and asked me to give him my reasons. I said that I could see no fundamental difference between it and the proposed Treaty, though here and there it might be an improvement. That being so, if it was passed and sent back to England as an alternative to the proposed Treaty, England would accept it as being practically the same thing, and I would not vote for any document or agreement which placed us in the position of a British Dominion.

He told me that I was all wrong, and that if I gave him an hour to discuss it he would prove to me that it was a document I could vote for. I agreed to give him the hour, but the only hour we could get before the debate was the lunch-hour. We decided to give lunch a miss, and sat there in the University, where he proceeded to explain how very wrong I was in deciding against de Valera's document. I cannot recall all the arguments he used, but one was that the King was in a very different position in de Valera's document, that he was in the position, more or less, of a managing director of a business. My answer to that was that he was there, and that the position of Dominion State remained unchanged. He continued his arguments, but I remained unconvinced. He was very disappointed at his failure to convert me to his viewpoint. He fully believed in de Valera's document, and said he was sure that de Valera would get unanimity on it. Was I prepared to break that unanimity? I said, ' I can't see him getting it, but if he does, I won't vote at all.'

When the Dáil met after lunch, de Valera proposed his document. Griffith got up and said that it was *ultra vires*, as the Dáil had been summoned to discuss the proposed Treaty and that alone. John Mac-Neill, who was Speaker of the Dáil, ruled de Valera's proposal out of order. The debate which followed was on the question of whether to accept or reject the proposed Treaty. Sitting through it was a trying experience, listening to men who had been as brothers a short time before indulging in the most venomous attacks on each other. It left me stunned; I got the feeling that every harsh word spoken would be a stumbling-block in our uniting to defeat England on any issue in the future, and decided that no matter how I felt, no harsh word would be spoken by me.[1]

When it came to my turn to speak, I said, 'I rise to support the motion of the President, to reject this Treaty. It is to me the simple question of right or wrong. To my mind it is a surrender of all our national ideals. I came to the first meeting of this session with the feeling strong upon me, and I have listened to all the arguments in favour of the Treaty. But the only thing I can say of them is: maybe there is something in them, I can't see it. Arthur Griffith said he had peace with England and freedom in Ireland. I can only say it is not the kind of freedom I have looked forward to. If this Treaty is ratified, the result will be a divided people. The same old division will go on, those who will enter the British Empire, those who will not, and so England's game of divide and conquer goes on – God, the tragedy of it!

'I was deeply moved by the Minister of Economics on Monday. Listening to him, I realised more clearly than ever before the very grave decision put to our plenipotentiaries. My sympathy went out to them. I only wish other members of the delegation had taken the same course. Having signed the Document, bring it home and let the Dáil reject or ratify it on its merits. We were told by one deputy on Monday, with a tremendous bellow, that this Treaty was a stupendous achievement. Well, if he means as a measure of Home Rule, I will agree. It is the biggest Home Rule Bill we have been offered, and it gives us a novelty in the way of a new kind of official representing His Majesty King George V, name to be yet decided. If England is powerful enough to impose on us Home Rule, Dominion, or any other kind, let her do so, but in God's name do not accept or approve it, no more than you would any other Coercion Act.

'I heard big, strong military men say here that they would vote for this Treaty, which necessarily means taking an Oath of Allegiance, and I tell these men there is not power enough to force me, nor eloquence enough to influence me in the whole British Empire into taking that Oath, though I am only a frail scrap of humanity. I took an Oath to the Irish Republic, solemnly, reverently, meaning every word of it. I shall never go back from that.

'Like the deputy, I too can go back to 1916. Between one and two o'clock on the morning of the 3rd of May, I, a prisoner in Dublin Castle, was roused from my rest on the floor and taken under armed guard to Kilmainham Jail to see my husband for the last time. I saw him, not alone, but surrounded by British soldiers. He informed me he was to be shot at dawn. Was he in despair like the man who spoke of him on Tuesday? Not he. His head was up, his eyes flashing, his years seemed to have slipped from him. Victory was in every line of him. "Tell the Irish people," he said, "that I and my comrades believe we have saved the soul of Ireland. We believe she will never lie down again until she has gained absolute freedom." And though sorrow was in my heart, I gloried in him. I gloried in the men who have carried on the fight since, every one of them. I believe that even if they take a wrong turn now, they will be brave enough to turn back when they discover it. I have sorrow in my heart now, but I don't despair. I never shall. I still believe in them.'

I never visioned a settlement which would mean complete separation from England at that stage of our struggle. I knew England was still too powerful to agree to such. I knew there would be some halfway house for a period, even though I could not agree to its acceptance, but the last thing I thought would happen was the agreement to Partition.

On Michael Collins's return from London, I met him in the Mansion House and had a talk with him about the agreement he had signed. 'Surely, Mick,' I said, 'you do not think people like me could vote for such an agreement?' 'No,' he replied. 'Nor would I like to see people like you vote for it. What I would like people like you to do would be to stand behind us and through your strength ensure that everything promised in the Treaty is got, and then we will work through it to complete freedom.'

When the vote was taken and the proposed Treaty carried by a majority of seven, de Valera stood up and tendered his resignation as President. This action was a complete surprise to me; I had had no idea he contemplated such a thing, and was very angry over it. The Dáil adjourned until next day, and those who voted against the Treaty retired to another room in the University and held a short meeting. I asked de Valera why he had resigned, and he said that he had had to when his proposal was defeated; I think he said something about its being constitutional practice. I said that those who supported him should have been consulted in the matter before he acted. He said that it really did not matter, as he was sure he would be re-elected; the vote was not against him personally, and he felt sure they would still want him as President.

I replied that I did not agree. I was sure the vote for President would be the same as that on the Treaty, that it would not be reasonable to assume that those who supported Griffith on the Treaty would vote against him for President. What I took exception to was that he had resigned his position as President of the Republic, and that even if he was elected as President, it would not be as President of the Republic. Had I been in his place, law or no law, I would not have resigned. They might vote me out, but then I would have gone down fighting. However, it was decided to have another meeting before the Dáil met again. I did not attend that meeting. I was too disgusted with de Valera's action in resigning, and his vanity in thinking he would be re-elected.

I decided to attend the meeting of the Dáil, and if de Valera was proposed for President I would vote for him. As I walked into the hall of the University Mrs Pearse met me. She seemed very excited, and asked why I had not been at the meeting, and that I must hurry, as de Valera had done me the honour of selecting me to propose him for President. I told her I would not propose him; I considered he had no right to resign. She was very insistent, but I remained adamant. Then she suggested I should see Seán T O'Kelly, who was Whip, and tell him. I told her I would do nothing of the kind. They had no right to nominate me in my absence, or without my consent.

I left her, and went to the room where the Dáil was to meet. Members were already beginning to assemble, but there was yet ten minutes or so to go before the Speaker took the Chair. I was not long seated when Seán T O'Kelly came to know if what Mrs Pearse told him was correct. I said Yes, that I was not going to propose de Valera. 'He had no right to resign without consulting those who had supported him.' He begged me to reconsider my refusal, but I said, 'It's no use, Seán, I will not propose him.' 'My God,' he said, 'what will I do? There is no time to select another person.' 'Well,' I said, 'you had no right to decide on me in my absence, or without my consent.' He left me, and went round from one member to another, then over to de Valera.

He then returned to say that they had all said I must do it. I said, 'Tell them I won't.' Off he went again and did the rounds, and came back again to me. 'The Speaker will be in the Chair in a minute, there is no time to arrange a change,' he said. 'Well,' I said, 'that is your affair, not mine.' Then he said, 'Mrs Clarke, I was a great friend of your husband, and he was a great friend of mine.' 'He was, Seán,' I said, 'he trusted you.' 'Well, you know the relations which existed between us,' he said, 'and now I ask you in his name to do this thing, will you?' 'You make it hard for me to refuse you, Seán, when you ask in his name,' I said. 'Well, I do ask, and I think he would wish you to do it,' he said. 'I suppose in that case I cannot refuse you, but it is with the utmost reluctance I consent,' I said. During all this time de Valera was looking over at me, and possibly his antagonism to me down the years since was born then, though it was only indulged in when he could do it without showing his hand.

In proposing him I was as brief as possible. I hated to be, in a sense, forced to do it. I felt very strongly over his resignation. I was sure he would be beaten and was sorry to see him so vain as to think, under the circumstances, he would be elected. When the election was over and Griffith elected President, the vote being the same as on the Treaty, the Dáil adjourned. The anti-Treaty members, as we were called, retired to another room in the University. De Valera was in the chair, and said that he wished to resign; he would go back to his teaching. He was prepared to be the leader of the Irish people, but did not wish to be leader of a party. I said that was all bunkum. He was never leader of the Irish people, he was leader of the Republican section of the Irish people, and he was still in that position. He did not resign. Perhaps I gave him the line he was seeking, and if I could have seen into the future I would have let him go back to his teaching.

The next meeting of the Dáil was very acrimonious. In an effort to settle our differences amicably, it was proposed and carried that six members of the Dáil, three from each party, be appointed to go into the question of how to get an agreement on an election and other things, which would keep us together. Those selected were Liam Mellows, Harry Boland, Seán MacKeon, Pádraig O Máille, Séamus O'Dwyer and myself. At the first meeting of this committee, which was held in the Mansion House, I was elected Chairman, and for about three weeks we sat constantly, often late into the night. The Treaty members proposed that there be an agreed election, but that the anti-Treaty members should surrender sufficient members to give them a good working majority.

The anti-Treaty members favoured the agreed election, but could not agree to sacrifice members of their party. It would in effect be penalising them for their vote against the Treaty. At one morning meeting, the Treaty members were urging agreement with their proposal very hard. Lunch-hour arrived without agreement being reached, so we adjourned. Harry Boland, as a rule, reported what progress, if any, we were making, and he asked me to go with him to report. I refused, saying, 'Harry, I want to keep my mind clear. If I go near that man [de Valera] he will get me confused. I'll get lost in the labyrinth of lanes and byways he will take me up and down.'

Harry was late that day in getting back after lunch, which was unusual. When he came in, he said he thought we could agree to give the majority that the Treaty side wanted. Liam Mellows said, 'I certainly will not agree,' and I supported him. Harry said to me in a whisper, 'The Chief says we can agree.' 'Are you sure, Harry?' I said. 'Positive,' he answered, 'I left him only a few minutes ago.' I turned to the other members and said, 'Our members do not seem to be in agreement on this question. I think if we adjourn for half an hour to get things straight, it would be best.' That was agreed to, and Harry, Liam and I left the drawingroom to hear from Harry exactly what de Valera had said to him. We went into the Round Room. Harry was very positive that de Valera had told him we could agree to give the majority of seven asked for. Liam Mellows said he would not agree, and I supported him. We returned to the drawingroom where the others awaited us, and I told them that we would have to get a meeting of all the anti-Treaty TDs to put the matter before them, as we could not take the responsibility of such a decision. The meeting then adjourned.

The meeting of anti-Treaty TDs was summoned, and took place that night in Suffolk Street. It was a stormy one, and the proposal to give the seven majority was turned down. Harry Boland maintained that de Valera had told him we could agree to give the majority. This de Valera hotly denied, and said Harry had misunderstood him. It was very late when the meeting was over. It was held in a room at the top of the house. The last tram to Clontarf had gone, so Harry Boland ordered a taxi and said he would give Madge Clifford and me a lift; the three of us lived in the same district. When the taxi arrived Madge Clifford and I got in, assuming Harry would join us in a few minutes. After waiting for what seemed a long time I got impatient, and went in to find out what was keeping Harry.

As I walked up the stairs I heard Harry and de Valera shouting at each other, whether in fun or anger I could not tell. Just as I reached the top landing, I heard Harry say, 'It's all right, Chief, you let me down, but I won't give you away.' I made a noise to let them know I was there, and Harry came out on the landing and down to the taxi with me, but he made no mention of what had been going on between himself and de Valera. All the way home my mind raced over what I had heard, and over recent events. I recalled that the plenipotentiaries had claimed that de Valera had known the terms of the proposed Treaty, and was in agreement with them. I thought at the time that it was a misapprehension on their part, but what if something had happened to them like what had happened to Harry Boland? I was in a sea of doubt and uncertainty.

Next day Liam Mellows, Harry Boland and myself again met the other members of the group in the Mansion House, Seán MacKeon, Pádraig O Máille and Séamus O'Dwyer, and informed them that the proposal to give the Treaty party the extra members was not acceptable to the anti-Treaty party, though an agreed election was desired. We could not agree to victimise any members for their vote against the Treaty. So the Pact, as it was later called, drawn up by us but not signed, was submitted to the Dáil as representing the nearest approach we could get to agreement. The Dáil directed that Collins and de Valera should meet and discuss the draft, and see if they could advance further towards our unity. Both men signed the draft, and called it a Pact.

A General Election was then declared. I was sent to Nenagh and Clonmel with Mrs Terence MacSwiney and Dr Brennan, Coroner for South County Dublin, to address meetings for the anti-Treaty candidates. The bitterness between the opposing parties was intense, and we got a rough time. When we got back to Dublin, I heard that de Valera would not be able to go to Co Clare for the election. On hearing this, I decided to go to Clare instead of staying in Dublin, where I was a candidate in the area I then represented, North City. John MacNeill was also a candidate for Co Clare, and I feared that if a big effort was not made for de Valera, MacNeill, who was a candidate for the Treaty party, might head the poll. That I was going to prevent, if possible. I told the people of Clare about MacNeill's action in 1916, and the view that my husband and his comrades had taken of it. I spoke at two or three meetings a day. I forget how many candidates there were, but Brian O'Higgins and de Valera were the two anti-Treaty ones.

I wrote to de Valera that I was going to Co Clare to work against MacNeill, and received the following reply: 'I shall of course be delighted if you can go to Clare. I am sure your presence would help here and in the USA. I am afraid, however, that if you were to attack MacNeill now, on account of my having formerly stood up for him, it would do more harm than good. We must not win him sympathy.'

I returned to Dublin when the election was over, well content that MacNeill did not head the poll. De Valera did, though I did not care who did when it was not MacNeill. My luck was out in Dublin, I was not re-elected. It did not worry me much; I was in the same boat as the other women TDs who voted against the Treaty, Countess Markievicz, Mrs O'Callaghan, Miss Mary MacSwiney, Dr Ada English and Mrs Pearse. Well, we all paid for our temerity in voting as we did. We were all women who had worked and suffered for the freedom of our country.

The election being over, I had temporarily very little to do. It felt strange having so little to do, as with all my other activities during the Black and Tan war I had attended all meetings of the Corporation Council, committee and subcommittee meetings, and many Board meetings as Corporation representative. One day during that period I had to see the Minister for Local Government, Liam T Cosgrave. I had to interview him in a cellar under a shop in Exchequer Street, as he was on the run like all the ministers. I went down through a trapdoor in the floor inside the counter. The minister and his assistant minister, Kevin O'Higgins, were in a very disturbed state of mind. I asked what was the trouble, and Cosgrave told me.

There had been a dance in Portrane Mental Hospital for the patients, and one of the attendants had got too much drink and became troublesome. He was put into a padded cell to sleep it off, but instead of sleeping he became mischievous and slashed the rubber wall with his penknife, causing great destruction. He was suspended by the hospital board, and the matter was reported to the Minister for Local Government, who dismissed him. When Mick Collins heard of the dismissal he kicked up ructions, and insisted the man be reinstated, as he was one of his (Mick's) best men in the area. This was what the minister and assistant minister were in such a way about. How could the minister reinstate him? What reason could he give?

When I heard the story I said, 'I'll tell you what can be done. I am on the Board. I'll go to the meeting of the Board this evening, and move that the Minister's decision be sent back for reconsideration, on the grounds that the punishment was too severe.' Kevin O'Higgins said that the meeting would be at three o'clock. I said I knew, that I would run home, get my dinner and go to the meeting. Meanwhile, he could have a motion drafted and sent to the hospital ready for me. I would move it and get it carried. 'My God,' both men said, 'it takes a woman. Here we have had hours of torment and could see no way out of our difficulty, and you show us a way out in a few minutes.' It was the first time I had met O'Higgins, and he struck me as a clever, forcible character. I went to the meeting, moved the motion and had it carried, and that was the last I heard of it.

Having little to do after the election, I decided to join my sisters and two of my sons, Tom and Emmet, who were in Ballingeary, Co

Cork, learning Irish. Before leaving Dublin I visited the Four Courts, where the anti-Treaty troops were in possession; I was anxious to know what they intended doing.[2] I met Liam Mellows and Oscar Traynor, and asked them what their intentions were, and why were they continuing in possession, a thing I was not in agreement with. They gave me no answer, and adopted an air as if it was no business of mine. This irritated me; I felt everything concerning Ireland was as much my business as theirs. I said I thought that staying there was a mistake, and likely to lead to trouble, that their presence there was a challenge, one which Mick Collins would tolerate only until such time as he had an army under his control. Then, I thought, he would fire them out of it. Did they want that? I got no reply from Liam Mellows, but Traynor hummed and hawed. I left them, feeling both annoyed and despondent. The holding of the Four Courts was surely going to lead to trouble, and I could not see what was going to be gained by it. I was surprised by the attitude of Mellows; he knew very well how closely I had worked with the leaders of 1916.

I left for Ballingeary that evening very troubled, and had been in Ballingeary a few days when news came that the Four Courts had been attacked on Mick Collins's order, and that there was fierce fighting in Dublin. My sisters and I left for Cork city as soon as we could. As there was a train leaving for Limerick when we got to Cork, my sisters, with my son Tom, left for Limerick at once. There were no trains running to Dublin, so I had to wait a day before I could get a conveyance to Dublin. My son Emmet and myself were provided with a motor car through the IRA, to take us to Dublin, and we were accompanied by a Cork lady who had messages to the IRA in Dublin. We had to go by Carlow and Kilkenny to avoid Treaty troops. We passed through an IRA post in Co Cork where I met Tom Hunter, a great friend of my husband, who had been in the Rising. He seemed to be in command. It was a great surprise and pleasure to meet him, as I had not seen him for a long time. I had had letters from him from prison; he had been one of the sentenced men.

We passed through Carlow without stopping. Some miles outside Carlow we met a group of marching men, seemingly armed. As they advanced towards us our driver slowed down, not knowing whether they were friends or otherwise. The car we were in was an open one, and as we came near I saw the men kneel down with their rifles at the ready, pointed at us. As they came nearer I recognised one of them, jumped up and waved at them. The man I recognised came over and said, 'Mrs Clarke, is it you? Well, I might tell you that you were never nearer death in your life than when you jumped up in that car.' I laughed, taking it as a joke, but he seemed quite serious. The man was Ernie O'Malley. He asked what had been the conditions in Carlow as we passed through. I told him we had passed through without interference, and as far as I could see there were no military there.

I had seen one or two men in uniform, but everything seemed to be normal. He said, 'It is lucky we met you. We got a report that there was a strong force of Treaty troops in Carlow, that the town was held by them, and we had been preparing to attack the town that night.' We said goodbye, and continued our journey.

When we reached Blessington it seemed occupied with a large force of IRA with some members of Cumann na mBan and Father Dominic [O'Connor, OFM Cap.]. Gerald Boland seemed to be in charge. He immediately commandeered our car, and made arrangements for Miss O'Sullivan, Emmet and myself to be accommodated for the night in Crooksling Sanatorium. The Chief Medical

Superintendent, Dr Harrington, received us very kindly and made us very comfortable. At the time I was Vice-Chairman of the committee in charge of the Sanatorium under Dublin Corporation.

Next day, we were driven into Dublin in an ambulance. I left Emmet at home and went to join Cumann na mBan. I was told that Central Branch had a dressing-station at the back of the Gresham Hotel. As I went along Killarney Street and Seán MacDermott Street, there was a good deal of firing. I did not know where it was coming from, but it was near enough to make me feel like running for shelter. As bullets whistled by me it took all my courage to continue my journey, and I was very glad when I located the house where Cumann na mBan were installed. There I was told that the fighting was practically over. They had a few casualties. I was sorry to hear it. I hate war, particularly civil war, though I realise one must fight for what one wants in this world.

When I arrived home I was surprised to find Harry Boland there, using it as his headquarters; he had not asked me if he could do so. Next day I went to the headquarters of the anti-Treaty party, Cumann na Poblachta, in Suffolk Street, where Miss MacSwiney was in charge. While I was chatting to her a swarm of Free State troops came in to raid the place, and arrested Seán T O'Kelly and some others. When they had left, I hurried home to tell Harry Boland; I had a feeling they would come there for him. I told him to destroy any papers he had; we had already made plans for his escape in case of a raid.

As I was speaking, I looked down the avenue and saw a party of Free State troops turning into it. 'Here they come, Harry,' I said, 'Run!' He did, and got away safely. He handed me a bundle of papers and told me to hide them until he came back; 'If I do not come back, you can do what you like with them.' I could not think of any place to hide them that the military would not think of also, and in a distracted way I kept saying, 'Where will I hide them?' The military were almost at the door when my youngest son, Emmet, said 'Put them here, Mama.' 'Here' was under his pullover. I said, 'It won't do, they would see the bulk and perhaps ill-treat you.' He said, 'They won't if I keep my arms like this on the table', and there he sat all through the raid at the kitchen table, during a raid by Irishmen.[3]

The troops had arrived by this time, and I told the maid to open the door to them, as I intended to appear very busy in the kitchen preparing dinner. When they arrived in the kitchen, I was a very surprised person indeed, and asked who had let them in, and what was their business. They said they had come for Harry Boland. 'Well,' I said, 'he is not here.' They searched the kitchen, but took no notice of the little boy sitting at the table.

When they had left the kitchen, I followed them upstairs to see what they were doing. As I went into the diningroom I saw one of them take up a bundle of papers from the sideboard which belonged to me. I told him to lay them down, that they were mine, but he said he was taking them, and he did not care who they belonged to. I said, 'You have stated you came here for Harry Boland. Those papers have nothing to do with Harry Boland, or even with the present, and you must not take them.' He said he would take what he liked. By then I was very angry, angry enough to kill him. Running through my mind was all I had suffered at the hands of the British, and now my own people were causing me more suffering, and it hurt more because they were my own. I tried to snatch the papers from him, but he put his hands behind his back. I boxed his face as hard as I could.

Another of the raiders, who had been standing at the door,

stepped forward and said, 'Now, now, what is all this about?' 'Don't be asking fool questions,' I said, 'you have been standing there some time and must have seen and heard what passed. I claim this man has no right to take papers belonging to me.' He took the papers, looked them over and then handed them to me. The matter was settled. But the papers, which were important to me, would have been taken only for the fight I put up. In the meantime, everyone who came to the house was arrested and questioned, but released when the raid was over.

Harry Boland was shot by Free State troops in a hotel in Skerries, on 30 July 1922, and died from his wounds in St Vincent's Hospital four days later, in the most terrible agony. I was present with his mother and sister when he died, and I shall never forget it. His poor mother fainted at the sight of his terrible suffering.

The civil war gradually terminated all over the country. The anti-Treaty forces were beaten everywhere, disarmed and imprisoned. Amongst those imprisoned was Liam Mellows, one of the purest patriots that ever lived. Cathal Brugha and Mick Collins, both patriots, went down in the fight.[4]

A meeting of the new Dáil was summoned for the 7 December 1922. Seán Hales, a Cork man, a lovely, gentle, distinctly Irish character, was in Dublin to attend it. He was in favour of the Treaty. As he and Pádraig O Máille left their hotel to go to the Dáil meeting, they were fired upon, it was presumed by some anti-Treaty person, and poor Seán Hales was killed. Lord, how sorry I was for him when I heard it. I did not foresee the terrible reprisal which followed by order of the government, but it in no way lessened my sorrow for Seán Hales. Liam Mellows, Rory O'Connor, Dick Barrett and Joe McKelvey, who were prisoners in Mountjoy Prison at the time and could not have had any possible connection with the attack on Seán Hales and Pádraig O Máille, were shot without trial as a reprisal. The whole country was shocked. It was a dreadful reprisal. They were four of our best men.

When the Civil War ended, early in 1923, I went to Limerick to see how my mother and sister fared. When I got to Nenagh, I learned that the train would go no further, as no trains were allowed to go into Limerick. The only thing available was a seat in a newspaper van going to Limerick with the evening papers, and I took it.

My mother and sisters had fared very badly indeed, I found. The Free State troops had taken possession of the bakery, and held it for some time, using the sacks of flour and feeding stuffs as sandbags. When they finally handed it back, it had been emptied of everything movable and of all their stock, which was considerable. Meanwhile customers had to go elsewhere for their bread, and it took a long time to get the trade back to what it had been. I returned to Dublin very heartsick at the vengeance taken on my mother and sisters by those they had often housed, at great personal risk, and helped with money and in every way they could.

I now turned my attention to business, and rented a shop in D'Olier Street. One day an American journalist called into the shop to ask me if I could arrange an interview with de Valera, who was on the run. I promised to see what I could do, so on my way to the bank to make a lodgement next morning I called into the office in Suffolk Street, to ask Miss MacSwiney if she could arrange the interview. I was only a few minutes talking to her when there was a raid by Free State troops, and everyone in the office was put under arrest. Miss MacSwiney and myself were held under arrest until late that night, then we were taken to Kilmainham Jail, a place that had such terrible memories for me.

On entering, we were asked by officials if we had anything on us. I was not clear what they meant, and said I had a lodgement of money for the bank, and had been on my way to the bank when arrested. I was asked to hand it over and did so, assuming that I would have no trouble in getting it on my release. We got a great welcome from members of Cumann na mBan already imprisoned there. It was not so gloomy as it had been in 1916; there was electric light. Before morning, we were released as being of no military importance, but my money was not returned to me. When I asked for it, I was told to make an application for it. I was not worried about it, thinking that was just a formality; I was glad to get away from that chamber of horrors and rejoin my children.

I wrote asking for the return of my money, and received this reply: 'I am instructed by the Director [of Intelligence] to acknowledge receipt of your letter...Before making a decision upon the matter of returning the monies asked for, he desires to be furnished with an explanation of how you come to have so much money in your possession. He considers it very extraordinary that anyone should carry around, as a matter of course, a sum so considerable as the amount found on your person.'

Answering him, I explained that it was shop receipts which I had been on my way to lodge in the Munster Bank, Dame Street, when arrested. Yet it was not returned to me for a considerable time, which was a great embarrassment to me as I had little capital, and was entirely dependent on the earnings of the shop; I had put all the capital I had into it. It is quite possible it would never have been returned to me, only for my friendship with the sister of a 1916 man who was secretary of a department, who knew the circumstances and vouched for the truth of my statement.

11
Dáil, Senate,
Lord Mayor

1925-1943

USA trip – Dáil – Senate – oath of allegiance –
1937 Constitution
– the founding of Fianna Fáil – Kathleen, first woman
Lord Mayor of Dublin – resignation from politics

As Dublin Corporation had been abolished by the Free State government [1924], and Commissioners put in its place to carry on the
direction of the work for the city, I had very little to do then in public
affairs. My main activity outside my business was the Dependants
Fund, at a meeting of which Madame O'Rahilly proposed that I
should be sent to the USA to collect money for the Fund. It was not a
job I cared for, but the longing to see my eldest son, Daly, who was in
Los Angeles for health reasons, overcame my dislike, so I consented.
Madame was the widow of The O'Rahilly, who had been killed on
leaving the burning GPO in 1916, and was one of the best workers

on the Dependants' Fund. She was very retiring, gentle and digni-
fied, and never got credit for the very fine amount of work she did for
the Fund. Miss Anna O'Rahilly and Mrs Humphries, The O'Rahilly's sisters, were also great workers for the Fund.

I arranged to leave my business in charge of a girl already
employed by me, a member of Cumann na mBan. Then I found I
was up against the snag of a passport. I was told by a friend who knew
that there was no use asking for one from the Free State government,
and advised me not to apply. I didn't, but it got my back up, and I
determined I would go out there somehow.

I went over to friends in Manchester, and booked a passage to
Montreal, Canada, on one of the Canadian Pacific Line ships. It was
a very calm and pleasant voyage, but when we arrived at St John's we
learned that the St Lawrence river was frozen, and we would have to
go on to Montreal by train. As I was about to board the train, a uni-
formed man came up to me and said I was wanted in the office. I was
quite alarmed, but kept cool. He conducted me into a large office
with two windows at one end, and a table in the centre. There was a
man seated at each side of the table. I was told to sit at the end of the
table, directly facing the window. Then the men started questioning
me, and I saw the reason for placing me facing the windows. My face
could be watched for any quiver or change of expression. I have a
good poker face, and they got little from it.

I had no idea of what it was all about. They first asked why I had
come to Canada, and I answered, 'On a visit to friends.' They said, 'Is
it not a strange time of the year to be visiting Canada?', but I said No,
that I did a lot of visiting, having plenty of leisure. They then asked,
'Are you Irish?' I said Yes, but that I had been living in Manchester (I
had, for a week). They kept repeating these questions in different

forms for what seemed an endless time, I being on guard all the time lest they trip me up. Then one of them said, 'There has been a good deal of trouble in Ireland.' 'Yes,' I said, 'I read of it.' Then they said, 'Things are better there now, there is a government set up.' I said I understood there were two. At this they jumped; they thought they had me. I smiled to myself, I meant them to think so. By then I had tumbled to what they were after. 'Oh,' they said, 'how do you mean, two governments?' 'Well,' I said, 'isn't there one for the north and one for the south?' That seemed to finish them, and one of them said, 'Apparently you are not the person we are looking for.' 'Well,' I said, 'thank goodness for that. I wonder what you want this namesake of mine for? I am quite sure when next I decide on a holiday I will give Canada a wide berth. It is not pleasant to be taken for someone who has committed an offence.'

They stood up then, and said I could go. I smiled at them and said, 'Would it be any harm to ask who this person you are seeking is?' They said, 'As a matter of fact it is a lady whose name and description are somewhat similar to yours, and we were asked by cable from the Free State government not to allow her to land.' 'Oh,' I said, 'and supposing you had decided I was the person, what would have happened?' They said, 'You would have been imprisoned until the next boat was going out, and deported.' I shuddered, and said, 'I am so glad I am not that poor lady.' I had travelled under my own name of Clarke, but had chosen one of my confirmation names instead of Kathleen. As I am a bit absent-minded, I feared that if I chose any name other than Clarke I might forget it.

I got on board the train leaving for Montreal. Arriving there very early in the morning, I took a taxi to the home of a lady whose address Mrs Sheehy Skeffington had given me, a Miss Sheridan, a very clever high-minded girl and a very active worker for Ireland, though Canadian-born. It was some time before there was an answer to my ringing, and I was just wondering if I had got to the right house when the door opened. On presenting my credentials from Mrs Sheehy Skeffington I got a very warm welcome, both from Miss Sheridan and her mother, a perfect little lady, and her uncle, a quiet, gentlemanly, studious man. Miss Sheridan had lots of friends, and with the help of one of them it was arranged that I would travel over to New York the next night. I was really being smuggled, as I had no passport. Mrs Sheehy Skeffington's sister and her husband came to see me that night, and we had a great evening talking about Ireland; they wanted to know every little thing that was happening there.

Next night I started for New York, but was not lucky. The man that was to have been on the train to get me through was not on it. I was taken off the train at the border and questioned, and though I had been well coached and had answers for all questions, and for everything, I was not let through. I was held all night at the border, sitting on a hard chair, and sent back to Montreal in the morning. Next night I ventured again, and got through. I went to my sister, Eileen O'Toole, who lived in Brooklyn, and gave her the surprise of her life when I walked in.[1] I was feeling a bit shaken, and for days after I could not get over the feeling of a hand on my shoulder.

I rested all that day, and went over to headquarters in New York next day. There I met Miss Comerford, who had been sent out to accompany me through the States. How she got to the USA I do not know, but I assume she got a passport. She only travelled with me to a few places. I don't know how she managed the change in the order, but she stayed around the East. I was sent West alone, a most tiring and weary business except for the joy of meeting my son in Los

Angeles. I was rather shocked at how frail and delicate he still looked.

At the first big meeting which Miss Comerford and I attended in New York, I was called on to speak first, and in stressing the importance of providing for the needs of the families of the men in prison, I said that none knew better than Mick Collins the importance of that. There was a hiss at the mention of Mick Collins. This shocked me, and I stopped and said, 'I do not like that.' Back came the question: 'Why? Was he not a traitor?' I said, 'No, Mick Collins was no traitor. I did not agree with him on the question of the Treaty, but I cannot agree that he was a traitor. He is dead; for the work he did for Ireland, let him rest.' I tried to go on, but the incident had shaken me, and I lost the thread of what I had been saying. In a panic, I took a step nearer the Chairman and said, 'I have forgotten what I was going to say – tell me something to say, quick.' In a cool voice, he said, 'You are doing very well, keep on.' With the cool words memory came back to me, and I was able to finish, but I fear I did not make a very good impression on the audience.

A priest spoke after me. I cannot remember his name, but he was a very fine speaker. He praised what I had said about Mick Collins, and said it was the most charitable thing he had heard since the Treaty was passed, and it was a pity more of that kind of charity was not evident amongst us. I had not been thinking along charitable lines, I was just resenting the injustice to Collins.

Things were very unpleasant among the Irish in the USA; the Treaty question divided them as at home. It was my usual luck to be there at such a time; it was difficult to get meetings, and more so to get money. The majority of the rich Irish took sides with the Treaty. The next meeting Miss Comerford and I attended, a very small one, was in Washington. Then I travelled to Los Angeles, taking in meetings on the way as arranged from headquarters in New York, where J J O'Kelly, known as 'Sceilg', was in charge. I was treated kindly wherever I went, but there was no enthusiasm. The split on the Treaty had killed it. The Irish seemed even more bitter with each other than at home. I think I was rather a failure there when I did not denounce vehemently those who accepted the Treaty.

I was very tired when I reached Los Angeles, but my son and Peter Murray were at the station to meet me. My son looked so frail I wanted to bring him home with me, but the doctor advised me to leave him there a little longer. He lived with Peter Murray, and Peter and his dad thought they could never do enough for him as the son of Tom Clarke. Both of them loved him for himself too, they told me. The whole Murray family were devoted to Ireland. They were very influential with the Irish in Los Angeles, and were always ready with their money and their help when a call came from Ireland.

I had some amusing, if trying, experiences in my travels. In Portland, Oregon, the organisers of the meeting for me had some difficulty in getting a Chairman, and invited a man who had never acted as such before. He was not familiar with procedure; instead of introducing the speakers, he seemed to think he was the speaker, and started telling the audience his life story. The audience stood it for a while, then they began to tell him to shut up, to sit down, they wanted to hear the speaker. It was no use, he went blithely on, charmed with himself, and heard none of the hullabaloo. Men on the plaform pulled his coattails to get him to sit down, and in the end he was forced down. I was then introduced, and began to speak. I was just warming into my subject when without warning the hall was cleared. The only persons left were those on the platform. We looked at each other; we could not understand it. What caused the audience to leave in a body like that? One of the men on the platform went to the back of the hall to enquire, and found that someone at the back of the hall had called 'Fire!' No-one waited to question, they just ran. When it was ascertained that there was no fire, they all sloped back, and the meeting ended successfully.

After the meeting, many came onto the platform to meet me. One lady threw her arms around my neck and hugged me, saying, 'You are a real revolutionary, and I love you for it. I never saw anything like this happen before – it's your spirit, it disturbs.' Her name was Dr Marie Equi; she was of Irish and Italian descent, and had been in prison at the entrance of the USA into the European war. She was one of the few women I met there that left an impression on me.

The last meeting I attended before leaving for home was in New York. It was a Convention of the American Association for Recognition of the Irish Republic (AARIR) and I was there only as a visitor. The meeting began very quietly, but after a while some members started a row. In a few minutes it had become pandemonium. J J O'Kelly (Sceilg), in the Chair, banged the bell for order, but the members were too busy banging each other to heed any bell – he might bang away for all they cared. When there was a lull for a minute, Sceilg got up and said, 'Mrs Tom Clarke will now address you.' Immediately, there was dead silence. I was aghast; I was quite unprepared for speaking, and made no move to go forward. Sceilg turned to me and said, 'Come on.' I went over to him and said, 'This is unfair, Sceilg. I did not expect to be called on to speak. I am only a visitor here. I don't know what to say.' 'Give them hell,' he said.

Well, I did what I was told. I said I was shocked at what I had witnessed, that for people who had the advantages of free education, in a free country, with every opportunity to learn how to conduct themselves in an orderly manner, I thought their conduct was disgraceful. I would be ashamed if the people at home acted as they had that day. I said, 'Ireland wants your help, and there are two ways you can help her, one with money, the other, instead of fighting each other over trivialities, turn your attention to the game England is playing here, and use your energies in working to defeat her. She is aiming to get the USA behind her, in case of another war. If she succeeds, it will be a bad day for Ireland, and possibly for the USA too.' There was a gasp of rage or surprise from the audience, I do not know which, nor did I care. When I sat down the Chairman announced an adjournment for lunch. After lunch the members returned in a different frame of mind; many were smiling. The trouble was over. Perhaps I had knocked some sense into their heads; still, I did not think it was fair of Sceilg to call on me, even to get himself out of a difficulty.

Before leaving for home, I went to see my old friend John Devoy. The visit made me sad. He was old, blind and deaf, but his mind was as clear and as strong as ever, and his heart as deeply interested in Ireland's fate as ever. His whole soul was wrapped up in Ireland. His blindness and deafness cut him off from contact with everyone except his closest friends, and on them he depended for keeping him posted on what was happening in Ireland.[2]

I left New York a few days later for Montreal, to return home on a Canadian Pacific Line boat. An American friend accompanied me to Montreal. On reaching there, I gave the keys of my bags to a representative of the hotel we intended staying in, for the Customs examination, and went to the hotel. We were just sitting down to a meal when a message came from the Customs for me to go over immediately. This alarmed me, as I had nothing of a dutiable nature in my bags. What on earth did they want me for? When I got there I was questioned and inspected, and then told I was not the person they were looking for. I did feel a bit shaken after it, and felt very glad I was going home. It was a lovely trip down the St Lawrence river to the sea. The boat docked at Southampton, and I went on to Dublin and Limerick without stopping, I was so eager to meet my son Emmet. I returned to Dublin with him and collected my son Tom, who was a boarder in Father Sweetman's college in Wexford.

Most of the prisoners of the Civil War had been released by then. The anti-Treaty members of the Dáil met occasionally.[3] I was summoned to these meetings, as were all the members of the Second Dáil who had not been elected to the Third Dáil. They were very solemn meetings, as the *de jure* government of the Republic, but sometimes we would adjourn the meeting of the government to hold a meeting of the political party called Cumann na Poblachta without moving out of our seats, the only change being the Chairman. This happened whenever something was introduced which was more suitable for discussion as a political party than a government. It sometimes struck me as a bit of playacting, and I said something to that effect one day, but de Valera assured me that under the circumstances it was necessary.

I was not satisfied that we could claim to be a government, *de jure* or any other kind, especially when the IRA, which had been under the control of the government of the Republic, informed us that in future they would act under the control of their own Executive and obey that only. Then the Republican Courts ceased to function, as those who had operated them split over the Treaty too. No-one, outside the four walls of the room we met in, acknowledged us as a government, not even our own supporters.

Considering the whole position at the time, it seemed to me that if we were to continue to live, even as a party organisation, we must change our policy from military to political. We must face up to the fact that the people gave the majority vote in the election in support of the vote in the Dáil to accept the Treaty, that the IRA had repudiated our authority, that we were disarmed. That being so, it seemed futile to me to try to continue a military policy; endeavouring to do so, we would in all probability die a natural death. The people had had enough of war for the time being. In our history we had had to change from one policy to another through force of circumstances, though never changing our objective, ie freedom from foreign domination.

I took my courage in both hands at one meeting and suggested the change, and to go all out on a campaign against the Oath of Allegiance.[4] The people would understand what a barrier the Oath was, and that it would not be reasonable to expect us to take it. They wanted settled conditions, but while we were debarred from entering the Dáil through the existence of the Oath, they knew conditions would remain unsettled. I believed public opinion would become strong enough to force the abolition of the Oath, and when the Oath was abolished we could then consider our next step towards the restoration of the Republic.

Many members were inclined to confuse change of policy with change of objective. Some would not enter the Free State parliament even without an Oath, as it was set up under a British Act of Parliament, so the change I suggested was met with a cold, hostile silence. De Valera was present, and though he looked at me as if he was considering the matter, he remained silent.

The next meeting of the Party I attended was about a month later.

I again urged an all-out campaign for the abolition of the Oath, and a change from a military to a political policy. I was met with the same cold hostility, though this time there was some attempt made to attack me. When the meeting was adjourned until the next day, and I was leaving with the others, some of them cut me dead, and some glared at me. I fully intended to be at the next day's meeting, and have a showdown on the matter, but unfortunately I was in the throes of 'flu next morning. I was ordered by my doctor not to leave my bed, and indeed I was not able to do so. I had a very vivid dream that night, which, despite my inability to rise, give me strength to act. In the dream I thought I was in bed and my husband came into the room, came up to me, laid his hand on my shoulder and said, 'Why do you lie there instead of getting up and pushing your idea of a campaign against the Oath? It is the only thing that will save the country.'

I woke with the dream having complete possession of me, and resolved to act. I sent a letter to de Valera, intending it to be read at the meeting, resigning from the Party and stating that I did not intend to retire from public life, but would try to get together a group who would work with me along the lines I had suggested at the meeting the previous day. In answer, he sent Gerald Boland with a letter to my home, which said: 'I mentioned the matter of your resignation to one or two *teachtaí* but did not bring the matter before the meeting. Might I ask you not to take the step you indicate until I have an opportunity of talking the matter over with you.'

I was in bed when Gerald Boland called, and still very sick, but I saw him. He gave me the letter from de Valera, and said that he had instructed him to say that he had taken the liberty of not putting my resignation to the meeting, as he was in agreement with me, and if I would give him time, and withhold my resignation, he would form a new policy on the lines suggested by me.

When I had recovered, I went to discuss the matter with de Valera. He said the great trouble would be to get unanimity. I agreed, but thought it was useless waiting to get it. He pointed out all the snags we would encounter; one was that if we were successful, all the self-seekers and chancers in the the country would flock into our organisation and corruption would creep in. To this I answered that as long as the heads of the organisation do not become corrupt, and are on guard against corruption, any attempts on it could be stamped on, with which he agreed.

However, when he did launch the new policy, it was not exactly the thing I had visioned or outlined when advocating a change, but I realised I could not get him to see with my eyes. I had not thought in terms of a new organisation, but of using the Sinn Féin organisation to work through. I was disappointed, but reasoned that it was a move in the right direction, and as such accepted it, though I still think my idea was a better one. From the time de Valera agreed with me a change was necessary, he made no attempt to consult further with me.[5]

My sisters were very much opposed to the new policy, and condemned me very harshly for linking up with it, not knowing I was very largely responsible for it. I kept quiet about my part in the changes. Not that I cared who knew, I did not fear criticism, I always did what I believed right regardless of consequences. My reason for keeping quiet was, in a sense, to shield de Valera. Some time before, he had been sneered at as being under petticoat government, that Miss MacSwiney was running him. I did not want that sneer repeated, with just a change of petticoat.

The proposal split Sinn Féin, why I could never understand. Our

objective remained the same, but the changed circumstances necessitated a change in our method of reaching it. The policy was still a
fighting one, though not military. The majority of Sinn Féin supported de Valera, which gave him the right to continue as Sinn Féin,
and I wondered why he surrendered it to the minority, who were very
bitter with him. He had to take all the blame of the change, when in a
sense I was the culprit. It is quite possible the change would have
come anyhow, but that is the way it did come.

Building up a new organisation without funds was hard work; I
know I put every ounce of energy and enthusiasm I possessed into it,
and up to a certain time believed in de Valera. I believed in the new
policy, and I think if he had adhered to it strictly, Fianna Fáil [Sol-
diers of Destiny] would have achieved much bigger things than it has
done.

After the start of Fianna Fáil, the Free State government became
more coercive, and things were becoming almost intolerable. De
Valera decided something must be done to stem the tide of coercive
legislation, and he sent a summons to every Fianna Fáil deputy.[6] It
was a full meeting, and at it de Valera proposed that we go into the
Dáil, fight the government there and put a stop to coercion. A long
debate followed his proposal, and when the vote was taken only two
voted against it; one was Mr Victory, the other was myself. De Valera
asked us to reconsider our vote. He explained that he was going to
move a vote of No Confidence in the government, and would need
every member to carry it. After some pressure, Mr Victory agreed to
go in with them. De Valera then turned to me and said in his sweetest
tone, 'What about you, Mrs Clarke?' I said I did not want to take the
Oath, and I did not want to vote for others to do so, but if, as he said,
it was in the best interests of Ireland, I would have to consider it from

that point of view, but I would like a few days to do so. Then he explained to me that we would not be required to take the Oath actually, but to sign a book which contained the printed form. At the end of a few days I decided to go in with them. I found it a very hard decision to come to.

De Valera said he was going to issue a statement to the press, explaining that the Oath was an empty formula. I objected, and said I could not see the necessity for that; if what we had decided to do was being done, as we believed, in the best interests of the country, why apologise? Even if we had to take the Oath, we could do as the Fenians did when they entered the British military and police forces with a definite object, do it with a mental reservation. Despite my objections, he issued his statement about the empty formula. It was interpreted as I feared, as an apology.

We went into Leinster House, signed the book as arranged, but took no Oath. After one meeting of the Dáil, it was dissolved. De Valera did not carry his motion of no confidence. A General Election followed in which I was defeated, and so ended my career as a Deputy.

At that election, North City, Dublin, was one constituency, with eight seats. There were eighteen candidates, and Cumann na Gaedheal had the majority vote in the constituency.[7] On the first count Alderman Alfred Byrne, Richard Mulcahy and Jim Larkin were elected. Next came Seán T O'Kelly and myself, not elected, that is we were fourth and fifth in the first count. The Returning Officer, Dr Lorcan Sherlock, came up to me to congratulate me. I said, 'I am not elected yet.' 'Oh,' he said,' you could not be beaten with such a first preference vote.' But I was beaten; since then I have had no confidence in proportional representation as a fair representation of the people's wishes.

Jim Larkin was subsequently disqualified on the grounds of being (technically) a bankrupt, and that necessitated a by-election in North City. Jim Larkin was again nominated by Labour, Cumann na Gaedheal put forward a candidate and I was nominated by Fianna Fáil. I had not the faintest hope of being elected, as Cumann na Gaedheal had still a very large majority in the area. Cumann na Gaedheal got the seat.

Some time later, a vacancy occurred in the same constituency, and the voting position was still the same. Oscar Traynor was selected by Fianna Fáil headquarters to contest it; he was not a member of Fianna Fáil, but Cumann Tomás O'Cléirig [Tom Clarke Branch] was asked to co-opt him as a member to justify his nomination. He had been a TD for Sinn Féin when we were going into the Dáil, and had been asked to come in with us, but had refused. He went forward as a Sinn Féin candidate in the election following our entrance into the Dáil, but was defeated.

A Senate election was due to take place some time after this; the Senate at that time did not go out with the Dáil. There was a Senate election every three years, and members were elected for three, six or nine years, according to the vote they received. From a number of Fianna Fáil Cumainn in Dublin, and many places throughout the country, my name was sent forward to headquarters as nominee for the Senate. So far, there were no Fianna Fáil Senators. I had not thought of going for the Senate until notified of these nominations, and was not sure if I would care for it. Meeting Alfie Byrne, or to give him his full title Alderman Alfred Byrne, TD, who was always very friendly to me, I asked his advice. He strongly advised me to accept the nomination; he said the work was less strenuous than in the Dáil, and would be interesting.

Remembering what had happened in the General Election and the following by-elections in North City, I decided I would not go forward unless I had the full support of the Fianna Fáil Party in the Dáil. The members of the Dáil and Senate were the electors of the Senate. I went to de Valera and explained the position to him, and asked for the pledged support of the Party. He said he could not speak for the Party, but he would put it before them. He did, and the Party readily agreed to support me, and I was informed of their decision.

De Valera sent for me soon after this, to ask me to withdraw from the Senate election in favour of Mrs Pearse. He told me that when Mrs Pearse heard that I was being nominated for the Senate, she asked to be nominated too, and the Party would not support two women as they would only be able to elect five members. I said that that was a very strange request, a very unfair one, and one that should not be made to me. I had been promised the full support of the Party, and presumed they would keep that promise. I could see no reason for the Party refusing to support two women, when women had played such a big part in the fight for freedom. P H Pearse, addressing the women in the GPO on the Friday before the surrender, said that if it were not for the women, the fight could not have lasted so long, and that when the history of that week came to be written, the highest honour and credit should be given to the women, whose bravery, heroism and devotion in the face of danger surpassed that of the women of Limerick in the days of Sarsfield.

I said I had gone forward on the promise of Party support, and having done so I could see no reason why I should withdraw. Of course, I said, he may talk the Party into rescinding its decision to support me, but I was not withdrawing. I got up to leave, feeling very indignant. He then said, 'This is your last word?' I said, 'Yes, it is.' I got the impression that I was being tested to find out if I was the pliable type de Valera seemed so fond of gathering around him. Well, I was not. I was not ready to acquiesce in things which I considered wrong, which was unfortunate for my success in public life.

Mrs Pearse did not go forward for election. I was elected with the highest number of votes of the Fianna Fáil candidates, and this elected me for nine years. Senator Mrs Wyse Power gave me her No 1 vote because I was the widow of Tom Clarke. She was a member of Cumann na Gaedheal, and in doing so must have given offence to her own Party. Her vote also enabled Fianna Fáil to get six seats instead of five.

I had not been long in the Senate when the Greater Dublin Bill was passed by the Dáil and Senate, under which the Dublin Corporation Council was re-established in 1930. This ended the Commissioners. An election was held for the Council, and I was elected to it. There was a businessmen's panel of seven on the Council, so on a vote for the Lord Mayoralty Cumann na Gaedheal, combined with the businessmen's group, gave the majority vote to Cumann na Gaedheal. They nominated Alderman Alfred Byrne for Lord Mayor and elected him, and elected him each year while they had the majority vote.

The Fianna Fáil Party nominated Seán T O'Kelly each year, until he became a minister in the Fianna Fáil government. As I was next in seniority, I was proposed for the Mayoralty at a meeting of the Party, in 1932. I asked for a few days to consider it. I did not like the idea of going up to be beaten every time, as I would be while we were in the minority. The next morning, the newspapers had a report that I had been nominated at a meeting of the Fianna Fáil members of the Corporation for the Mayoralty, and had accepted it. I had to go on with it or repudiate the report, so I decided to accept. In due course I was proposed at the Council, and like Alderman Seán T O'Kelly beaten. This went on for a few years; I was nominated without question each year.

While Fianna Fáil were the opposition in the Dáil, I had little fault to find with their actions. I believed all they said behind closed doors, and agreed with all they said they intended doing should they ever become the government. We had, of course, minor differences now and then. Then Fianna Fáil became the government in March, 1932, and a change took place. Things which they had condemned as wrong for W T Cosgrave's government to do became right for them. I had understood (perhaps foolishly) that the things which they, as the opposition, claimed were wrong would remain wrong. Instead, most of the things they had condemned, they adopted. They had condemned attendance at the League of Nations, as a body controlled by England, yet de Válera attended there and received very flattering attention from the British representatives. They had condemned the setting up of the Appointments Commission, as a body set up for ministerial patronage, the control of the Corporations and County Councils. They were to reorganise the civil service, to make it more suitable to the needs of a small nation, rather than the arm of a big empire. All these I was in agreement with. They were also to change the system of education. All these promises were abandoned when they took over control.

Then de Valera stated that he would never pay a penny of the land annuities to England. That sounded very grand, it caught the imagination of many, a wonderful gesture. He was so full of this grand gesture, it seems not to have occurred to him that there might be reprisals, and there were. The British government put a tax on all cattle landed in England from this country. He then went over to England and made an agreement with the British government to pay them £10 million at once, as a final settlement of the land annuities, on their agreeing to withdraw the tax, and he floated a loan here for £10 million to pay them.

This was all very disturbing to me, and I started asking questions which were not always answered. Gradually I came to realise that the programme being followed by the Fianna Fáil government was not the Fianna Fáil one with which I was in agreement, but one I would call a Government Programme. I found I was becoming a great nuisance to them with my questions. They certainly seemed to annoy de Valera. In answer to a question I asked one day, he said, 'Fools ask more questions than wise men can answer.' It was meant to squash me. It did not. I did not ask questions to annoy him or anyone, but to get information, and with the desire to get them to fulfil their promises to the electorate. Perhaps they were fool questions, but I did not think so.

Things were becoming strained between me and the government and the Party, and even the organisation, at least with those members of it who were ambitious to get on through government favour, but still I had faith in the organisation, as I knew many members who felt as I did. Partition and the Irish language were the first things they were going to tackle when they became the government, but nothing was being done about either, and many other members of the organisation were asking why. They got very little satisfaction. Mr McGinley and Eamon Donnelly were always asking about the language and partition, and urging that something should be done; both men were from the North.

The first Easter that Fianna Fáil were in government, they issued invitations to the relatives of the men executed in 1916 to attend the Arbour Hill ceremonies, which had been established by the Cosgrave government. In answer to the invitation, I wrote what I had written to the invitation of the Cosgrave government, that the men buried there had died for Ireland, therefore the graves belonged to the people of Ireland, not to a group or a party, even a government one. Until such time as those graves were opened up to the people every day of the year, so that they could be visited without permit or invitation, I or my family would not attend. The answer I got was that they were too near the military detention barracks, and that it could not be done. I suggested that the barracks could be put to another use, but my suggestion was ignored. Well, while Fianna Fáil remained in government, and the graves were kept locked up, neither I nor my family attended the ceremonies.

George V, King of England, died on 20 January 1936, and the Speaker of the Dáil moved a motion of condolence with the British royal family, which meant of course that it was a government motion. It was passed without a dissentient voice. This seemed a terrible thing to me; the Dáil represented the whole country, and this motion was committing the whole country to an expression of sympathy with the family who were head of the state which had crucified our country, and who even still maintained their right to hold the northern part of our country against our wishes.

I was sorry not to be in the Dáil then, to be even a voice in the wilderness against the motion. I assume the Speaker moved the motion on instructions from the government. Had de Valera, as Minister of External Affairs (as he then was), sent a message from himself as such,

I would not have taken exception to it. He had a right to his opinion, but he had no right to commit the whole country, through the Dáil, to his opinion. It made me wild, and it was not fair to the country.

Shortly after, a meeting of the Senate was summoned, which I attended. While waiting in the members' room for the bell to ring summoning us to the Senate chamber, Senator Joseph Connolly came up to me and said, 'I have been selected by the government to move that motion.' 'What motion?' I asked. 'The motion of condolence with the royal family on the death of the King.' 'Surely, Connolly,' I said, 'you are not going to bring that thing into the Senate?' 'Oh yes,' he said, 'the government selected me to do it.' He seemed rather smug and pleased with himself. 'Well,' I said, 'I thought it was bad enough when it was moved in the Dáil and passed without a dissentient voice. To bring it in here is monstrous. It looks as if the government means to commit the whole country through the Oireachtas to this slave motion. Remember, Connolly,' I said, 'our grievances with England are not in the dim and distant past. The partition of our country is a crime of today.'

I do not remember all that I said. I know I was furious. I had attended a Party meeting that morning and did not get even a hint that such a motion was to be moved in the Senate that evening. Had I got the slightest hint, I would have fought it there. I told Connolly I would oppose it. He said, 'You can't do that.' 'Oh,' I said, 'Who will stop me?' 'Well,' he said, 'if you feel so strongly about it, better not come into the meeting.' I said, 'I'm coming. You have sprung this thing on me, and left me little time to think, but if it is moved I am going to object somehow.' The time was so short and I was so agitated that I found it hard to get my thoughts in order, or to think how to deal with the matter.

Senator Joseph Connolly moved the motion, and it was seconded. Then the Chairman rose to put it to the house. I rose and said, 'Chairman, before you put this to the house, at the risk of being classified as ungracious, ungenerous, bitter, and all the adjectives which may be flung at me, I wish to be recorded as dissenting from this motion.' The Chairman directed the Clerk to record my objection. This was done, and the motion was then put to the house. 'Motion declared passed, all members present, with the exception of Mrs Clarke, rising in their places' (Senate record, Wed. 12 Feb. 1936). The whole house gasped at my objection, and there was a stunned silence. I was trembling; it is not easy to do a thing which you know will be misunderstood, misinterpreted and condemned, but I felt I would be untrue to our dead who died for Ireland if I allowed that motion to pass unchallenged.

The Senate adjourned almost immediately, till next day, and all the Senators went into the members' room. They stood about in groups, apparently discussing and condemning my action, but none came near me, I stood a bird alone. Why? Some of the members may have had an uneasy conscience; they and their families had been victims of British tyranny, and at one time they would have done the same as I had done, but Party discipline and other reasons made them act contrary to their natural inclinations.

While I was standing by one of the windows in the members' room, curious to see if any member of my Party would come to talk to me, and feeling very contemptuous towards them, Senator Bennett, Chairman of the Senate, came out of his office and came up to me. 'Mrs Clarke,' he said, 'that was a dreadful thing you did. You shocked me. I went into my office to think it over, and in thinking it over I have come to the conclusion, knowing your family history, that you could do nothing else.' I thanked him for coming to tell me his conclusions, despite the fact that my action had shocked him; I said it was the act of an honourable and upright gentleman.

I knew some of the members might be thinking like me, but would not do what I did, fearing that they might be considered petty or narrowminded. It was so much better to appear magnanimous, and pretend to forgive and forget. That attitude might be condonable if our enemy showed any sign of sorrow or regret for the sins committed against us, but our country is still partitioned, the greatest wrong that can be done to a small island country, and the freedom we have in the twenty-six counties we would not have if our people had not kept up the fight for freedom, despite the ruthless war our enemy waged against us.

Three months later de Valera abolished the Senate, on 12 May 1936. He had previously got power to do this from the Party, but in asking the Fianna Fáil Senate and Dáil Party to give him this power, he gave an undertaking to this effect: 'Knowing there is divided opinion in the Party on the question of one or two houses, and the abolition or reorganisation of the Senate, though I am asking for this power, I will not act on it without coming back to the Party and taking a vote on it.' Believing him, I was satisfied; it was not always easy to follow his twists and turns.

Imagine my surprise when, coming down from the Senate one evening on my way to the restaurant for tea, I met a Cumann na Gaedheal deputy rushing up the stairs. He stopped and said, 'You're squashed.' 'What do you mean?' I asked. 'Who's squashed?' He said, 'De Valera is just after getting a motion passed to abolish the Senate.' It was indeed a surprise; I had had such confidence in the undertaking de Valera had given. He had always seemed so meticulous about keeping a promise. I had been at a Party meeting that morning and not a word had been said about abolishing the Senate; I did not even get a hint that such was contemplated. I knew, of course, that had he asked the Party to support the motion, the majority would have agreed to do so.

Well, with the Senate abolished I was out of the only paid job I ever got.[8] It was a crippling financial loss, but it was not the first time I had to pay for trying to do what I believed to be right. I did not sit down to grieve over my loss, and I had plenty of unpaid activities, but I did think it strange that of the first six Fianna Fáil Senators, five of them got paid positions on the closing of the Senate, and I was not one of the five. I still had faith in the Fianna Fáil organisation, if not in the Party, and worked as usual in the *Cumann* and the Executive, and also with the Fianna Fáil Party in the Corporation, but as time went on I began to feel the weight of Party influence moving against me.

Still I stuck, believing it was a small party or group that was acting in self-interest. I was sadly disillusioned. The whole weight of Fianna Fáil No 2 area were out to down me. From their actions I gathered that I was considered more or less of a danger, something to beware of. Perhaps I was, to Party interests; country came before Party. To me a thing was right or wrong no matter who sponsored it, and on that I acted. Many mean or underhand things were done to me; they are not worth recording.

Later in the year, King Edward VIII of England abdicated. After the abdication, all British Dominions had by law to approve of the proposed new King before he could be crowned. To get the approval of this country, a meeting of the Dáil was summoned. The motion of approval was moved and carried, like the vote of condolence, without a dissentient voice. This motion was to my mind a definite recognition of a British King as our King. Recognition of a British King had hitherto been imposed on us by force, and it was unthinkable that we should now accept him voluntarily. It was only then I began to see why the Senate was abolished, and I wondered what had become of our rebels.

When de Valera announced his intention of bringing in a new Constitution in 1937, I could see no reason for it. He questioned me as to why I objected, and I told him that it seemed to me that if he brought in a new Constitution, it would have to be within the four walls of the Treaty. In doing that, he was accepting the Treaty, whereas Fianna Fáil had only accepted the fact that the Treaty had been carried by a majority of the Dáil, and supported by the majority of the voters in the General Election, and a government set up in accordance with it. In other words, we accepted the Treaty position as established. If he went outside that position, it would mean a clash with England. If that was his intention, I would stand in with him; if not, I would oppose him. I said it would be time enough to bring in a new Constitution when we had re-established the Republic, which I understood was the aim of Fianna Fáil. He listened to me, but made no comment.

At this time, I had no idea what the proposed Constitution would be like. The morning it appeared in the press, I was assured by Seán MacEntee in his most unctuous manner that through it we had the Republic in all but name. This I thought was dishonest. It was a pretence that when the new Constitution was passed, it would change the whole position, that we would no longer be a Dominion of England. We had our Republic on the strict QT, unbeknownst to England. I was not going to be a party to what seemed to me a piece of political trickery, but I was in a difficulty. The proposed new Constitution was to be voted for or against on the same day as the General Election, and though opposing the new Constitution, I did not want Fianna Fáil to be defeated.

I had a letter from Mrs Sheehy Skeffington, pointing out that the proposed Constitution placed women in a much lower position than that accorded to them in the 1916 Proclamation, and asking me to write to the press stating this. I considered it, and decided to write to the press on the lines suggested by Mrs Sheehy Skeffington. It would do less harm than the one I had intended to write, but would let people know I was critical of the proposed Constitution. I trusted Mrs Sheehy Skeffington, and had a great admiration for her.

My action was very much resented by the leaders of Fianna Fáil. This was passed on to the rank and file, and a small group, in whose way I seem to have been standing, took full advantage of the position. The first to take action was the Tomás O Cléirig Cumann, Fianna Fáil, of which I had been Chairman since the start. I had founded it. The following motion was proposed to a meeting on 29 July 1937, by Harry Colley: 'That this *Cumann* strongly disapproves of the action of its Chairman, Mrs Tom Clarke, in opposing the Constitution sponsored by the Government elected by this organisation, and by the Fianna Fáil organisation itself.' The motion was passed by twenty-four votes to five. I was not there. I do not remember getting a notice; I am sure if I did I would have been there to defend myself, and explain my attitude, and I feel if I had been there, voting would have been slightly different.

At a meeting of the North City Comhairle Ceanntair on 23 September 1937, the following resolution was proposed by Thomas A O'Reilly, Chairman, O'Hanrahan Cumann, Fianna Fáil: 'That this

Comhairle Dáil Ceanntair of North East, Dublin, Fianna Fáil, dissociates itself from the published opinions of one of our public representatives, Councillor Mrs T Clarke, with reference to the Constitution of Eire, sponsored by President de Valera, agreed to by the Fianna Fáil Party, and enacted by a free vote of the people. We repudiate such utterances, believing they have a demoralising effect on our organisation in part, and the public at large as a whole.' The resolution was passed.

The North Dock Cumann, Fianna Fáil, also proposed: 'That the members of the North Dock Cumann, Fianna Fáil, take a serious view of the persistency of Mrs Kathleen Clarke, TC, in claiming the right to publicly repudiate what must be regarded as Party Policy.

'It is the considered opinion of the members of the North Dock Cumann that the National Executive would be within their rights to call upon Mrs Clarke to publicly withdraw her published repudiation of the Constitution of Eire, which appeared in the Public Press a few days before the polling date of the last General Election. Failing such withdrawal, the National Executive, Fianna Fáil, should thereupon request the resignation of Mrs Kathleen Clarke, TC, from the Fianna Fáil organisation.'

The Tomás O Cléirig Cumann then wrote to the National Executive: 'This *Cumann* finds it hard to credit that the National Executive could justify Mrs Clarke's action in opposing the Constitution, thereby denouncing, by implication, the many voluntary workers who night and day worked to carry out the instructions of the same Executive, in favour of the Constitution. Some of these workers never saw bed for a week, mainly due to the propaganda of this organisation in support of the Constitution. Feelings amongst these workers is very strong on this question, and to put the matter to the test I am to ask the National Executive for their approval of the attached Resolution.'

I attended a meeting of the National Executive on the 8th November, and when these letters were read I pointed out to the Chairman that the President, Mr de Valera, had stated publicly that everyone was free to act as they wished on the question of the proposed new Constitution, and that I had asked for a direction before taking any action at a meeting of the National Executive. I had been told from the Chair that the proposed new Constitution was not an organisation matter, it was entirely a government one, and members were free to act as they thought best. Had I been told I was bound by the organisation to support the proposed Constitution, I would have resigned, in order to be free to act as I thought right on a question I felt very strongly about. I also reminded him that the Chairman of the meeting, when I asked for a direction, was a Minister of State.

The National Executive was forced to admit that Mr de Valera had stated publicly that everyone was free in the matter, and also that I had asked for a direction. In face of that, they could do nothing. And so the heroes of North East Dublin and Cumann Tomás O Cléirig, Fianna Fáil, had to bottle their wrath. Later, the moving figures in both resolutions arrived in the position of TDs and Senators. After that I resigned from Cumann Tomás O Cléirig, but remained on the [Fianna Fáil] Executive. I attended it regularly, but felt I was not very popular there.

In 1939 I was still a member of the Fianna Fáil Executive, and a Fianna Fáil member of Dublin Corporation. Oscar Traynor was co-opted to the Corporation in place of a member who had died, and from the time he came into the Fianna Fáil Party in the Corporation he did all he could to prevent me from being nominated for the Lord

Mayoralty. He tried in various ways to get me to withdraw, but did not succeed. I had not been very keen on getting the nomination hitherto, but when I saw Oscar Traynor's efforts to change the order of things I got angry. He became so insulting to me when I refused to withdraw, at a meeting in Alderman Tom Kelly's shop, that Councillor Dr Joseph Hannigan protested; he said he resented Oscar Traynor's attitude to me. They nearly came to blows over it. It made me smile when Alderman Kelly, fearing they would do so, said in his usual dry way, 'Now, boys, if you want to fight go out into the street – don't smash up my little shop.'

Despite Traynor's efforts, I was elected Lord Mayor in June, 1939. There was no-one in Ireland more surprised than I was when I found myself elected. I received letters, telegrams, cablegrams, from Ireland and from all over the world, congratulating me; it seemed to give the Irish at home and abroad great pleasure that the widow of the first signatory to the 1916 Proclamation should be so honoured.

As soon as I got the Mansion House over from the outgoing Lord Mayor, Alderman Alfred Byrne, I set to work to carry out a wish I had had for many years. That was to put a large painting of the late Queen Victoria of England, which occupied a very prominent position in the entrance hall, out of it. I felt I could not sleep in the house until she was out of it, she had been so bitterly hostile to Ireland and everything Irish. In order to avoid interference with my action, I made arrangements with a few men I could trust to come at six o'clock in the morning to remove her. I sat up all night, with my sister Laura, to await the coming of the men. I found on going through the house that there were other paintings of British monarchs also hung up there, and decided they should go too. They had all been heads of the country which had scourged us.

The men arrived on time and proceeded to remove the monarchs, a job which seemed to give them great pleasure. The pictures were very big, I think about eight feet long. They were ranged along the front wall of the Mansion House when the first tram of the day came down Dawson Street. From observation, it caused some little excitement amongst the passengers. By the time the next tram came along the pictures were gone and I was very happy. Among the many letters of congratulation I received for my act was one from an Irishman in Pennsylvania, USA, saying: 'I was delighted when I read of you putting that old B.... out of the Mansion House. Many a time I walked down Dawson Street and saw her looking out from the hall, and wished I could put her out, but why in hell didn't you burn her?'

Some months after my election, the Second World War was declared. The Corporation was ordered by the government to organise Air Raid precautions, erect Air Raid shelters, etc. over which there was great friction. There were endless meetings, which were of course only routine work for me. I was too familiar with them to cause me any worry, having been a member of the Corporation since 1919, and having acted as *locum tenens* Lord Mayor often during the Black and Tan period.

What constituted the real strain on me was National things. Before the war was declared, the then IRA decided to make war on England, and were busy bombing there. I was not connected in any way with the IRA at the time, nor with Cumann na mBan. New brooms who had come into the Cumann na mBan organisation after the Treaty flung me out when the split occurred in Sinn Féin and I took de Valera's side, or when I took my seat in the Dáil with de Valera; I forget which of these crimes I was punished for, perhaps for both.

I had no sympathy with the bombing policy carried out in England, as I could see no gain to Ireland arising out of it. Under the existing circumstances I thought it rather stupid, and when war was declared I thought they would have sense enough to abandon it, but they kept on. It led to arrests, imprisonments, deportations, executions, and while thoroughly out of patience with it, but knowing the purity of their motives, my sympathy went out in full measure for those involved and their dependants.

I could understand the British government, with a war on their hands, punishing the IRA for their action in England at such a time. What I could not understand was the action of the Irish government in punishing men for doing what they themselves had been doing in opposition to the Cosgrave government. Military courts were again set up, followed by raiding, arresting, imprisoning and even executing men. It nearly drove me insane, as I was a member of the Fianna Fáil organisation. Of course, the organisation was not consulted in the matter; appealing to the ministers or the government was useless, it was appealing to deaf ears. It is extraordinary the change that comes over men, or most men, when they get a little taste of power; they seem to become so intolerant.

Many of those men imprisoned by the Fianna Fáil government were men who had given long and faithful service to Ireland. Some had 1916 records, but could not see that a parliament set up under a British Act of Parliament was either Irish or free, and were endeavouring to keep on the fight until the Republic was re-established for the thirty-two counties. I was in complete accord with their ideal, but thought the proper course to take, once war was declared, was to call off all military activity for the time being, and place all their strength behind the government of the twenty-six counties, which had declared neutrality, to see that neutrality was strictly adhered to.

It is quite possible that had the government met these men in a comradely spirit, instead of the big stick, a working agreement could have been arranged for the duration of the war. They had been comrades-in-arms. One man, Patrick McGrath, was arrested and went on hunger-strike. The government would not release him, and the hunger-strike continued day after day. I knew he was the type like Terence MacSwiney, that would not give in, and feared each day would bring the tragedy of his death.

With many others I went on deputations to the government to plead for his release. I used all the influence the Lord Mayor is supposed to possess to get the government to release him. At last, when I had given up all hope, he was released. He was sent to Jervis Street Hospital to recover, and there I went to see him. I was overjoyed at his release. He told me he would have gone through to a finish. I had never met him before, and was very much impressed with his nobility. He recovered from the effects of his hunger-strike, and resumed the activities he had been engaged in.

The annual pilgrimage to the grave of Wolfe Tone in Bodenstown churchyard was banned by the government, for some unknown reason. It led to a number of tragedies. There was a police raid on a house where a meeting was being held; McGrath was one of those present. A struggle ensued and a policeman was killed. McGrath was arrested and charged with shooting the policeman. He was brought up before the Military Tribunal set up by the government for the purpose of trying such cases, instead of the ordinary court, and was convicted and sentenced to death. It came as a shock to most people, and everything was done to prevail on the government to reprieve him. It was no use, the government was adamant.

I got on to the acting Minister for Justice, Gerald Boland, late on the night before McGrath's execution, and pleaded with him for a reprieve. It was in vain. He said the matter was out of his hands; it was a Cabinet decision, McGrath had to die. It crossed my mind at the time that the Fianna Fáil government was showing as little mercy to those who opposed them as the Cosgrave government had, and Fianna Fáil had denounced them in no uncertain terms. To show my sympathy with the relatives, and my disagreement with the government's action in refusing to reprieve him, I ordered the blinds in the Mansion House to be drawn and the flag to be flown at half-mast, then ordered the City Manager to have the flag flown over the City Hall at half-mast.

As a member of the government's political organisation, this was a dreadful thing to do, but then I had to do what I thought right, even though I gave great offence for which I think I was never forgiven. McGrath's execution to my mind was a crime, and I had to make a protest. Then I never could see why as a member of a party or organisation I was bound to approve of everything the leaders did; I could not put Party interests before my ideas of right and wrong. I don't claim I am always right, but I act in accordance with what I believe to be right. It seemed to me that in executing men like McGrath, the government were carrying out the old British policy of killing or exterminating in one way or another all the best of our people.

Then there was Tomás MacCurtain, whose father, the late Lord Mayor of Cork, had been assassinated by the Black and Tans. This boy was arrested and charged with shooting a policeman. He was brought before the Military Tribunal, found guilty and sentenced to death. This came as another shock to many, and a committee was set up to work for his reprieve. I placed a room in the Mansion House at their disposal. That committee worked late and early, with the result that the pressure of public opinion was so great, the government was forced to yield and a reprieve was granted. It was a terrible thing to be meeting the lad's mother daily while he was under sentence of death, and at the hands of an Irish government, remembering as she did her husband's murder. He had been a comrade-in-arms of those who now composed the government, and for a crime that was a continuing part of the split on the Treaty. One would need to have a heart of stone to look unmoved at that mother's grief.

One thing I feel very happy to have established while I was Lord Mayor is the Irish Red Cross. I chaired the first meeting in the Mansion House, and was elected President, so I can claim to be the first President of the Irish Red Cross. It was not then a paid job. I remained with it until it was established.

The office of Lord Mayor is a very busy one, and there is little time for relaxation. I had one form of relaxation which was always at hand, and that was a talking parrot. He was an amazing bird, and gave me many hours of real pleasure. He could repeat anything he had heard a few times, and in the exact tone of voice. His cage was in the room where I usually sat when work was over, standing in front of a large portrait of an English earl. At eleven o'clock every night he mounted to the top of his cage, strutted around for a while and then stood in front of the painting and said, 'You are a pup.' He then would take another turn around the top of his cage, again stand in front of the painting and in his most impressive manner say, 'You are a bold pup.' Then he went into the cage and said 'Good night', which was the signal for me to cover him up.

When my term of office as Lord Mayor was finished, in 1941, I decided to end my association with Fianna Fáil at the first suitable opportunity. To remain with them might end in my succumbing to the natural selfishness and greed which is in most of us, the desire, when one has reached place and position of power and consequence, to hold it at any cost, as I have seen colleagues whom I thought were incorruptible do. So, like a good coward, I decided to show a clean pair of heels. Had I yielded to such temptations I would not dare face my husband in the next world, where I hope to meet him, nor would I dare be untrue to the lessons learned from parents, uncle, aunt and grandmother, to be true to Ireland, first, last and all the time, no matter what the cost.

Another General Election was due, and I was nominated by Fianna Fáil in the North East Dublin constituency. I refused to accept, and resigned from the organisation. I was sorry to have to do so; I liked public life, and liked having a say in the affairs of my country, and felt I had earned the right to do so, but the qualities which made for success in the war for independence were no longer needed. I wrote a letter to de Valera, as President of the Fianna Fáil organisation, tendering my resignation, stating my reasons and regret at having to do so after our long association: 'I held on so far in the hope that you would eventually make an effort to carry out the Fianna Fáil policy or that the Organisation would assert itself and force you to do so. That hope is now dead. You are going farther and farther away from the Fianna Fáil policy. I regret having to part from a group I worked with and to whom I gave faithful service, a group I had such a high opinion of and who I thought appreciated integrity, honour and straight-forwardness' (3 May 1943).

In answer, I received a note from Miss Kathleen O'Connell, de Valera's secretary, saying that the President had received my letter and that it would come up for consideration at the meeting of the

Fianna Fáil Executive. Following that, I received a letter, dated 17 May, informing me that my resignation had been accepted. And so ended my association with Fianna Fáil. Later, I was called on to resign from Dublin Corporation, in accordance with some pledge I had been asked to sign when I was elected. As I had already severed my connection with them when the request was made, I just ignored it.

At the next election for Dublin Corporation I went forward as an Independent candidate, though I knew there was little chance of my being elected, having three big organisations, Labour, Fianna Fáil and Cumann na Gaedheal, to compete with, and little money. I did get a fair first preference, but none others. Later I was nominated for the Senate by the Technical School Board, and though having no hope of being elected I felt bound to accept the nomination, as it was intended to honour me. The result of the election was that I did not receive even one first preference vote. I received letters from some of the Fianna Fáil deputies, apologising for not being able to vote for me, as they were party-bound. So were all the other parties.

And now I am left with one hope, that the bitterness resulting from the difference of opinion on the question of the Treaty will be allowed to die, and once more Irish men and women will stand together as unbreakable on the abolition of partition of our country and the complete freedom from foreign domination of our thirty-two counties, as they did before the Treaty split them.

EPILOGUE

Kathleen Clarke's autobiography, written mainly in the 1940s, deals in great detail with her life up to the Easter Rising and the War of Independence. It becomes much less detailed after that, and her public life is covered in only a few pages. She wrote the memoir in order to secure Tom Clarke's position in the pantheon of republican leaders, and to make sure his ideals were passed on, and she was less interested in recording her own political life – her time as a TD (member of parliament) and as a senator, and her many years on Dublin Corporation, culminating in her election as Ireland's first woman Lord Mayor in 1939.

Writing about this election, an achievement of which she was extremely proud, Mrs Clarke gives very little information about the office itself and how she spent her time. In fact, the excitement caused by this breakthrough for women was intense, and she was interviewed by numerous journalists – women, of course, for the 'women's page'. Speaking to the public, she emphasised her belief in women's abilities: 'I am terribly keen on the fact that women, if given the opportunity, could do as well in positions in public life as the men. I have great faith in my own sex' (*Irish Press*). Interviewed by the *Herald*, she said, 'I am definitely national, and elements that are not national I will not support in a personal or an official capacity'.

Although she now held an official position, Kathleen Clarke

continued to be outspoken in her views. In July 1939, as war clouds gathered, she stated to the *Stand*: 'It is very well for England to denounce Herr Hitler, and to talk of the atrocities and brutalities, but it is up to us to point out to Irish children that atrocities and brutalities began in Ireland by England and by the people England sent across to Ireland'. Such remarks upset many Dublin ratepayers, who were largely unionist in sympathy, and protesting letters were sent to newspapers by 'Liberty, Equality and Fraternity', 'Patriotic Anti-Fanatic', 'A Supporter of Royalty', 'Plain Citizen' and 'One Who is Pained' (pseudonyms were then allowed). The Irish motto on her mayoral crest translates as 'I bring peace'. However, her action in removing royal portraits from the Mansion House ('No crowned heads will remain hanging in the Mansion House while I am in residence') unleashed a torrent of criticism. The Lord Mayor was accused of having a 'pettish, school-girl mentality', but argued that her uncle, John Daly, had removed the royal coat of arms from Limerick Town Hall when he was Mayor of Limerick (1898-99).

Kathleen Clarke's two terms as Lord Mayor coincided with the outbreak of the Second World War (the 'Emergency'). Dublin suffered rationing and fuel shortages, with the rest of the country, and its large population of poor people needed more help than ever. Mrs Clarke was a founder and strong supporter of the Irish Red Cross, and used her position to head appeals for charities and hospitals. She appealed to the striking Municipal Employees' Union to continue to provide essential services, and also apparently mediated in a milk strike. A Mansion House Coal Fund provided fuel for the needy, and the Red Cross helped to look after the victims of German bombs that fell in Dublin in 1941.

She strongly supported Ireland's neutrality, and indeed suspected that de Valera was 'more neutral to the British' than she approved of. A letter to her from Professor Rudmose-Brown of Trinity College complains of de Valera's action in sending the Dublin Fire Brigade to help a bombed Belfast in April 1941, an act of generosity for which he has always been commended. He writes, 'While of course, like all Irishmen, I have great sympathy for the unfortunate Belfast victims of British policy, I do think that our government should be made to take our neutrality seriously, and not risk unnecessarily offending the other great belligerent,' and he obviously believed she agreed with this.

Kathleen Clarke suffered a long illness after an operation in March 1940, reducing her activities. Nevertheless, she was re-elected on 2 July 1940, and served for another year. In June 1941 she announced that she would not seek re-election, and later resigned from Fianna Fáil, as she describes in Chapter 11.

Mrs Clarke played an active part in Irish life for many years, even after this resignation. In 1946, Sean MacBride and other modernist politicians, some of them ex-IRA members, founded Clann na Poblachta, a republican party with a policy of social reform. Kathleen Clarke joined the Clann after it won two bye-elections in 1947, and stood for it in the general election of 1948, unsuccessfully. Younger candidates, without a background in the earlier upheavals of the century, felt that older republicans such as Kathleen Clarke were using them relying on the transfers of their younger running-mates to get elected. Captain Peadar Cowan complained in his unpublished autobiography that his role in Dublin North-East was to help to elect 'senile Mrs Tom Clarke' (she was about seventy). As it happened, the younger candidates won the Clann na Poblachta seats in that election, not the old guard.

As a member of Dublin Corporation until 1945, Kathleen Clarke was an active participant in Corporation activities, and sat on a large number of boards. She was nominated as a board member for St Ultan's Hospital (1930-31), the Grangegorman Mental Hospital Board (1933-8, 1942-4), the Berwick Home, Rathfarnham (1935-8), the Rotunda Maternity Hospital (1936-8) and The Dublin Orthopaedic Hospital (1936-8, 1942), and was an Executive Committee member of the board of the National Maternity Hospital, Holles Street, from 1941 to 1944. She sat on various committees: the City of Dublin Child Welfare Committee (1931, 1936-8, 1942), the City of Dublin Old Age Pensions Committee (1931-2, 1942-44), the Lane Pictures Committee (1931), the Playground Committee (1932), the City of Dublin Vocational Education Committee (1933-4, 1942), the Estates Committee (1934), the City of Dublin National Monuments Committee (1942), and the committee on building a new City Hall (1938). She also spent some time on the boards of the Irish Tourist Association and the Royal Irish Academy of Music. Outside her Corporation work, she was involved with the National Graves Association and the Wolfe Tone Memorial Fund.

Kathleen Clarke's memoir does not provide much detail about her time in Dáil Éireann, apart from the Treaty debates, but during her time in Seanad Éireann (1928-36) she contributed to debates on various issues, not solely concerned with nationalism. Among topics she spoke on were the Workmen's Compensation Act (1933), the Juries (Protection) Bill (1929), the Importation of Bacon Bill (1930), the powers of the Electricity Supply Board, and the Road Traffic Acts (1933). She would often exemplify a woman's point of view; while the Road Traffic Acts were being discussed, for example, and the question of police wearing uniform for traffic duties was at issue, she pointed out that as a woman driver she would be very unwilling to stop for a man who signalled her to do so, if he was not in uniform.

During the debate on the Local Government (Dublin) Bill, 1930, Kathleen objected to the proposal that five members of Dublin City Council should be elected by 'commercial electors', 'creating amongst the people a privileged class in a country that suffered so much in the past from a privileged class... My fear is that the principle of this Bill, which only affects Dublin, will eventually be applied to other things, such as the Parliamentary franchise, and that there will be created a still larger privileged class.' Three years later, when the subject was debated again, she repeated this concern: 'I have worked [in Dublin Corporation] with those who were elected on the commercial register... I have no fault to find with them as men, but I have not found in any one of them anything outstanding, anything that would say to me that these men are entitled to privilege'. She objected to an impression given during the debate that the previous Dublin Corporation had been abolished because of corruption, and she implied that the Corporation had been abolished because the Corporation majority had been anti-Treaty, and had protested vigorously against executions of IRA members.

Mrs Clarke was always quick to take issue with any friendly references to Britain, and in 1929 objected strongly to the appropriation of £25,000 for British military graves in Ireland. Active in the National Graves Association, she spent much time trying to raise money for the graves of the patriot dead, and resented that British graves should apparently be more respected. During a debate on the Irish Nationality and Citizenship Bill, in April 1935, she leapt immediately on a reference to 'the friendship which exists between this country and England'. She protested, 'I would like to see that friendship established, but England must earn our friendship. So far she has not made any attempt to earn it, and where she has not bullied us, she has tricked us. Until she has learned to cease her bullying and trickery and to be generous to this country, and restore the rights she took from us, there will be no friendship between us and England...'

Here she was opposed by Senator Miss Browne, who accused her of speaking for 'a limited number of very extreme people...Whatever may have been the history of the country in the past, there is no use in dragging it up time and time again in order to hinder further the progress of this country.' Senator Counihan agreed: 'I think it is very bad policy and propaganda to put forward in a responsible body, and I can say that she is not speaking on behalf of any responsible section of the community of this country', but Senator Ó Maille declared that 'Senator Mrs Clarke gave expression to the sentiments of the great majority of the Irish people'. After further lively discussion, the President brought the debate to a close, saying during his speech that 'Senator Mrs Clarke, wisely in my opinion, laid stress on the fact that though we desire these friendly relations [between the two countries], there are things at the present time which militate against these desires becoming effective.'

She was very interested in social issues, and depended a good deal on 'common sense', even when dealing with matters rarely spoken of in a puritanical society. During a debate in February 1935 on the banning of contraceptives in Ireland, she opened her statement by saying that when she had asked for the prohibition to be deleted from the Bill, 'my reasons were very much misinterpreted in the Press', and it certainly took nerve to join publically in such a debate at that time. While she was fully in agreement with Church and State in condemning the use of contraceptives, she felt that prohibition was the wrong way of going about it. She drew on her knowledge of the alcohol prohibition laws in the USA, pointing out that she had rarely seen anyone drunk while she lived there between 1901 and 1907, but that travelling through the country in 1924 she had found that 'prohibition had driven these people from a state of sobriety to a state of drunkenness – that even the children were not free from it'.

She opined that '...human nature is a peculiar thing, and the minute you prohibit anything the human being is inclined to rebel against it...I think that there should be some other method by which we would be able to appeal to the higher and nobler and more spiritual side of the human being than that of prohibition'. Senator Oliver St John Gogarty later said that 'it was very courageous of Senator Mrs Clarke to adopt the attitude she has adopted...upon this highly debatable question. She made a most sincere contribution to the debate.'

Kathleen Clarke was very interested in the position of women in the home, and their financial situation. In a debate on the Widows' and Orphans' Pensions Bill, 1935, she was critical of the level of income being discussed (5 shillings per week, plus 2/– for the eldest child and 1/– each for the others): '...in order to bring up children with right ideas and as decent citizens of the State, it was necessary to have the mother...provided with sufficient money to enable her to remain in her home, to keep her home together and look after her children... [W]hen the mother has not sufficient money to remain at home...she naturally has to go out to work, and when she is at work the children are on the streets... ' She herself had always been a working mother, even when her husband was alive, but she knew that few women were in a position to combine work and childrearing comfortably.

Again, she was vigorous in support of the Nurses' and Midwives' Pension Bill in 1935, particularly of nurses who were not attached to hospitals and could not save enough for a pension when they were no longer physically able to work: 'They may get a case on which they would have four or five weeks' work, and when they leave that case they have to spend four or five weeks more waiting for another case, which brings the rate of their remuneration down very low alto-gether...I know an elderly doctor in a hospital who gave this advice to a young nurse: "Missy, get married if you can. Do not get old in the profession. The patients do not want you; they want a bit of fluff"... When they reach the age of 45, they have to look forward to 25 or 30 years more of terrible poverty.'

Senator Mrs Clarke was active in the defence of a woman's right to work, and took a strong line on the 1935 Conditions of Employment Bill. She attacked the Labour Party's view, saying that James Con-nolly would never have agreed with it, 'when they can think of no other means of giving the poor men who are being shoved out of work a job except by bringing in legislation which is going to debar women from certain classes of work...' In regard to the argument that men's pay would gradually be depressed to that of women, 'If a woman goes into a particular form of industry...at the same rate of pay as the men receive and says that she will accept nothing less, and if the men's trade unions stand behind her on that, I do not see how employers could face what that means'.

She continued, 'Take all the people in this Chamber...They have boys and girls. If legislation was brought in prohibiting their girls from entering, say, the commercial or the professional world, what would they think of it? Here you are bringing in legislation to do that in the industrial world...If the only reason that Labour can put up for being in favour of this is that women are driving men out of the labour market, then I think that is a very poor reason.' She was opposed by Senator Foran, who stated, 'The modern machine is adaptable to the flapper and, consequently, the male is being thrown out on the scrap heap...Do the feminists want here what occurs in certain industrial centres across the water where the men mind the babies and the women go into the factories? Do they want that, in this holy Ireland of ours? I do not, and I was in favour of votes for women.'

Mrs Clarke assured the Senator that she had never been associated with the feminist movement, but had always been in sympathy with it: 'I helped it if it did not clash with the work in which I was always engaged – work for the freedom of my country'. Her opposition to the limitations on women was based on the Proclamation of 1916, which gave every citizen equal rights and opportunities. In relation to men rearing children, she said, 'If men could do that job as well and as successfully as women, I do not see why they should not do it. It is most important work for the nation, though rather sneered at by men... I do not think it would detract from their dignity in any way.'

The measure was too wide in application: 'Why does the Minister not name the particular industries he is aiming at? A lot of my objection would be met if the particular industries were named...The present Minister may have the most holy, the most idealistic and the most beautiful ideas about what he is going to do with the women, but he is only here for today or tomorrow....and it is putting a weapon into his successor's hands which he may use ruthlessly against the opposite sex... I would be perfectly in agreement...if he said "I am going to prevent women from ever scrubbing floors and I will make men do it instead". With that aim, I would be in absolute agreement, because scrubbing floors is an ugly, hard and badly paid job, and men do not want it'. Senator Mrs Wyse Power was equally cutting: 'The Senator who spoke held forth about the glories of the home and said the home was the place for women. Well, I hope he will set up a bureau to supply women with husbands and homes. That is his place.'

Seanad Éireann was abolished in 1936, and Mrs Clarke, as she says, 'was out of the only paid job I ever got'.

In 1966, during the celebrations for the fiftieth anniversary of 1916, Kathleen Clarke and other relatives of signatories of the Proclamation were conferred with honorary doctorates of law by the National University of Ireland. These were presented by Eamon de Valera, then Chancellor of the NUI, and President of Ireland. In 1967, Mrs Clarke opened a Fenian Exhibition at Kilmainham Jail, where her husband had been imprisoned and executed, saying, 'It was the Fenians who aroused in Tom Clarke that intense love for Ireland's freedom for which he was ready to make any sacrifice'.

She lived for many years in Serpentine Road, Sandymount, close to her eldest son, John Daly Clarke, then in 1965 moved to Liverpool to live with her youngest son, Dr Emmet Clarke, and his family. Many of the Irish community in Liverpool went out of their way to entertain her, and she led as active a social life as her health would allow. She died on 19 September 1972, aged ninety-four.

Kathleen Clarke was given a state funeral in the Pro-Cathedral, Dublin, with military honours, and her coffin was escorted by the Army No 1 Band, the procession halting for one minute opposite the General

Post Office. There was a firing party at the graveside, in Dean's Grange cemetery. The funeral was attended by the President, Eamon de Valera, the Taoiseach (Prime Minister) Jack Lynch, and members of the Government and Opposition.

Tom and Kathleen Clarke had three surviving children. John Daly Clarke, who married Mary Byrne in 1952, worked with the Irish Hospital Sweepstakes and died in 1971, aged sixty-nine, without issue. Tom Clarke junior married Maureen Kennedy in 1939, and managed Daly's Bakery in Limerick for many years, later becoming a director of the Irish Life Assurance Company. During the late 1940s he stood unsuccessfully for election in Limerick as a Fianna Fáil candidate. He died in 1988, without issue. Dr Emmet Clarke, a consultant psychiatrist practising in Liverpool, married Ellen Mullaney in 1955, and left two sons and two grandsons at his death in 2005, aged ninety-five.

In 1938, Dublin Corporation voted to change the name of Mountjoy Square to Tom Clarke Square, but a plebiscite of the house-owners voted down the suggestion. A plaque commemorating Tom Clarke's part in the preparations for the Rising was later erected on the wall of his shop at the corner of Parnell Street and O'Connell Street, Dublin. Clarke Tower in Ballymun, County Dublin, one of a number of 1960s tower blocks named after 1916 leaders, has recently been demolished as part of the renewal of that area, but it is hoped the names will be passed on to the new housing being developed. When, in 1966, the names of the 1916 leaders were given to railway stations, Tom Clarke's name was given to Dundalk station, and Edward Daly's was given to Bray station.

NOTES

Chapter 1

1. The founder of this branch of the Daly family came to Limerick from Galway, after the failure of the 1798 rebellion. His son, John, married Margaret Hayes of Fedamore, and they had seven children, two of whom died of cholera in the Great Famine (1845-9). The two older boys, James and Michael, emigrated to Australia in the 1850s. Another brother, John (born in 1845), became an active member of the Fenians when he was twenty, and in the 1870s was a National Organiser for the Irish Republican Brotherhood (IRB), founded in 1858. Kathleen Clarke (née Daly) was the third of the nine surviving children of the fourth brother, Edward, also a republican activist, who married Catherine O'Mara; the other children were Eileen, Madge, Agnes, Annie, Caroline, Laura, Nora and Edward (Ned).

2. When John Daly thought he was dying, in 1886, he said: 'I wished to see Mr Egan because ... I wished to say with my dying breath, almost in the presence of the unknown God, and in the presence of witnesses, that during the time I lived in his house in Birmingham, he never at any time had my confidence. He had no share in my political sentiments, no more than the child unborn . . . I had several reasons for wishing to live in his house; amongst them was economy, his beautiful garden and the society of his admirable wife and his own, but before God as a dying man, I wanted to say I had no political reason whatsoever.' ('Blue Book' c.6016 p.182, quoted in Le Roux, 'Life and Letters of John Daly', unpublished, now held in University of Limerick (UL) archives. Louis Le Roux, a Breton journalist who settled in Ireland, published a life of Tom Clarke in 1936, and a life of P.H.Pearse in 1932.)

3. The trial of Daly and Egan took place at Warwick. 'The prosecution stated that Daly, who had been living with Egan near Birmingham, and who had gone under the name of "Denman", was arrested at the Birkenhead Railway Station on the 9th April, 1884, with four parcels of bombs in his possession; that letters were found in Egan's house from Daly, and a bottle of nitroglycerine in the garden of

the house near Birmingham.' (Mark Ryan, Fenian Memories, Dublin: M H Gill
and Son, 1945, p 114.) The letters were identified as being in Daly's handwriting
by Dr Denis W Donovan, who had worked in the mental home at Burgess Hill
where Daly had been an attendant, and John Moran of Tubbercurry, who had
turned 'approver' (informer), testified that while a member of the Fenians he had
seen Daly with P J Sheridan, Head Centre for Tubbercurry district, in April 1880.

4. In 1896, an ex-official of Scotland Yard is said to have given the following
answer to queries on John Daly's arrest:

Q: 'Do you say the whole business was due to Agents Provocateurs?'

A: 'I would also go that length. There is no man who was concerned in the question but who would not, in his calmer moments, admit that all these men imprisoned were more sinned against than sinning....It is late now to recall all the
incidents, but this much I do say, the information which has leaked out slowly and
by degrees, year after year, has shown, nay proved, to us, that the so-called dynamite conspiracy was largely fomented and forced to an artificial head by Agents
Provocateurs and a good many of us look back with sorrow to think we had a hand
in the dirty business.' (Quoted by Le Roux, 'Life and Letters of John Daly').

5. Published by Maunsel and Roberts Ltd., Dublin and London, 1922, with an
introduction by P.S. O'Hegarty.

6. Catherine Daly (née O'Mara) was one of two sisters whose mother (a de Lacy)
had eloped with a steward who worked in her parents' home. Edward and Catherine Daly had no children for the first few years of their marriage, and lived with his
parents and his sister, Lollie. Both Catherine and Lollie were trained dressmakers,
and had a thriving business with Limerick high society, but when John Daly was
imprisoned this clientele vanished. Edward Daly, a timber measurer, worked in
Spaight's Timber Yard.

7. Three Fenians, William Allen, Michael Larkin and Michael O'Brien, were executed on 23 November 1867 for the murder of a policeman when two Fenian
prisoners were rescued from a police van. There was a good deal of public disquiet
about the conduct of their trial; one of their fellow accused later had his death sentence commuted and another was granted a Free Pardon.

8. After Edward Daly's death, a collection was made to help his family and the
money raised was invested in a small pub in Shannon Street, Limerick. This was

not a success, and it closed after about a year.

9. Following the notorious O'Shea divorce case, in which Charles Stewart Parnell, leader of the Irish Parliamentary Party, was cited as co-respondent, the Party split in December 1890. Parnell refused to relinquish the leadership, and 46 members of the Party, led by Tim Healy, withdrew, leaving him with 28 followers, including John Redmond. The split divided the country, and for some time there were several factions in the House of Commons fighting for Home Rule, but the Party reunited in 1900.

10. John Devoy was the leader of Clan na Gael, an Irish-American revolutionary organisation which provided support for the IRB after the failure of the Fenian rising of 1867.

Chapter 2

1. However, Louis Le Roux states that he was not met by his brother, and that Daly and Egan went to London ' to keep a vow...they had made in Portland, that on the day of their release they would treat themselves to a hot punch together.' (Le Roux, Tom Clarke and the Irish Freedom Movement, Talbot Press 1936, p. 53.)

2. Tom obtained his certificate of naturalisation on 2 November 1905. (Le Roux, Tom Clarke, p.69.)

Chapter 3

1. Theobald Wolfe Tone, a Protestant barrister, helped to found the United Irishmen, who started a rebellion in 1798 with French assistance. The rebellion failed, and Wolfe Tone committed suicide before he could be executed. He was committed to a policy of social equality and religious liberty.

2. The Dublin Lockout, 1913, resulted from a struggle between employers and the Irish Transport and General Workers' Union, founded in 1909 by James Larkin. When workers refused to undertake not to join any union, they were dismissed. Between August and September, 25,000 employees were locked out, with consequent misery for themselves and their families. By January 1914 many decided to go back to work, provided they did not have to sign an anti-union undertaking, and in February the British TUC announced that their Dublin

Relief Fund would be wound up; this effectively brought the Lockout to an end.

3. The Ulster Volunteers were founded in 1913 by the Ulster Unionist Council to resist Home Rule, which was scheduled to become law in 1914 (it was postponed on the outbreak of World War I). They were able to operate openly, as drilling was legal when authorised by two magistrates, and they had financial support from Ulster businessmen and from English Unionists. The Irish Volunteers were founded in emulation, on Eoin MacNeill's suggestion.

4. 'Then we had Commandant Daly, later executed, a brother of Mrs Tom Clarke. He was very withdrawn, I thought, but a man you would never forget. He would come in and sit around and talk to some people who knew him and with Commandant [r. Captain] O'Sullivan, who later married his sister.' (Recollections of Brigid Lyons Thornton, in C K Griffith and T E O'Grady, Curious Journey, Hutchinson 1982, p.24.)

5. Cumann na mBan (Women's League), the women's division of the Irish Volunteers, pledged itself to work for an Irish Republic 'by organising and training the women of Ireland to take their places by the side of those who are working for a free Ireland.'

6. Sir Roger Casement worked in the British Foreign Service between 1892 and 1913, where he earned his knighthood. Becoming interested in the Irish nationalist movement, he joined the Gaelic League and, later, the Irish Volunteers.

7. In his speech, Redmond called on the Irish Volunteers to join the British Army and fight against Germany. The majority went with him, and were thereafter known as the National Volunteers.

8. Liberty Hall, on Dublin's quays, was the headquarters of the Irish Citizen Army, a workers' defence corps established during the 1913 Lockout.

9. O'Donovan Rossa joined the IRB in 1858, and was sentenced to life imprisonment for revolutionary activities in 1865. An inquiry into his dreadful prison conditions led to his release in 1871, and he went to New York with John Devoy. He broke with Clan na Gael in 1880.

Chapter 4

1. An addition to Kathleen Clarke's original manuscript reads: 'For some years after the Rising I had been reluctant to mention this, as I thought there was

no-one to substantiate my claim. [In the 1920s] an old friend of Tom's and mine, called Jim Gleeson, of Liverpool, called to see me. He had been the Liverpool delegate to the Supreme Council of the IRB...he told me he had been at the meeting when it [my responsibility] had been proposed by Seán MacDermott and passed unanimously, and that Dinny McCullough had been there...I approached Dinny McCullough on the matter, and he...gave me to understand that he was willing to sign a statement to that effect. Later, when I asked him to sign a statement I had typed out, he refused, or rather wrote that he could not remember. It is however an historical fact, and as such I think should be mentioned.'

2. John Mitchel (1815-75), a member of the Young Ireland Nationalist movement, founded a paper, The United Irishman, in 1848, and advocated militant resistance to landlords. He was sentenced to fourteen years' transportation in May 1848, but later escaped and made his way to the USA.

3. Kathleen brought with her a letter from Ned Daly to his mother.

4. MacNeill had been persuaded of the need for a rising by the 'Castle Document', which purported to give details of a planned British military occupation of Dublin; he was also reassured by the promise of the arrival of the Aud, with German arms. He inserted a notice in the Sunday Independent cancelling the planned 'manoeuvres' when he learned that the 'Castle Document' was a forgery (possibly by Plunkett) and that the Aud had been destroyed.

5. Casement, along with Robert Monteith and Sgt Julian Bailey, arrived at Banna Strand, Co Kerry, on 21 April (Good Friday) in a German submarine, but Casement and Bailey were immediately arrested. A German U-boat, the Aud, which had a cargo of arms, was challenged by a British naval patrol on 20 April, and was then scuttled by its captain.

Chapter 5

1. Robert Emmet (1778-1803), believing there was to be a Napoleonic invasion of Ireland, planned a Rising to coincide with this. He built up an arms depot in Dublin, but an explosion there, as France and England went to war, forced him to rise prematurely on 23 July 1803. Promised help failed to arrive, and fewer than 100 men rose in Dublin; the rising collapsed within a day. Emmet was executed on 20 September.

2. It was Bulmer Hobson who had discovered the plans for an armed Rising, and informed MacNeill. When MacNeill confronted Pearse, MacDermott and Mac-Donagh, they reassured him that German arms were about to arrive, and he agreed to let things go ahead. However, the Military Council, fearing that Hobson might continue to urge MacNeill to countermand the rising, placed him under arrest until it was under way.

3. Nora Daly married Eamonn Dore in May 1918.

4. Fianna Eireann, a youth movement, had been founded by Countess Markievicz in 1909 to train young people for the fight for Irish independence.

5. Griffith did not take part in the Rising, but was nonetheless arrested, as the authorities erroneously connected Sinn Féin with the Rising.

6. The casualties of the Rising were as follows: insurgents, 64 killed, 120 wounded; British forces and police, 132 killed, 397 wounded; civilians, 300 killed, 2,000 wounded.

7. Nurse Edith Cavell had been shot by the Germans in 1915 for aiding Allied fugitives, and her execution had caused a great outcry.

8. 'We were marched into a little patch of green in front of the Rotunda Hospital, an oval patch, and we were made to lie down there … we were kept there all night and a British officer amused himself by taking out some of the leaders. He took out poor old Tom Clarke and, with the nurses looking out of the windows of the hospital, he stripped him to the buff and made all sorts of disparaging remarks about him. "This old bastard has been at it before. He has a shop across the street there. He's an old Fenian", and so on.' (Recollections of Joseph Sweeney, in K Griffith and T E O'Grady, Curious Journey, p.79.)

Chapter 6

1. 'My sister Kathleen saw us at once and was awaiting us at the door. I hope never to see in any human face such absolute desolation. She looked as if life could do no more to her, as if some vital part of her was dead, and yet she was calm, but the most violent grief would have been easier to look at.' (Recollections of Madge Daly, unpublished, UL archives, p.121.)

2. General Maxwell had written to Dr Dwyer, Bishop of Limerick, requesting the removal of two diocesan priests from their duties, as they were 'a dangerous

menace to the peace and safety of the Realm'. Dr Dwyer refused, saying: 'They are both excellent priests who hold strong Nationalist views, but I do not know that they have violated any civil or ecclesiastical law....you appeal to me to help you in furtherance of your work as military dictator of Ireland. Even if that kind of action was not outside my province, the events of the past few weeks would make it impossible for me to have any part in proceedings which I regard as wantonly cruel and oppressive...'

Chapter 7

1. Kathleen 'came to live with us in Limerick...She felt quite miserable and only stayed for a year. She had no occupation, and this gave her too much time to think and fret. Her house in Richmond Avenue had been let furnished to Mr P S O'Hegarty...so she took a furnished house in Dundrum.' (Recollections of Madge Daly, UL archives, p.182.)

2. 'When the soldiers left it (the shop), it was cleared of all the valuable stocks of tobacco, cigars etc., and left open for the looters to finish the job. A few days after, a neighbour nailed up the door; but later, during my sister's illness in Limerick, the landlady took forcible possession of it. The action of this lady...deprived my sister of the only means of making a living for herself and her children – her husband had built up a prosperous business there, so she had a vested interest. The rent was paid up to the week before Easter....When she recovered sufficiently to return to Dublin...she got no redress – in fact, the tenant refused to give her some mahogany fittings which Tom Clarke had made himself...Later on, Mrs Clarke could have forced her claim more successfully, but the constant strain of the years following and her bad health put the matter into the background.' (Recollections of Madge Daly, UL archives, p.148.) Since the contents had been looted, nothing remained with which to pay the business debts after Tom's death, and Kathleen paid everything owing out of her own resources. The receipts for these payments are still extant. (Family sources)

3. There is no street named after Tom Clarke in Dublin (1991). There is a Clarke Tower among the tower blocks at Ballymun. In 1966, Dundalk railway station became Clarke station.

4. Although de Valera was sentenced to death after the Rising, this was commuted to life imprisonment. It was later conjectured that this was because of his American

citizenship (he was born in New York in 1882), but a more likely reason is that great revulsion had been caused by the executions, and no more took place after those of Connolly and MacDermott on 12 May.

5. Laura Daly married Séamus O'Sullivan on 4 May 1918. The marriage took place at midnight because he was 'on the run' at the time, and was living concealed in the Dalys' attic.

Chapter 8

1. Kathleen wrote out her will and sent it to Limerick: 'I, Kathleen Clarke, appoint my sisters Madge Daly and Agnes Daly guardians and trustees until the age of 18 years for my three children, John D. Clarke, Thomas Clarke and Emmet Clarke. All the money or property I possess to be used for them as my sisters think best. To Daly his papa's watch, tools, American and Limerick [illegible] papers, the watch to go to Emmet in case of Daly's death. To Tom, the piece of Moore Street house wall and I.V. Commission. To Emmet, the doorway from Moore Street, my watch and his papa's tickets-of-leave. The rest of my personal property to be divided equally between them by my sisters. Signed in the presence of Constance de Markievicz, Maud Gonne MacBride: Kathleen Clarke, June 26th, 1918.' (Kathleen Clarke to Madge Daly, UL archives.)

2. 'Whereas, Mrs Tom Clarke is a person within the area in respect of which the operation of Section One of the Defence of the Realm (Amendment) Act 1915 is for the time being suspended, And whereas on the recommendation of the Competent Military Authority appointed under the Defence of the Realm Regulations, it appears to me that for the securing the public safety and the Defence of the Realm, it is expedient that the said Mrs Tom Clarke should, in view of the fact that she is a person suspected of acting, having acted and being about to act in a manner prejudicial to the public safety and the Defence of the Realm, be subjected to such obligations and restrictions as are herein after mentioned, I hereby order that the said Mrs Tom Clarke shall be interned in Holloway Prison, and shall be subject to all the rules and conditions applicable to persons there interned and remain there until further orders...' (Family sources.)

3. A letter from Countess Markievicz to Madge Daly reads: 'Kathleen has suffered a great deal since she has been here with internal trouble and bad back. This was worst during the earlier days. This got better but unfortunately during that very

cold weather before they lit the fires she was chilled to the bone and got very bad rheumatic pains, which centered in her chest. When the doctor painted her with iodine, wrapped her in cotton wool and gave her a filthy bottle she got relief and began to rally. She is now singing little songs and I have to restrain her from dancing jig steps. You know her wonderful spirit – she never loses heart …' (C Markievicz to M Daly, 11.11.1918, in UL archives.)

4. 'We started for home next day and were met by a huge crowd – a repetition of the wild scenes when the prisoners returned in 1917. Mrs Clarke was very ill, but the excitement of the warm reception stirred her, and she insisted in going to a banquet given in her honour that night. Next morning she collapsed, and was taken to a Nursing Home where she lay very near to death for weeks …' (Recollections of Madge Daly, UL archives, p.217.)

5.'I miss you very much, especially in the evening, and I keep forgetting and beginning to babble all sorts of nonsense to you. I am very well and quite cheerful and am painting away harder than ever…I wonder whose head you are snapping off now!' (C Markievicz to K Clarke, 18.2.1919, UL archives.)

Chapter 9

1. Under the Defence of the Realm Act (DORA), suspected persons could be seized and imprisoned at any time. This Act was also used widely against the Suffragettes in England.

2. The first Dáil Eireann, 'Parliament of Ireland', consisted of elected Sinn Féin representatives who refused to take their seats in the British House of Commons. Only 27 out of 69 were able to attend the first meeting on 21 January 1919; most of the rest were in prison. De Valera, who had escaped from Lincoln Jail, was elected President of the Dáil, and he made Countess Markievicz Minister for Labour. The first session approved the Constitution, the Declaration of Independence and the Democratic Programme. On 10 September 1919 the Dáil was declared a dangerous association and banned; subsequent meetings were held in secret.

3. The Royal Irish Constabulary was supplemented by a new force, recruited in England among demobilised soldiers, during the War of Independence (1919-21). They were known as the Black and Tans because of the colour of their uniforms.

4. De Valera had gone to the USA in June 1919, against the wishes of his cabinet, to float a Dáil Eireann loan and to secure recognition of the Irish Republic. A rift developed between himself, Devoy and Daniel Cohalan, which split the Friends of Irish Freedom (FOIF), and de Valera founded the American Association for the Recognition of the Irish Republic (AARIR) in June, 1920. He returned to Ireland in January, 1921.

5. The first Dáil established Courts to replace the British Courts, and decrees were enforced by police provided by the Dáil. At first the Courts sat in public, but they were constantly attacked, and were forced underground. The British Courts gradually fell into disuse, and the Dáil Courts operated more openly after the War of Independence Truce (July 1921).

6. On Sunday 21 November 1920 (Bloody Sunday), Michael Collins's intelligence 'Squad' killed fourteen British secret service agents. The Auxiliaries (a volunteer force allied to the RIC) took reprisals by killing Clancy, McKee and Clune, who were being held prisoner in Dublin Castle. Later that day, Black and Tans shot and killed twelve people during a football match at Croke Park.

7. '...Her whole nervous system was upset. For years after, she suffered from fierce headaches, and could not get a proper night's sleep. Every time a lorry passed our house at night, she dashed out of bed screaming. Eventually, the doctor advised us to leave that house and by degrees she recovered.' (Recollections of Madge Daly, UL archives, p.258.)

8. Kevin Barry was executed in November 1920 for involvement in an IRA raid which caused the death of a British soldier.

Chapter 10

1. In a passionate and emotional letter to Madge Daly on 19 December, Kathleen says: 'Great God did I ever think I'd live to see it, to see men who were the bravest, now fooled and blinded by a juggle of words into the belief that this treaty means a realization of our highest ideals. If you heard the speeches in private you'd be sick. Collins has mesmerised them all into thinking it's the high road to everything we dreamed, and he has been fooled into believing it himself, and Dev. to a large extent is to blame, for one thing his lack of experience which I always feared, and another, his habit of trying to work things out alone in his own way taking no one entirely into his confidence, and also trusting too much in the goodness of other

people....I am to speak tomorrow, and my heart fails me at the thought. On Dev's advice we are all retraining ourselves, but it's difficult. I'd just love to rip the duds off some of them...' (UL archives).

2. The Four Courts, centre of the judiciary, were seized by a battalion of the anti-Treaty IRA's Dublin Brigade on 14 April 1922. The Provisional Government did not immediately try to remove them, but the general election of 16 June placed the Treaty supporters in a strong position. When the garrison refused to surrender on 28 June, the building was shelled; the Civil War had begun. The records office was destroyed, and the garrison surrendered.

3. 'I said that I would put them under my jersey but she said they would notice the bulge. So I suggested that I would sit at the table with my arms folded ... the military rushed in to search the ground floor and then rushed down to the kitchen and were busy searching cupboards and pantries. Then some went out to the garden which was up some stone steps. My mother came and relieved me of the load and found a secure place to hide them...She had brought in fresh plaice for all of us so that I had to eat the extra in case the soldiers would notice. For years after I did not like plaice.' (Emmet Clarke, personal comment to the editor).

4. Brugha died after the Four Courts fell, in a heroic last stand after ordering his men to surrender. Michael Collins was shot in an ambush at Béal na mBláth, Co Cork, on 22 August 1922.

Chapter 11

1. Eileen and Ned O'Toole had moved to the United States in 1923 with their two sons.

2. John Devoy died in 1928, aged 86.

3. The Republican (anti-Treaty) Teachtaí Dála (TDs, members of Parliament) refused to recognise the newly-elected Third Dáil, which met in September 1922, and called it the Provisional Dáil. The Free State came into existence in December 1922 when the Third Dáil became the Provisional Government. Meanwhile, the anit-Treaty TDs (now a party called Cumann na Poblachta, 'Republican League') continued to meet separately.

4. This Oath had been specified in the Treaty, and in the 1922 Constitution, and promised fidelity to 'HM King George V, his heirs and successors.' The

Republican members of Dáil Eireann refused to sign it, and thus could not take their places as TDs.

5. De Valera resigned as President of Sinn Féin and set up a new political party, called Fianna Fáil ('Soldiers of Destiny'); 44 Fianna Fáil deputies were elected in June, 1927. The Electoral Amendment Act, 1927, forced them either to take the Oath or be disqualified, so he signed the book containing the Oath, calling it 'an empty formula', and led his Party into the Dáil.

6. Kathleen Clarke won a Fianna Fáil seat in June 1927, and lost it the following September. She was defeated again in a by-election in April, 1928, and was nominated to the Senate.

7. Cumann na nGaedheal (the 'Irish League') was a Party for the supporters of the Treaty, and had been founded by W T Cosgrave in 1923.

8. Kathleen Clarke was in receipt of a pension, which was tax free, given to all the relatives of the signatories. Later, the tax concession was abolished.

INDEX

Daly, Caroline (Carrie), 247–8

Daly, Catherine (mother), 10, 14,
15, 18–19, 23, 45, 102, 275
Annie's birth, 15–16
beaten by Black and Tans, 245
and Clarke, 32, 34
Edward's birth, 21
Edward's execution, 154
home burned, 250–2
home raided, 242–9

Daly, Edward (brother), 21, 53, 87,
90, 161
and Easter Rising, 101–2, 105
execution, 137, 147–50, 154, 155
Howth gun-running, 67–8
joins Volunteers, 61–2
memorial, 323

Daly, Edward (father), 10–11,
15–16, 18, 19
death of, 20–1, 22

Daly, Eileen (O'Toole), 9–10, 11,
21, 23, 157, 242, 280

Daly, Father, 105, 106

Daly, James, 22–3, 25, 27, 40

Daly, John, 14, 15, 45, 49, 164, 234,
247
bakery, 26–7
and Clarke, 31–2, 35, 50, 52, 53,
56, 94, 154–5
death of, 173
and dependants' fund, 168
and Devoy, 41

and Easter Rising, 137, 138,
154–5
and Griffith, 76
health, 15, 19–20
home raided, 155–6, 157
imprisonment, 10–13, 24–5
and Irish Volunteers, 63–4
mayor of Limerick, 28–9, 314
parliamentary candidate, 21–2

Daly, Laura, 104, 114–16, 152, 154
attacked, 244
Edward's execution, 147–50
home burned, 250–2

Daly, Lollie, 10, 11, 13–14, 21, 32,
121
home burned, 250–2
prison visits, 15, 19

Daly, Madge, 21, 45, 50, 52, 53,
164, 219, 234
bakery horses, 247
and dependants' fund, 157–8,
167–8, 169, 176
and Easter Rising, 147–50, 152,
154, 155
Edward's execution, 147–50
home burned, 250–2
home raided, 155–6, 242–9

Daly, Margaret (grandmother), 10,
13, 19–20, 21

Daly, Michael, 22

Daly, Nora, 114–17, 173

Daly's Bakery, 26–7, 61, 323
Civil War, 275

P

Pact election, 267–8

Parnell, Charles Stewart, 174

partition, 65

Pearse, Mrs, 175, 176, 186, 263,
268, 292–3

Pearse, P H, 58–9, 70, 83, 87, 94–5,
190–1, 292

and Easter Rising, 101–2, 106,
110, 113–14, 115, 138, 139

execution, 137, 147, 153

in IRB, 60

loan to, 90–1

O'Donovan Rossa funeral, 80

as President, 188, 224

Proclamation, 99–100

Perolz, Marie, 129–33, 134, 140

Pim, Herbert, 185

Plunkett, Count, 153, 187

Plunkett, Countess, 187

Plunkett, Joseph Mary, 87, 91, 106,
153

execution, 137

Plunkett, Miss, 92

Plunkett, Mr, 139

Portland Prison, 31, 136, 186

Portrane Mental Hospital, 269

Powerscourt, Lord, 229–30

Prendergast, James, 26–7

proportional representation, 290–1

R

Rathdown Union, 33

Rathmines Police Station, 129

Reddin, Mrs, 69

Redmond, John, 63, 68–9, 72, 75,
167, 176

Republican Courts, 235–7, 285

Reynolds, John R, 160–1, 165,
215–16

Reynolds, Molly, 160

Richmond Barracks, 136, 158, 163

Road Traffic Acts, 1933, 316–17

Robinson, David, 232

Rogers, Mrs Thomas, 69

Rotunda Maternity Hospital, 60–1,
139, 238, 316

Royal Irish Academy of Music
(RIAM), 316

Royal Irish Constabulary (RIC), 59,
78

Rudmose-Brown, Professor, 315

Ryan, Misses, 98

Ryan, Mr, 111

S

St Enda's School, 90, 119, 153

St George's Private Lunatic Asylum,
10

St Lawrence's Cemetery, Limerick,
16–17, 20

St Ultan's Hospital, 316

St Vincent's Hospital, 274

Sarah (maid), 122, 123–5, 128–9,
146, 158, 161, 166, 171

Sarsfield, Patrick, 292